EIGHTEENTH-CENTURY SCOTS

Thomas Boston 1676–1732
John Colquhoun 1748–1827
Thomas Chalmers 1780–1847
Robert M. M'Cheyne 1813–43
Robert S. Candlish 1806–73
John Duncan 1796–1870
James Buchanan 1804–70
George Smeaton 1814–89
Alexander Whyte 1836–1921

NORTH AMERICAN LEADERS

Archibald Alexander 1772–1851
William Nevins 1797–1835
J. H. Thornwell 1812–63
Robert L. Dabney 1820–98
W. G. T. Shedd 1820–94
Clement R. Vaughan died 1911
B. B. Warfield 1851–1921
A. W. Tozer 1897–1963

BRITISH EVANGELICAL LEADERS

John C. Ryle 1816–1900
C. H. Spurgeon 1834–92
John Murray 1898–1975
D. M. Lloyd–Jones 1899–1981

'Clean the grand old pictures of the divine masters; hang them
up in new frames; fix them on the walls of your people's
memories, and their well–instructed hearts shall bless you.'
C. H. SPURGEON

THE OLD
EVANGELICALISM

By the same author:

The Forgotten Spurgeon

The Puritan Hope: Revival and the Interpretation
   of Prophecy

The Life of Arthur W. Pink

D. Martyn Lloyd-Jones: The First Forty Years

D. Martyn Lloyd-Jones: The Fight of Faith
   (the two-volume authorized biography)

Jonathan Edwards: A New Biography

The Life of John Murray

Australian Christian Life from 1788

Revival and Revivalism: The Making and Marring of
   American Evangelicalism 1750–1858

Spurgeon v. Hyper-Calvinism: The Battle for Gospel
   Preaching

Pentecost – Today? : The Biblical Basis for
   Understanding Revival

Evangelicalism Divided: A Record of Crucial Change
   in the Years 1950 to 2000

Wesley and Men Who Followed

THE OLD
EVANGELICALISM

Iain H. Murray

THE BANNER OF TRUTH TRUST

THE BANNER OF TRUTH TRUST
3 Murrayfield Road, Edinburgh EH12 6EL, UK
P O Box 621, Carlisle, PA 17013, USA

★

© Iain H. Murray 2005

ISBN 0 85151 901 6

★

Typeset in 12/13 pt Bembo at
the Banner of Truth Trust
Printed in the U.S.A. by
Versa Press, Inc.,
East Peoria, IL

CONTENTS

Preface   xi

1. PREACHING AND AWAKENING: FACING THE
   MAIN PROBLEM IN EVANGELISM   1
   No One Will Become Concerned about Himself until
      He Learns about God   8
   Under Conviction Individuals Commonly Endeavour a
      Change of Behaviour   9
   By the Law Men Learn Their Helplessness   11
   The Initial Need in Evangelism Is Not to Win an Acceptance
      for Christ   15
   Regeneration and Conviction   18
   Conclusions: 1. The Case Demonstrated by History   24
                2. What Preachers Need   28

   ADDITIONAL NOTES:
      John Brown of Wamphray: *What Preparation Is Not and
         What It Is*   33
      Thomas Scott: *The Offence of the Cross Ceasing*   35
      Alexander Whyte: *Preaching to the Conscience*   36
      D. M. Lloyd-Jones: *The Law*   37

2. SPURGEON AND TRUE CONVERSION   39
   Conversion, Profound and Mysterious   42
   Where Conversion Has to Begin   46
   How the Law Came to Be Put Aside   49

2. SPURGEON AND TRUE CONVERSION (cont.)

Why Law Preaching? 52
What is Regeneration? 54
Preaching for Conversion 60
Conclusions: 1. True gospel preaching is multi-faceted 64
2. When there is a wrong conversion model
a sense of sin and the fear of God disappear 65

ADDITIONAL NOTES
D. M. Lloyd-Jones: *Evangelism and Conviction of Sin* 69
A. W. Tozer: *'Conversion' without Regeneration* 70

3. 'CHRIST OUR RIGHTEOUSNESS' – GOD'S WAY
OF SALVATION 71

The Importance of the Doctrine 73
All Mankind in Darkness 76
Why 'the Righteousness of Christ' is Good News 82
Imputation –the Old Testament Gospel 86
Conclusions: 1. The danger of modifying the doctrine 89
2. Justification not to be preached alone 90
3. The doctrine always in need of recovery 92
4. Justification opposes man's root sin 94
5. The solution to contemporary weakness 95

ADDITIONAL NOTES:
George Herbert: *Judgement* 97
John Bunyan: *My Righteousness in Heaven* 97
Charles Simeon: *Conversion Testimony* 98
Martin Boos: *Words He Never Forgot* 99
Frances Ridley Havergal: *Personal Testimony of 1864* 99

4. THE CROSS – THE PULPIT OF GOD'S LOVE 101

Two Truths 106
At Calvary We Learn of Forgiveness Consistent with Holiness
and Justice 108

4. THE CROSS – THE PULPIT OF GOD'S LOVE (cont.)

By Christ Crucified the Love of God Is to Be Made Known
to All People   110

Particular Love and General Love   115

Conclusions: 1. Not all truth is equally important   123

2. The unexplainable not to be 'explained'   124

3. The practical, not the theoretical, is
paramount   125

4. Care needed in controversy   127

5. The priority of love   127

ADDITIONAL NOTES:

John Calvin: *Gospel Preaching*   131

Thomas Chalmers: *God Is Love*   131

William Nevins: *The Extent of the Atonement*   132

John Bonar: *The Universal Offer and the Compassion
of God*   132

5. WHAT CAN WE LEARN FROM JOHN WESLEY?   135

Wesley Is a Necessary Reminder of How Upbringing and
Education Prejudice Our Minds   139

Wesley Has Something to Teach Us on the Relationship
between Zeal for the Gospel and Church Government,
Procedures and Practices   143

In Wesley and Methodism We Are Taught that Persuasion
of the Love of God for Men Makes Churches Truly
Evangelistic   151

A Parallel Witness from Scotland   158

Wesley Challenges Us on the Focus of Our Doctrine of
Sanctification   162

6. ASSURANCE OF SALVATION   167

The Truth and Usefulness of Assurance   170

The Holy Spirit and Assurance   172

The Twofold Basis of Assurance   175

6. ASSURANCE OF SALVATION (cont.)

'Legalism'   179
A Third Way to Assurance?   181
Unbalanced Teaching   190
Conclusions: 1. Assurance and feelings   194
              2. The non-Christian has no right
                 to assurance   195
              3. Assurance and service for Christ   196
              4. The importance of assurance   198

7. CHRISTIAN UNITY AND CHURCH UNITY   201

Denominations and Unity   204
When Church and Denomination Are Confused   207
The Unity That Comes First   210

ADDITIONAL NOTES:
    John Owen of Thrussington: *Uniformity and Unity*   215
    William Gibson: *Unity and the Holy Spirit*   215

Index   217

PREFACE

A number of the happiest days of my life have been spent in the company of brethren at conferences for preachers and missionaries in different parts of the world. The contents of this book are made up of addresses given on some of those occasions over the last thirty years and later revised. Although the original audiences were usually made up of men in the Christian ministry, I believe the subject matter will be found to have a wider bearing and be of help to others.

I have entitled the book *The Old Evangelicalism,* not because that is explicitly the theme, but because the material consistently shows that, on a number of fundamental truths, the evangelicalism of the last hundred years contrasts unfavourably with what went before. One of the older evangelicals who forecast the coming change was C. H. Spurgeon; another was William Booth. When Booth was asked by an American newspaper what he regarded as the chief dangers ahead for the twentieth century, he replied tersely: 'Religion without the Holy Ghost, Christianity without Christ, forgiveness without repentance, salvation without regeneration, politics without God and heaven without hell.'[1] Such a decline in the biblical message has indeed taken place and a weaker evangelicalism has been unable to stem the tide.

My thesis, however, is not that the remedy lies simply in the recovery of all the older tradition. For one thing, the older tradition was not so uniform that it can be taken on as

---

[1] *The War Cry*, 5 January 1901, p. 7.

a single whole. There were significant variations, as the inclusion of John Wesley in these pages reminds us. The *whole* truth has never been with any one group in church history. That there were mistakes in the older evangelicalism I do not doubt for a moment. For instance, in the emphasis formerly given to the role of preachers and preaching it could too easily be assumed that revival in the churches depends exclusively upon the pulpit or upon ordained ministers. The truth is, as the last hundred years have demonstrated from China to Cuba, that Christianity can still advance where preachers are imprisoned and silenced. J. C. Ryle wrote long ago:

> It is high time that the old tradition, that the clergy alone ought to teach and spread religious knowledge, should be exploded and cast aside for ever. To do good and diffuse light is a duty for which all members of Christ's Church are responsible.[2]

At the same time I do not mean to hide the fact that on such doctrinal and experimental subjects as conversion and assurance the English Puritans provide a greater wealth of help than any other school in the English language, and probably in any language. I have quoted heavily from that source. In addresses, unlike sermons, I think there is place for such citations. They will show the books that have helped me (as they have so many others since the seventeenth century) and their re-appearance in print at the present day is a hopeful sign. For far too long the attitude depicted by Spurgeon has been too common:

> It seems odd, that certain men who talk so much of what the Holy Spirit reveals to themselves, should think so little of what he had revealed to others . . . A respectable acquaintance with the opinions of the giants of the

---

[2] *Expository Thoughts on St Mark* (1857; reprint, Edinburgh: Banner of Truth, 1985), p. 69.

past, might save many an erratic thinker from wild inter-
pretations and outrageous inferences.[3]

Spurgeon was ever telling his students for the ministry, 'To
be effective preachers you must be sound theologians.'
William Williams, one of those students, reported, 'Week by
week we were advised what books to buy,' and he related
how they were introduced to 'Augustine, Owen, Baxter,
Brooks, Charnock, Manton, Sibbes, and a host of other illus-
trious names'. My hope is that these pages will help stir
young men to give themselves and their time to these proven
authors
Yet my frequent reference to authors belonging to the
older evangelicalism is not a substitute for scriptural evidence.
Let all teachers be judged by Scripture. 'You have one
Teacher,' our Lord warned the disciples (*Matt.* 23:10, NIV).[4]
It is because the Puritans took that so seriously that there is
such a biblical flavour and depth to their writings.[5]
The original addresses that make up this book were delivered to men who, for the most part, were already sympathetic
to the old evangelicalism. Our own faults and failings lie
in areas rather different from the ethos of modern evangelicalism and in some of these addresses I have tried to speak
to some of those areas, particularly the weakness often asso-
ciated today with Calvinistic belief when it comes to

[3] *Commenting and Commentaries* (1876; reprint, London: Banner of
Truth, 1969), p. 1.

[4] I am aware that my quotations from Scripture in the addresses in this
book do not follow a consistent source. They are drawn from several versions (AV, NKJV, NASB, NIV and ESV), and sometimes represent my
own rendering of the original. I hope readers will allow for this, and
appreciate that my intention was to convey the force of the original rather
than to follow any particular version exclusively.

[5] For those just beginning to read in this field, much help will be found
in J. I. Packer, *A Quest for Godliness: The Puritan Vision of the Christian Life*
(Wheaton: Crossway, 1990).

evangelistic effort and effective outreach. There is a perception abroad that such belief has no dynamic for reaching a
lost world. I think it is better to concede that there is cur-
rently some reason for this perception, and to consider why
it exists, rather than to deny it any validity. Whitefield's Tabernacle in the eighteenth century and Westminster Chapel in
Lloyd-Jones' day could be described as 'soul traps' but the
designation cannot be given to many churches of that tradition at the present time.

For the Puritans, a saving conversion to Christ was *the* pre-
eminent subject for study and for the pulpit. That is the point
that needs a new priority among us. But I am not advising
that we restrict ourselves to seventeenth-century mentors as
though we had nothing to learn from others. Wherever gospel preaching has been much owned of God it has always had
one great characteristic, and John Wesley can show us that as
well as George Whitefield and the school to which the latter
belonged. Should we fall into a narrowness of spirit that for-
gets that the Holy Spirit has been given for *all* the body of
Christ, we shall be unlikely to receive the fresh anointing that
we need. Knowledge is a vital thing, but more love is the
greater requirement. To be better Christians is the main
need.

Once again I have to say that, next to my wife, my chief
debt is to my colleagues and friends in the work of the
Banner of Truth Trust.

IAIN H. MURRAY
Edinburgh,
February 2005

I

Preaching and Awakening:
Facing the Main Problem
in Evangelism

'Let no man think to understand the gospel, who knoweth nothing of the law.'

JOHN OWEN, *The Doctrine of Justification by Faith, Works* (1850–3; reprint, London: Banner of Truth, 1965–8), vol. 5, p. 189.

'Those that lived under the Pharisees' teaching would never have been convinced that the thoughts and affections of the heart were breaches of God's law; they did not understand that there was heart-adultery, and heart-murder, as our Saviour instructed them. What a world of sins a people live in for want of a sound and powerful ministry!'

ANTHONY BURGESS, *Spiritual Refinings,* Part II (London, 1654), p. 189.

'How is it that the preaching of the gospel has so little effect in the work of conversion? I cannot but come to this conclusion, that there never will be a revival in this country until *the law* is preached in all its full power to the conscience of the unconverted sinner, convincing him of sin, undermining all his refuge of lies, unfolding to him his native depravity, and unveiling the tremendous consequences of living and dying in an unrenewed state.'

MARY WINSLOW, *Heaven Opened* (reprint, Grand Rapids: Reformation Heritage Books, 2001), p. 278.

The danger of contrasting our own days with former times is a real one. It is easy to romanticize a past period with which we would compare ourselves, and then to judge our deficiencies by conditions that never existed as we imagine them. This admitted, the fact remains that there has been an element present when the gospel has made its swiftest advances in the world that is notably uncommon today, namely, the fear of God. Not only the experience but the very words have all but disappeared. Yet its place in Scripture is unmistakable. Christ directed his disciples to 'fear him which is able to destroy both soul and body in hell' (*Matt.* 10:28), and this fear was clearly part of the health of the apostolic churches. It was to be seen in the disciples themselves and then in those who heard their message: 'Walking in the fear of the Lord' (*Acts* 9:31); 'Knowing the fear of the Lord' (*2 Cor.* 5:11). When Peter preached at Pentecost 'fear came upon every soul'. In Ephesus, we read, 'Fear fell on them all' (*Acts* 19:17); in the court-room at Jerusalem it is not Paul who trembled but Felix, the judge, when he heard the prisoner speak on 'righteousness, temperance and judgment to come' (*Acts* 24:25).

Lest we suppose that the fear of God was a peculiarity of New – not to say Old – Testament Christianity, there is a consideration to check any such thought. It is that the same spirit has ever reappeared in times when the gospel has been seen in its power. Before the eighteenth-century Awakening, as Samuel Blair, a minister of that period wrote: 'It was thought that if there was any need of a heart-distressing sight of the soul's danger, and fear of Divine wrath, it was only needful for the grosser sort of sinners.' Instances of conviction of sin, Blair went on to say, had come to be regarded merely as mental depression and as something to be avoided. 'People were very generally through the land careless at heart and stupidly indifferent about the great concerns of eternity.'[1] In New England, Jonathan Edwards spoke similarly of people who regarded hell as 'nothing but a mere fiction to fright folks'.[2]

This general condition changed with the Evangelical Revival. When Isaac Watts and John Guyse wrote a Preface to the first edition of Jonathan Edwards' *Narrative of Surprising Conversions* in 1737, they noted the transformation in Northampton and observed, 'Wheresoever God works with power for salvation upon the minds of men, there will be some discoveries of a sense of sin, of the danger of the wrath of God.'[3]

The same has been true in every revival. An eye-witness who, in 1910, recalled the 1859 revival in Scotland, said:

> Then, the one deep dominant note was an overpowering sense of sin. The sense of sin is not found in anything like the same degree today. . . . There were old, greyheaded men and women, young men and maidens, weeping and sobbing as if their hearts would break with sorrow . . . the realisation of the presence of the Spirit of God was such as to overawe us so much, that we dare not to speak except in whispers, as we tried to point those in agony of soul to the Saviour.[4]

Of the great revival that began in Pyongyang, Korea, in 1907, an eyewitness wrote:

> Every man forgot every other. Each was face to face with God. I can hear yet that fearful sound of hundreds of men pleading with God for life, for mercy. The cry

---

[1] John Gillies, *Historical Collections Relating to Remarkable Periods of the Success of the Gospel* (1754; reprint, Edinburgh: Banner of Truth, 1981), p. 343.

[2] *Works*, vol. 10 (New Haven: Yale University Press, 1992), p. 370.

[3] *Works*, vol. 1 (1834; reprint, Edinburgh: Banner of Truth), p. 345.

[4] *Reminiscences of the Revival of '59 and the Sixties* (Aberdeen: University Press, 1910), pp. xii, 90.

went out over the city till the heathen were in conster-
nation . . . Looking up to heaven, to Jesus whom they
had betrayed, they smote themselves and cried with bitter wailing: 'Lord, Lord, cast us not away for ever!'
Everything else was forgotten, nothing else mattered.[5]

Times of revival are invariably times of widespread spiritual
concern, and that concern is ever related to a recovery of the
fear of God. The assertion of W. G. T. Shedd is not stronger
than the evidence when he writes:

All great religious awakenings begin in the dawning of
the august and terrible aspects of the Deity upon the
popular mind, and they reach their height and happy
consummation in that love and faith for which the
antecedent fear has been the preparation.[6]

This consideration must lead to the question of the agency
that brings about such a change. Does it come from heaven
so directly that it can be accounted for only as the immediate work of God? Is the fear of God that comes upon
individuals and communities a mysterious emotion that
defies rational explanation? The question is not simple. As
the Westminster Confession of Faith says, God is free to work
without, above, and against means, at his pleasure (5:iii). So
men and women may come into conviction of sin through
no human agency at all. But the same section of the Confession reminds us that 'God in his ordinary providence makes
use of means' and this is patently evident in the history of the
gospel. Even in revivals, which are sudden and extraordinary
events, it is true. Our English word for that phenomenon is
akin to the French, *réveille*, and provides an illustration.
Réveille, the morning hour of wakening in the army, is
announced by a bugle. When times of awakening occur in

[5] William Blair and Bruce Hunt, *The Korean Pentecost & the Sufferings
Which Followed* (Edinburgh: Banner of Truth, 1977), pp. 73–4.
[6] W. G. T. Shedd, *Sermons to the Natural Man* (Edinburgh: Banner of
Truth, 1977), p. 331.

the church the preaching of the Word serves that same function, as was once said of John Knox: 'The voice of this one
man is able in one hour to put more life in us than five hundred trumpets continually blustering in our ears.'[7]

Truth preached is the means of awakening. It was as John
the Baptist preached that men began to 'flee from the wrath
to come'. It was as Peter preached at Pentecost, and again at
Caesarea, that 'the Holy Spirit fell on all them which heard
the word'. It was when Paul preached that Felix trembled. To
say that revivals are ushered in by preaching is not to lessen
what we attribute to God; it is only to confirm the scriptural
principle that God is normally pleased 'by the foolishness of
preaching to save them that believe'(1 Cor. 1:21).

Preaching is thus connected with spiritual awakening. Yet
there is preaching under which the disinterested and the indifferent are never startled and awed. It brings no recovery of
the fear of God. Wherein lies the difference? In one respect
it may be accounted for in terms of divine sovereignty. Not
all preachers are appointed the same mission, nor are all given
to see the same results (1 Cor. 3:5–7). But to stop there would
be a mistake for there are definite responsibilities on the
human side. It is of preachers that God says: 'If they had stood
in my counsel, and had caused the people to hear my words,
then they should have turned them from their evil way, and
from the evil of their doings' (Jer. 23:22). Timothy was responsible to save himself and those who heard him (1 Tim. 4:16).

Biblical truth has to be preached, and more particularly,
the truth most adapted to awaken men and women. John
Duncan, one of the wisest Christians of the nineteenth century, once said that he believed no extensive awakening had
ever been produced except 'by awakening the conscience and
setting forth Christ'.[8] The sequence in his statement is surely

---

[7] The English ambassador in Scotland, quoted in A. Taylor Innes, *John Knox* (Edinburgh: Oliphant, 1896), pp. 89–90.

[8] A. Moody Stuart, *The Life of John Duncan* (1872; reprint, Edinburgh: Banner of Truth, 1991), p. 210.

scriptural. There is an order in which the truth is to be preached – the conviction of conscience first, or, as Jesus told Nicodemus, man must first hear 'earthly things', that is, the evidence of his ruin from his first birth, before 'heavenly things' (the love of God in sending his Son). And Jesus made clear the reason for that order: it is impossible for anyone to appreciate the provision until they first know why it is needed. Hence the force of his question to Nicodemus: 'If I have told you earthly things and you believe not, how shall you believe if I tell you of heavenly things?' (*John* 3:12).

Christ's personal dealings with individuals follow the same starting point, and the reason is laid down in the principle, 'Those that are well have no need of a physician, but those who are sick' (*Matt.* 9:12).[9] New Testament preaching, from John the Baptist preaching in the wilderness of Judea, to Paul in the first three chapters of the Epistle to the Romans, follows this order.

Dealing with the conscience must come first, 'that every mouth may be stopped, and all the world may become guilty before God' (*Rom.* 3:19). This being true, the conclusion of J. H. Thornwell has to follow, 'The most successful method of preaching is that which aims at thorough and radical convictions of sin.'[10]

This argument I will seek to elaborate in the sub-headings that follow.

[9] 'It is an easier thing to persuade a well man to go to the physician for cure, than it is to persuade a man that sees not his soul-disease, to come to Jesus Christ.' *Works of Bunyan* (1854; reprint, Edinburgh: Banner of Truth, 1991), vol. 1, p. 295. All the Puritans deal with this theme. John Flavel writes: 'There is no need of rhetoric to persuade a condemned malefactor to accept his pardon, a hungry man to sit down at a full table; but, alas! Sin is not felt, Christ is not known; therefore the one is not bewailed, nor the other desired.' *Whole Works* (1820; reprint, London: Banner of Truth, 1968), vol. 4, p.131. More particularly, see vol. 2, pp. 306–17.

[10] *Works of J. H. Thornwell*, vol. 2 (reprint, Edinburgh: Banner of Truth: 1974), p. 100.

No One Will Be Concerned about Himself until He Learns about God

Only in the light of the moral perfections of God – his infinite excellence and goodness – can man learn his true condition. For God's character is the opposite of our own. He created us in his moral image, to be like him, to live for him as the centre of our being, and to love him with heart and soul and mind and strength. But sin has reversed the purpose of creation and man has become the contradiction of what he ought to be. Withholding from God what belongs to him, men serve themselves and love themselves: 'They exchanged the truth about God for a lie and worshipped and served the creature rather than the Creator, who is blessed forever' (*Rom.* 1:25). The charge brought against Belshazzar applies to the whole human race: 'You have lifted up yourself against the Lord of heaven . . . And you have praised the gods of silver and gold, of bronze, iron, wood and stone, which do not see or know, but the God in whose hand is your breath, and whose are all your ways, you have not honoured' (*Dan.* 5:23).

This is not a discovery that man is willing to recognize, hence God's word to Jeremiah: 'And when you tell this people all these words, and they say to you, "Why has the LORD pronounced all this great evil against us? What is our iniquity? What is the sin that we have committed against the LORD our God?" then you shall say to them: "Because your fathers have forsaken me, declares the LORD, and have gone after other gods and have served and worshipped them, and have forsaken me and have not kept my law" ' (*Jer.* 16:10–11). At the same time God spoke to Jeremiah of another day, when 'nations come from the ends of the earth and say: "Our fathers have inherited nothing but lies, worthless things in which there is no profit" ' (*Jer.* 16:19–20). Such is the darkness of the human heart that the lie has been deliberately chosen. 'They did not see fit to acknowledge God' (*Rom.* 1:28). 'There is no fear of God before their eyes' (*Rom.* 3:18).

God is disowned and worthless things put in his place. Lloyd-Jones was not going beyond the scriptural evidence when he said, 'The sinner is an abomination, he is a monstrosity in God's universe, he is altogether hateful and vile.'[11]

The revelation of God in Scripture is intended to lead us to this discovery about ourselves. It is focused particularly in the standard God requires in his law, given in the ten commandments, for 'by the law is the knowledge of sin' (*Rom* 3:20). It is there that we learn that we are to love God with the totality of our being, and our neighbour as ourselves. The law enlightens us to a universe in which God in his majesty is at the centre. The Son of God, instead of appointing another standard and setting aside the ten commandments, perfectly exemplified them and expounded them in searching detail. No greater mistake can be made than to suppose that preaching the law is just Old Testament preaching: it is no less the law of Christ (*Matt.* 5:17) and the effect is the same. When, through the person and words of Jesus, Simon Peter was brought to that light, he had to say, 'Depart from me, for I am a sinful man, O Lord' (*Luke* 5:8).

The knowledge of God does not therefore first come to sinners with comfort, rather it is intensely disturbing. Mouths are shut, or if they speak at all it is to say such words as: 'Against you, you only, have I sinned' (*Psa.* 51:4). 'Woe is me, for I am lost' (*Isa.* 6:5); 'You have set our iniquities before you, our secret sins in the light of your presence' (*Psa.* 90:8). 'I had heard of you by the hearing of the ear, but now mine eye sees you; therefore I despise myself and repent in dust and ashes' (*Job* 42:5).

UNDER CONVICTION INDIVIDUALS COMMONLY ENDEAVOUR A CHANGE OF BEHAVIOUR

All men possess a conscience, and when the conscience is awakened it demands a reversal in behaviour: 'By the fear of

---

[11] D. M. Lloyd-Jones, *Romans: Exposition of Chapter 5, Assurance* (London: Banner of Truth, 1971), p. 123.

the LORD men depart from evil' (*Prov.* 16:6). This brings us to a subject on which the old evangelism differs markedly from the modern. Today it is often assumed that because the witness of conscience cannot save, it has no part in the work of conversion. To alarm and direct the conscience is not seen as part of evangelistic teaching, and if anyone shows any sign of trouble of conscience the direction is at once given that there is no need for concern, the person's only responsibility is to believe on Christ.

This teaching is so common that any alternative procedure is almost unthinkable. But the fact is that old-school evangelism believed that the call to faith is not the *one* direction necessary as soon as there is any sign of interest or concern. Rather the preacher should join with conscience, and press home its witness, by insisting on *obedience* to all that God commands. The truth is that an awakened person's sense of obligation to change his life-style is right. There is a reversal of conduct required, and the individual needs to be told so, as John the Baptist and the Apostle Paul told their hearers (*Luke* 3:8–14; *Acts* 24:25).

But this is not enough. The awakened sinner does not know the extent of what is required of him. The repentance God demands is no partial change, no temporary feeling of sorrow, but an entire change of life. Perhaps a particular sin troubles the individual, and he thinks that reformation and forgiveness in connection with that offence may be enough. It is by no means enough: the command is that he must stop *all* sinning – sins of life, heart and thought: 'Let the wicked forsake his way and the unrighteous man his thoughts' (*Isa.* 55:7). 'Cast away from you all the transgressions that you have committed, and make yourselves a new heart and a new spirit!' (*Ezek.* 18:31).

In short, the duty God requires is to be holy as he is holy, and to love him above all. Therefore he that does not hate his own life, says Christ, 'cannot be my disciple'(*Luke* 14:26). 'Strive to enter through the narrow door. For many, I tell you, will seek to enter in and will not be able' (*Luke* 13:24).

Is it coincidental that in a day when conviction of sin is comparatively rare, directions on the necessity of holiness to the unconverted are scarcely to be heard? Were they to be heard they might well be described as 'legalistic,' and rejected as a move away from the gospel to a form of salvation by works. But this criticism misses the whole point of the Scriptures I have quoted, and others that could be quoted. If the criticism was true, then Christ himself would have to be condemned for telling the rich young ruler, 'If you would enter life, keep the commandments' (*Matt.* 19:17).

This was indeed 'law preaching', but the purpose of thus summoning a man to full obedience was not to qualify him for salvation, it was rather to prove to him just how far he was from it. Our Lord gave that counsel, not because he thought the man could be obedient, but because the man thought he could. And every natural man in his self-confidence thinks the same. So the law says in effect, 'Make trial of obedience! Set about it as earnestly as you can – "If your hand or foot causes you to sin, cut it off and throw it away"' (*Matt.* 18:8)! The unconverted man is called to do this because the more he sets about it, the more the quest will be found to be hopeless. He finds that not only his conduct but his nature itself is wrong. The standard required is unreachable. By nature he cannot love, he cannot be holy, he cannot delight in God. 'Who then can be saved?' asked the astonished disciples, hearing Christ's absolute demand of the rich young ruler, and they received the answer that remains true today, 'With man it is impossible, but not with God' (*Mark* 10:27).

But if this is the case, is there not some kind of deception being played out, directing people to do what they cannot do? Not at all. For what is commanded is what they ought to do and what God created man to do. Because the sinner has lost the capacity to obey, God has not lost his authority to command what is 'holy, and just, and good'.[12] Incapacity is

---

[12] On the command to love God with all the heart, and soul, and strength and mind, John Duncan wrote: 'Obligation to discharge this duty

no excuse for disobedience, if it were, then the more sinful anyone became the less responsible they would be. <u>God's law is to be preached to the lost so that their conscience will register the rightness of what he commands.</u> Where a soul is being led to salvation it is not with the law that he will find fault but with himself. Before the law his own conscience condemns him, and he confesses himself not only guilty but powerless to do what he ought. If there is no other way to God, then he is truly lost. This is the distress to which Paul refers when he said, 'I was once alive apart from the law, but when the commandment came, sin came alive and I died' – died to his previous self-confidence and pride (*Rom.* 7:9).

The preaching of holiness and the law to the unregenerate – to natural men and women – if rightly done, does not lead them to a dependence on their own works. It does the very opposite. In the words of Jonathan Edwards:

> Such earnestness and thoroughness of endeavours, is the ordinary means that God makes use of to bring people into an acquaintance with themselves, to a sight of their own hearts, to a sense of their own helplessness, and to a despair in their own strength and righteousness . . . It is experience of ourselves, and finding what we are, that God commonly makes use of as the means of bringing us off all dependence on ourselves . . . It is therefore quite a wrong notion that some entertain, that the more they do, the more they shall depend on it. Whereas the reverse is true; the more they do, or the more thorough they are in seeking, the less will they be likely to rest in

––––––––––––––––

is not founded upon grace. Inclination to discharge this duty comes from grace, but obligation to discharge it does not come from grace, but of eternal and immutable law, as founded on the eternal loveliness of God.' *Rich Gleanings after the Vintage from 'Rabbi' Duncan*, ed. J. S. Sinclair (London: Thynne, 1925), p. 41.

their doings, and the sooner will they see the vanity of all that they do.[13]

BY THE LAW MEN LEARN THEIR HELPLESSNESS

Where there is an absence of this knowledge there is a fundamental obstacle to salvation. It was confidence in their spiritual ability which led the Jews to reject Christ. To his invitation to freedom they objected, 'We were never in bondage to any man'(*John* 8:33). Unless this mind-set is corrected Christ's work cannot be understood. Those who do not know that they are bound and prisoners, have no desire for the 'redemption' that sets free from the power and captivity of sin. Those who do not know they are law-breakers will not look to One who has honoured that law in the place of sinners. Those who do not know the displeasure of God will not listen to a message of 'propitiation' – of wrath turned aside and forgiveness provided in Jesus Christ.

Where the gospel is presented solely as forgiveness, only as a change of status before God, it may appeal to the self-interest of the unregenerate. A person may 'believe' that message and still be content to live an unchanged life; he becomes a 'Christian' and yet knows no moral, ethical revolution. But where the conscience is more thoroughly dealt with by the law of God, a larger need comes into view and one which forgiveness alone would not answer. There must also be a change of nature, a deliverance from self, a new life. The desire of a true convert is that he may never sin again;

---

[13] Edwards, *Works* (Banner of Truth edition), vol. 1, pp. 656–7. Elsewhere Edwards says of Christ's dealing with the rich young ruler: 'It may be, if Christ had directed him only to give away a considerable part of his estate, he would have done it; yea, perhaps, if he had bid him part with half of it, he would have complied with it: but when he directed him to throw up all, he could not grapple with such a proposal. Herein the straitness of the gate very much consists.' Ibid., p. 658. For a fuller treatment of the whole subject, see the same author, Ibid., vol. 2, pp. 830–8.

such a person will pray, as William Wilberforce once prayed, 'O God, deliver me from myself!'[14]

It is true that under any type of preaching, conversions will occur that do not last. But the danger of the superficial and the temporary is vastly increased when the message of holiness is treated as though it has no relevance to conversion.[15] It was a bad day for the churches when 'evangelistic meetings' and 'holiness meetings' were separated, as though the latter could come at some later stage of discipleship. This happened when the preaching of the law ceased to be regarded as part of evangelism, and with that omission came a disappearing sense of sin. That, in turn, led to the idea of conversion, not as deliverance from the power of sin, but as something much less. And when conviction of sin was found to be absent in gospel hearers, other reasons too often came to be proposed to justify their need of faith in Christ. The result has been 'converts' who never knew that 'the fear of God is the beginning of wisdom' (*Psa.* 111:10), and who never learned to say, 'Oh, how I love Your law!' (*Psa.* 119:97). As the numbers of such people grew, so the churches became little different in life from the world.

The words of Richard Sibbes provide a good summary. He wrote:

> The Spirit that testifies to a man that his sins are pardoned him, doth it first by convincing a man of his sins. Now, you know there is more in conviction than bare discovery . . . It makes a man to see there is no sweetness in sin; it makes a man to find that sin is the greatest

[14] R. A. and S. Wilberforce, *The Life of William Wilberforce,* vol. 1 (London: Murray, 1838), p. 98.

[15] Samuel Walker of Truro, a leading evangelical of the Evangelical Revival, wrote: 'We see the true cause why of the multitude that seem for a time to make some shew of religion so many fall away, namely, because their hearts were never soundly convinced of sin, nor consequently prepared for receiving Christ.' *Practical Christianity, Illustrated in Nine Tracts on Various Subjects* (London: Dilly, 1766), pp. 237–8.

burden, the greatest misery, of this life. For that which makes a man delight in sin, is because it is presented to him in false shapes; but now when the Spirit of God comes to manifest sin, and makes a man to look upon it in its own shape and nature, then he finds it to be the most unprofitable burden he ever bore in his life . . . Sin, being discovered thus to a man, he comes to seek, above all things in the world, to be rid and eased of it.[16]

THE INITIAL NEED IN EVANGELISM IS NOT TO WIN AN ACCEPTANCE FOR CHRIST.

Where 'receiving Christ' is made the first object in evangelism, then the primary concern may be to do nothing to hinder that result. Nothing should be said to antagonize or to awaken resistance. So man's impotence and helplessness, his being 'dead in trespasses and sin,' his condition as an individual who 'is not subject to the law of God, neither indeed can be' – come to be regarded as truths likely to put off those who are to be won. For the same reason the wrath of God (a truth spoken of ten times in the Epistle to the Romans) is often considered to be a hindrance to the reception of the message.

The problem with this thinking is the assumption that somehow, after all, salvation is ultimately in the sinner's own hands, and that nothing must be done to provoke his resistance. But such thinking is really to deny that man is in the condition that God has revealed. Either it is true or it is not, that 'the natural person does not accept the things of the Spirit of God' (*1 Cor.* 2:14). If it is true, then conversion does not come about by the preacher gaining the sinner's acceptance of his message. Paul's whole argument in the passage in 1 Corinthians, where he asserts the impossibility of the natural man receiving spiritual things, is that all men are

---

[16] *Works of Richard Sibbes,* ed. by A. B. Grosart (1862–4; reprint, Edinburgh: Banner of Truth, 1973–82), vol. 7, p. 274.

offended by the preaching of the cross – 'a stumbling block to Jews and folly to Gentiles'. It is that fact that makes the intervention of divine grace and power essential: 'Faith is not of your own doing; it is the gift of God' (*Eph.* 2:8). Instead, then, of hiding their helplessness from men, and avoiding what might offend, the preacher needs to show the full extent of their predicament and their dependence on the mercy of God. The unregenerate are as unable before the invitations of the gospel as they are before the claims of the law, yet their lack of faith is no more to be excused than their disobedience to the law. Indeed unbelief heightens guilt (*1 John* 5:10).

What this means in practice is well illustrated in the life of Benjamin Morgan Palmer, a much-owned herald of the gospel in the Southern States in the nineteenth century. It happened that a young man was staying in Palmer's home in Savannah during a time of revival. Many services were being held and the young man's host let him know that he could please himself whether he attended or not. Having nothing else to do, he did attend and soon by his irritation revealed that he did not like what he was hearing. The crisis came on a Monday when, entering Palmer's study, the visitor protested, 'You preachers are the most contradictory men in the world; you say, and you unsay, just as it pleases you, without the least pretension to consistency.' Palmer, who was working at his desk, has recorded what followed:

> Somehow I was not surprised at this outbreak; for though no sign of religious feeling had been evinced, there was a restlessness in his manner which satisfied me that he was secretly fighting against the truth. I thought it best to treat the case in an off-hand sort of way, and with seeming indifference so as to cut him off from all opportunity to coquette with the Gospel. Without arresting my pen, I simply, answered, 'Well, what now?'
>
> 'Why, yesterday you said in your sermon that sinners are perfectly helpless in themselves – utterly unable to

repent or believe and then turned square round and said that they would all be damned if they did not.'

'Well, my dear E—, there is no use in our quarrelling over this matter; either you can or you cannot. If you can, all I have to say is that I hope you will just go and do it.'

As I did not raise my eyes from my writing, which was continued as I spoke, I had no means of marking the effect of these words, until after a moment's silence, with a choking utterance, the reply came back: 'I have been trying my best for three whole days, and cannot.' 'Ah,' said I, laying down my pen: 'that puts a different face upon it; we will go then and tell the difficulty straight out to God.'

We knelt together and I prayed as though this was the first time in human history that this trouble had ever arisen; that here was a soul in the most desperate extremity, which must believe or perish, and hopelessly unable of itself, to do it; that, consequently it was just the case of calling for Divine interposition; and pleading most earnestly for the fulfilment of the Divine promise. Upon rising I offered not a single word of comfort or advice . . . So I left my friend in his powerlessness in the hands of God, as the only helper. In a short time he came through the struggle, rejoicing in the hope of eternal life.[17]

Across the Atlantic, a whole generation of gospel preachers in Scotland held to precisely the same biblical conviction. In the course of an Address on Preaching the Gospel before the General Assembly of the Free Church of Scotland in 1844, John Duncan said:

Some, indeed, would have man to do all, though he could do nothing; and others would have him to do

[17] T. C. Johnson, *Life and Letters of B. M. Palmer* (Edinburgh: Banner of Truth, 1987), pp. 83-4.

nothing, because all was done for him. As long as I am told that I must come to God, and that I can come, I am left to suppose that some good thing, or some power of good remains in me, and I arrogate to myself what belongs to Jehovah. The creature is exalted and God is robbed of his glory. If, on the other hand, I am told that I cannot come to God, but not also that I must come, I am left to rest contented at a distance from God, I am not responsible for my rebellion. But if we preach that sinners can't come, and yet must come, then is the honour of God vindicated and the sinner is shut up. Man must be so shut up that he must come to Christ, and yet know that he cannot. He must come to Christ, or he will look to another, when there is no other to whom he may come; he cannot come, or he will look to himself. This is the gospel vice, to shut up men to faith.[18]

REGENERATION AND CONVICTION

What has been left unconsidered so far is the relation of conviction of sin to regeneration. There can be no clarity on this point without a right understanding of what regeneration means. For some, it means the change produced by scriptural truth *as* sinners believe it. In other words, accepting the truth is regarded as the *means* by which regeneration is accomplished. But this definition confuses two different things, while belief rests on truth it is not faith that gives *the capacity* to believe. Faith is represented as 'the gift of God' just because the natural man, being at enmity to God, does not have that capacity (*Eph.* 2:8). The new birth has to precede faith as its *cause* although it has no priority in *time*. We do not 'see' and then are reborn; we are reborn and then we 'see' (*John* 3:3). It is 'the dead' who hear the voice of the Son of God (*John* 5:25); there is a divine call that secures justification

---

[18] *Rich Gleanings*, p. 392. Also *'Just a Talker': The Sayings of Dr John ('Rabbi') Duncan*, Edinburgh: Banner of Truth, 1997, p. 253.

(*Rom.* 8:30). [19] Thus Scripture represents regeneration as the immediate act of God; it is the giving of a new life, a being made alive from the dead, a new birth. Truth has no such creative power. [20]

When, then, does regeneration occur in the process of conversion? Is it at first conviction of sin, later during a deepening concern, or when? The answer is that no one knows, for the time of regeneration is hidden from the human consciousness. It is a change that occurs unseen in the depths of the human personality. 'The wind blows where it wishes, and you hear its sound, but you do not know where it comes from or where it goes. So it is with everyone who is born of the Spirit' (*John* 3:8).

Of course, when regeneration is considered as taking place at the decision of the individual there is no such mystery about the time. Obviously no one makes 'a decision' without knowing it. The idea that a Christian must know the time of his rebirth is based on this view of regeneration. Christian experience is against that understanding. Richard Sibbes did not hesitate to say, 'No man can see the conversion of another; nay, no man can discern his own conversion at first.'[21] The latter statement is probably too strong,[22] but on

---

[19] Many other Scriptures show the same sequence: e.g. *John* 6:44; *Acts* 13:48; *Acts* 16:14.

[20] The words in James 1:18, 'Of his own will *begat he us* with the word of truth' (AV) are better translated, '*brought us forth . . .* ' (ESV), for the reference is the maternal, not the paternal act. In 1 Peter 1:23, the 'incorruptible seed' that produces birth is the Holy Spirit; 'the word of God' is 'the sphere within which the birth takes place.' See W. G. T. Shedd, *Dogmatic Theology,* vol. 2 (Edinburgh: T. & T. Clark, 1889), p. 509n. 'The new life is not implanted because a man perceives the truth, but he perceives the truth because the new life is implanted.'

[21] Sibbes, *Works*, vol. 2, p. 332.

[22] 'I will not deny,' writes Owen, speaking of the time of conversion, 'that when it is known, it is of great use, tending to stability and consolation; but yet it is still a circumstance, such as that the being of the thing itself doth not depend upon.' *Works*, vol. 6, p. 599.

the teaching, 'All that are new born know the time of their new birth,' Giles Firmin was stating a characteristic Puritan conviction when he exclaimed, 'What divine, that did deserve the name of a Gospel-minister, did ever deliver such a doctrine?'[23] Richard Baxter speaks of a meeting of eminent Christians and ministers where it was asked that everyone should give an account of the time and manner of his conversion, 'and there was but one of them that could do it'. To which Baxter added, 'I aver from my heart, that I neither know the day, nor the year, when I began to be sincere.'[24]

To this it may be objected, if faith is the result of regeneration, then those who have faith must know when their faith began, and does that not make the time of rebirth easily recognizable? The answer is no, and for more than one reason. For one thing, while regeneration creates the habit of faith, the believer's first conscious exercise of faith may be so weak that he is by no means certain of its existence. Saving faith and the assurance that I am believing are not identical. Further, while true faith follows regeneration, there is another 'faith', which for a time may look the same, and yet finally proves never to have been the result of regeneration at all. Examples of this kind of faith are clear enough in the Scriptures, as in *John* 2:23–25, *Acts* 8:13, 21. This is the 'temporary faith' of which Jesus speaks when he speaks of the gospel hearer who 'receives it with joy, yet he has no root in himself, but endures for a while, and when tribulation or persecution arises on account of the word, immediately he falls away' (*Matt.* 13: 20–21). Sometimes the discovery of a non-saving faith is not made until eternity (*Matt.* 7:22; 22:11–14). 'That which has kept many from obtaining Christ, is the conceiving they have had him too soon.'[25]

[23] Giles Firmin, *The Real Christian* (London: Newman, 1670), p. 13.

[24] Quoted by Increase Mather in a Preface to Solomon Stoddard, *A Guide to Christ* (1714). Stoddard's work has been reprinted (Ligonier, PA; Soli Deo Gloria, 1993) but without this Preface.

[25] Thomas Watson, *The Doctrine of Repentance, Useful for these Times* (London, 1668), p. 197. (Reprint, Edinburgh: Banner of Truth, 1987.)

It is for such reasons that the wisest evangelists of the past never regarded *professions* of conversion as a safe guide to the true number. George Whitefield's biographer writes that Whitefield did not pretend to know when persons are justified. 'It is a lesson,' the evangelist said, 'I have not yet learnt. There are so many stony-ground hearers which receive the word with joy, that I have determined to suspend my judgment, till I know the tree by its fruits.' Similarly, when Whitefield heard cases of a sudden change in individuals under his preaching, he would say, 'I shall wait, until we see how the physic works.'[26] Commenting on reported 'results', Spurgeon was to say, 'Lay aside such numberings of the people, such idle pretence of certifying in half a minute that which will need the testing of a lifetime.'[27]

To return then to the question raised above, how is conviction of sin related to regeneration? The answer has to be that there is no *direct* connection. Conviction has to do with the application of truth to the conscience of the unregenerate. Such 'legal conviction' does not in itself dispose men to believe in Christ, still less does it qualify them to receive mercy. I have said that an attempted obedience to the law of God generally attends conviction but such obedience is in no way to be understood as a half-way stage to salvation. Men can have such experience and yet never be saved. 'Remember,' M'Cheyne told his hearers, 'you are not saved because you have a sight of your sins. It is not the awakened sinner that is a saved man.'[28]

Regeneration does not stand *causally* connected with conviction, and it occurs in no uniform way in the experience of those who come to Christ. There is no set pattern, no required duration of conviction, no particular degree of

[26] Robert Philip, *Life and Times of George Whitefield* (London: Virtue, 1838), p. 398.

[27] C. H. Spurgeon, *The Soul-Winner; or, How to Lead Sinners to the Saviour* (London: Passmore & Alabaster, 1895), p. 15.

[28] R. M. M'Cheyne, *A Basket of Fragments* (Aberdeen: King, n.d.), p. 202.

concern that has to be known first. There are wide variations in experience, as the examples of conversion in the New Testament make plain. Sometimes distress and fear are acute. Sometimes men who were to be greatly used as evangelists, such as Thomas Hooker, John Bunyan, George Whitefield and C. H. Spurgeon, experienced prolonged conviction, yet such an eminent preacher as Caesar Malan of Switzerland could say, 'My conversion to the Lord Jesus might, with propriety, be compared to a mother rousing an infant with a kiss.'[29]

If this is so, may it not be argued that any insistence on conviction is wholly needless? No, because, in the words of W. G. T. Shedd, 'The Holy Spirit does not ordinarily regenerate a man until he is a *convicted* man.'[30] Convictions do not save, but it is not going beyond the New Testament to say that salvation does not occur without them. No one was converted without knowing that he needed to be. Regeneration normally occurs when individuals are under conviction, and the presentation of the gospel therefore needs to be in accordance with this fact. The preacher knows that while God may at any time savingly intervene in regeneration, it is when an individual is in conscious need that grace generally interposes.[31]

To know that the turning point in conversion is God's work of regeneration does not mean that there has to be any holding back of gospel truth.[32] Even while the preacher

---

[29] *The Life, Labours, and Writings of Caesar Malan* (London: Nisbet, 1869), pp. 37–8.

[30] Shedd, *Dogmatic Theology,* vol. 2, p. 514.

[31] For helpful treatment of this subject, see Archibald Alexander, *Thoughts on Religious Experience* (1844; reprint, London: Banner of Truth, 1967), pp. 15-20. Before regeneration all repentance and humiliation are only 'legal'; after regeneration they are evangelical, i.e., a response to the believer's union with Christ.

[32] Those who think it must have this result usually overlook the fact that *responsibility* to believe the truth does not depend on *ability* to do so.

makes known the demands of the law, he is also to show that it is by *faith in Christ* alone that those demands can be met. When the illumination that accompanies the new birth occurs, the individual is amazed that he did not see this before. Now the same truths that formerly repelled him are full of appeal. A willingness to leave all for Christ, previously an impossibility, is now his own great desire.

The difference between the natural man and the Christian is indeed a supernatural one. It is only a regenerate person who truly prays, 'O God, deliver me from myself.' The real convert loves God, wants an end to all alienation from him and a full deliverance from the defilement of sin. This is certain because of what regeneration means: 'That which is born of the flesh is flesh, and that which is born of the Spirit is spirit' (*John* 3:6); 'For those who live according to the flesh set their minds on the things of the flesh, but those who live according to the Spirit set their minds on the things of the Spirit' (*Rom.* 8:5). 'For this is the love of God, that we keep his commandments. And his commandments are not burdensome. For everyone who has been born of God overcomes the world' (*1 John* 5:3-4).

The regenerate man loves God, loves holiness, loves the Bible, loves the godly, because it is his nature to do so. He now delights in the law of God written on his heart, and he looks to heaven as the world where he will love with all his being. While the difference between this person and the temporary convert may not immediately appear, it is profound. Of the latter, Joseph Alleine wrote: 'When they have as much as will save them, as they suppose, they look no further, and

---

Inability is the result of the sinfulness for which man himself is responsible. 'The gospel of grace addresses itself to our responsibility in the demand of repentance and faith. . . . The rule for us in every case is the revealed will presented to our consciousness, not his mysterious operations below the level of our consciousness.' John Murray, *Collected Writings* (Edinburgh: Banner of Truth, 1977), vol. 2, p. 199.

so show themselves short of true grace, which always sets men aspiring to perfection (*Phil.* 3:13; *Prov.* 4:18).'[33]

CONCLUSIONS

1. *While authority for the above teaching on the need for conviction of sin has to rest on the Bible, it gains strong confirmation from the evidence of church history.* We think it will be found that in every period where gospel faith has been strong and vigorous the necessity of conviction of sin has been unquestioned by evangelical leaders. Martin Luther regarded its presence or absence as providing a sure means of discriminating between the true and false. When Philip Melanchthon was hesitating over the profession of certain individuals, Luther advised him:

> In order to explore their individual spirit, too, you should inquire whether they have experienced spiritual distress and the divine birth, death and hell. If you should hear that all [their experiences] are pleasant, quiet, devout (as they say), and spiritual, then don't approve them, even if they should say they were caught up to the third heaven. The sign of the Son of Man is missing, which is the only touchstone of Christians and a certain differentiator between the spirits.[34]

Throughout the Reformation and Puritan periods in England this same belief prevailed. The seriousness of sin was confessed in parish churches every Lord's day in the words of the General Confession. Robert Bolton, a leading Puritan preacher, could assert: 'All the men of God and master-builders, who have ever set themselves to serve God in their ministry, and to save souls, have followed the same course; to wit, First, to wound by the Law, and then to heal

---

[33] Joseph Alleine, *An Alarm to the Unconverted* (1671; reprint, London: Banner of Truth, 1967 [retitled *A Sure Guide to Heaven,* 1989]), p. 75.

[34] *Luther's Works,* vol. 48 (Philadelphia: Fortress, 1963), p. 364.

by the Gospel. We must be humbled in the sight of the Lord; before he lift us up.'[35]

In the later seventeenth century, when evangelical religion and spirituality were again in decline, John Owen in 1674 looked back on a time when convicting preaching had marked 'many learned divines and faithful ministers of the gospel'. He continued:

> They had a useful and fruitful ministry in the world, to the converting of many to God. But we have lived to see all these things decried and rejected . . . all conviction, sense of and sorrow for sin; all fear of the curse and wrath due unto sin; all troubles and distresses of mind on account of these things, – are 'foolish imaginations, the effects of bodily distempers, enthusiastic notions, arising from the disorders of men's brains' . . . and the whole doctrine concerning these things is branded as novelty, and hopes expressed of its sudden vanishing out of the world.[36]

But, at the very point when such preaching was 'vanishing out of the world', it suddenly came back with power in the Evangelical Revival. Whitefield observed a new generation of preachers who 'wound deep before they heal, they are careful not to comfort overmuch those who are convicted,' and he concluded, 'I fear I have been too incautious in this respect, and have often given comfort too soon. The Lord pardon me for what is past, and teach me more rightly to divide the word of truth for the future.'[37]

---

[35] *Instructions for the Right Comforting of Afflicted Consciences* (London: Weaver, 1640), p. 135. 'Poor, ignorant souls,' he writes, 'for want of light in God's Law, they look upon their sins, as we do upon the stars in a cloudy night; they see only the great ones of the first magnitude; and here one, and there one: But if they were further enlightened, and informed aright, they might behold them as those infinite ones in the fairest, frosty winter's midnight' (p. 102).   [36] Owen, *Works*, vol. 3, pp.234–5.

[37] L. Tyerman, *Life of George Whitefield* (London: Hodder & Stoughton, 1866), vol. 1, p. 393.

Such convictions were not confined to Calvinists. John Wesley could write:

> I think the right method of preaching is this. At our first beginning in any place, after a general declaration of the love of God to sinners and His willingness that they should be saved, to preach the law in the strongest, the closest, the most searching manner possible; only inter-mixing the gospel here and there, and showing it, as it were, afar off. After more and more persons are con-victed of sin, we may mix more and more of the gospel, in order to beget faith, to raise into spiritual life those whom the law hath slain.[38]

After the revivals that marked the Second Great Awaken-ing in America, in the early nineteenth century, Archibald Alexander wrote in 1844, 'As far as I know, the opinion of the necessity of legal conviction has generally prevailed in all our modern revivals.' It also prevailed in 1859, as already noted, but in the last half of the nineteenth century the need for conviction of sin again began to pass out of sight. 'Revivalism' too often became a means of obtaining 'decis-ions' from individuals who knew no conviction. In 1882 C. H. Spurgeon wrote:

> Sometimes we are inclined to think that a great portion of modern revivalism has been more a curse than a bless-ing, because it has led thousands to a kind of peace before they have known their misery; restoring the prodigal to the Father's house, and never making him say, 'Father, I have sinned.' The old-fashioned sense of sin is despised . . . The consequence is that men leap into religion and then leap out again. Unhumbled they came

---

[38] *Letters of John Wesley*, ed. John Telford, vol. 3 (London: Epworth, 1931), pp. 79–80. Of self-styled 'gospel preachers', who denied this approach, he alleged they 'corrupt their hearers; they vitiate their taste, so that they cannot relish sound doctrine' (p. 84).

into the church, unhumbled they remain in it, and unhumbled they go from it.[39]

Spurgeon's warning was unheeded. Spiritual decline followed. As gospel was preached without law, faith without repentance, and heaven without hell, a careless spirit increased.

In connection with a Home Mission Report of the Methodist Church in 1957, W. E. Sangster said: 'We are appalled at the granite indifference of the artisan masses. The simple truth is that these people feel no need for the goods they think we are offering. We offer in Christ's name forgiveness, and at present they feel no need of it. We talk about peace and joy and they say, "I get along all right".' [40]

Two years later a very different approach was to be read in the first major publication of Martyn Lloyd-Jones, who was then exercising a very different and prophetic ministry in Westminster Chapel, London. In his *Studies in the Sermon on the Mount*, he differed from the whole contemporary scene in insisting, 'The essence of evangelism is to start by preaching the law.'[41]

In the same preacher's later-published series on Romans he was often to demonstrate from that epistle how the meaning of evangelism was being lost:

The business of evangelism is not just to solve people's problems; psychology does that, the cults do that, many things do that. The thing that separates the gospel from every other teaching is that it is primarily a proclamation of God and our relationship to God. Not our particular problems, but the same problem that has come to all of us, that we are condemned sinners before a holy God and a holy law. That is evangelism.[42]

[39] *The Sword and the Trowel* (London: Passmore Alabaster, 1882), p. 545.
[40] Paul Sangster, *Doctor Sangster* (London: Epworth, 1962), pp. 228–9.
[41] *Studies in the Sermon on the Mount*, vol. 1 (London: IVF, 1959), p. 235.
[42] *Romans, Exposition of Chapter 1, The Gospel of God* (Edinburgh: Banner of Truth, 1985), p. 95.

The response to this on the part of many was to say that Dr Lloyd-Jones was not an evangelist and they would not advise young converts to go to Westminster Chapel!

2. *Preaching for conversion, far from being a simple matter, is the most demanding of all responsibilities.* While the gospel minister knows that it is God's work to change hearts, his is the responsibility to present truths of the greatest magnitude. To fail to do so accurately and appropriately may have eternal consequences. The conversion of sinners should therefore be the subject for study. It can never be understood sufficiently. In the words of Thomas Hooker, 'The almighty power of God in the conversion of a sinner is the most mysterious of all the works of God, it shakes the hearts of the ablest divines upon earth.'[43]

Solomon Stoddard, who like Hooker had much experience in this area, wrote: 'Those whose business it is to lead souls to Christ need to furnish themselves with skill and understanding to handle wounded consciences in a right manner . . . There is great variety in the workings of the Spirit, and men that have had to do with many souls in their distresses may afterward meet with such difficulties as may puzzle them very much.'[44]

A first need, therefore, is for more wisdom. Dr Andrew Bonar had carved on his church door in Glasgow, 'He that winneth souls is wise' (*Prov.* 11:30). What is required for preaching the law is much more than an occasional series on the ten commandments. There have been times in the churches when law preaching has been common enough, and yet by an exaggeration of some aspects, or by an unwise understatement of others, little or no good is done. There is a wisdom that is necessary that cannot be learned from books

[43] T. Hooker, *Application of Redemption,* Books, 1–8 (London, 1657), p. 137.

[44] Stoddard, *A Guide to Christ* (reprint, Ligonier, PA: Soli Deo Gloria, 1993), pp. xx–xxi.

or from tradition. Times and situations change. Sometimes a tradition of preaching inherited from an earlier generation, and exemplified by powerful spokesmen, has been continued long after a change of emphasis was needed. Law preaching is especially needed where a nominal belief prevails, and when faith and worldliness walk hand-in-hand. But there have been situations where, under long-continued law preaching, Christians are so disheartened that joy and assurance disappear and a church gives no triumphant testimony to the world. 'A man may be held too long under John the Baptist's water,' Thomas Goodwin once observed, and so may congregations.

The emphasis needed is not invariably the same: always law and always gospel, but there is no uniform proportion to be followed, and when one emphasis becomes a settled tradition – as too often happens – the health of the church and of individuals is bound to suffer. The needs of no two congregations are identical, and, of course, within the same congregation there are often many differences in age and experience. While the danger today does not lie in too much preaching for conviction, yet wisdom is needed to stop us swinging from one extreme to another. Vital though the law is, it is not 'the whole counsel of God'.

But there is a greater problem for preachers than matters of understanding. To preach to hearts and consciences the speaker's own heart needs to be in harmony with his subject. The state of the messenger is little less important than the message, for if the one denies the other who will listen? The men used of God to awaken sinners are men who know something of sleepless nights and of a distressing concern for their hearers. Those who decry the place of fear in preaching to the lost are blind to eternal realities. But to speak severely on such a theme is no less reprehensible. Preachers are to go into their pulpits not to speak harshly but tenderly as fellow-sinners. There is a sympathy of heart, and a holiness of life, without which no good can be expected. As Spurgeon once said: 'Extremely pointed addresses may be delivered by men whose hearts are out of order with the Lord, but their results will be small . . . God connects special success with special states of heart, and if these are lacking he will not do many mighty works.'[45]

Further, while law awakens by directing to the holiness and majesty of God, it is the proclamation of the love of God that must draw the anxious to peace. In the words of William Gurnall, 'Sinners are not pelted into Christ with stones of hard provoking language, but wooed into Christ by heart-melting exhortations.'[46] Or to put a similar thought in more theological language: 'Love is the great attraction. Without the sternness of holiness and justice it would be the love of an unholy and unjust God; yet the holiness and justice of God repel the sinner.'[47]

The preacher faced with such demands can only say, 'Who is sufficient for these things?' (2 Cor. 3:16). No man is, yet 'we have received not the spirit of the world, but the Spirit who is from God' (1 Cor. 2:12). Convicting men and making Christ known is the Spirit's work. It is in prayer and in fellowship with him that God uses others to share in that work. 'We will give ourselves continually to prayer' (Acts 6:4), said the apostolic preachers. They knew that without the Spirit, given in answer to prayer (Luke 11:13), they could do nothing effectual. But by his aid a *reveille* was sounded in corrupt Jerusalem that awakened the thousands. Where the practice of the apostles remains the first priority, preaching will not be in vain. David Brainerd, the man who did so

[45] C. H. Spurgeon, *Lectures to My Students*, Second Series (London: Passmore and Alabaster, 1877), p. 190.

[46] W. Gurnall, *The Christian in Complete Armour* (1662–5; reprint, London: Banner of Truth, 1964), 2 vols in one, vol. 1, p. 507. It was said of Archibald Alexander that he set forth 'a felicitous mixture of doctrine and experience . . . the steel links of reasoning being often red with the ardours of burning love.' J. W. Alexander, *Life of Archibald Alexander* (New York: Scribner, 1854), p. 687.

[47] John Duncan, *The Pulpit and Communion Table*, ed. D. Brown (Edinburgh: Edmonston and Douglas, 1874), p. 47.

much to open the modern missionary era, noted in his diary: 'I longed for the Spirit of preaching to descend and rest upon ministers, that they might address the consciences of men with closeness and power.' And in accordance with these words, Brainerd, shortly before his death, exhorted his brother to 'an earnest endeavour to gain much of the grace of God's Spirit,' telling him: 'When ministers feel these special influences on their hearts, it wonderfully assists them to come at the consciences of men, and as it were to handle them with hands; whereas, without them, whatever reason or oratory we may make use of, we do but make use of stumps instead of hands.'[48]

A recovery of the fear of God, and of the greatness of his displeasure against sin, is the need of our times. The prayer has to be, 'Put them in fear, O LORD! Let the nations know that they are but men' (*Psa.* 9:20). And repeatedly through history God's answer has been to send men in whom his fear was a reality. Thus it was John Bunyan's testimony: 'In my preaching of the Word, I took special notice of this one thing, namely, that the Lord did lead me to begin where his Word begins with sinners . . . this part of my work I fulfilled with great feeling; for the terrors of the law, and guilt for my transgressions, lay heavy on my conscience. I preached what I felt, what I smartingly did feel.'[49] Just so was the eighteenth-century awakening in Wales led by Daniel Rowlands, of whose preaching at the outset his biographer says:

> The substance of his preaching was man's condemnation through sin, and the dreadful consequences of living and dying without a renewal of the heart and reconciliation with God. There was such seriousness, vigour, flaming energy, and melting sympathy in his preaching, that his

---

[48] Edwards, *Works* (Banner of Truth edition), vol. 2, p. 383. See Stoddard on 'Ministers need to have the Spirit of the Lord upon them in order to the reviving of religion among his people.' *Guide to Christ*, p. 72

[49] *Works of Bunyan,* vol. 1, p. 42.

words, like the sharpest arrows, penetrated into the hardest hearts, and produced deepest convictions.[50]

When God anoints such men again there will be awakening, and prayer will again be heard similar to the words with which Calvin concluded a sermon in Geneva:

Now let us cast ourselves down before the majesty of our good God, in acknowledging our faults, and praying him that he will make us in such sort to feel them, that it may be to humble us before him, and for to make us to ask pardon of him, and also for to make us hate ourselves; and pray him that it would please him in such sort to reform us, that we would grow up more and more in all holiness and obedience of his righteousness.[51]

---

[50] John Owen of Thrussington, *Memoir of Daniel Rowlands* (London: Routledge, 1848), p. 81.

[51] *Thirteen Sermons, Election and Reprobation* (reprint, Audubon, N.J.: Old Paths, 1996), p. 281.

ADDITIONAL NOTES

JOHN BROWN OF WAMPHRAY, C. *1610–79*: WHAT PREPARATION IS NOT AND WHAT IT IS

'In some sense, I do not allow of preparatory works, and, in some sense, they are to be admitted. Negatively, I say,

1. There are no such natural abilities in unregenerate persons, which a man can improve, and which, rightly used and improved will certainly prove effectual to the attaining of grace . . .

2. There are no such preparations as have any actual influences to produce the work of grace and conversion in the soul . . .

3. There are no preparatory works that can properly be said to please God . . .

4. Nor do we allow of such preparations as take off any part of the guilt that is lying on the sinner . . .

5. Nor do we grant any such preparations as are any part of the work of conversion, as if such were the beginnings of grace, though they be *gradus ad rem*, steps to the business, yet they are not *gradus in re*, or any beginnings of the work; the digging of the ground is no part of the building, though it prepare for it.

6. Nor do we acknowledge any such so prepared by the law, and humbled in the sense of their sin and guilt, did merit grace at God's hands . . .

8. Nor grant we any such preparatory works as have a promise of grace made unto them, for there is no such promise . . .

9. Nor are there any such preparatory works, as have a certain connection with faith and conversion, as if such, and all such as are so and so preparatorily wrought upon, shall certainly be converted. . . . It is true if we speak of such of whom the Lord is about to bring home in this way, there is a secret unseen connection; but that is not because the preparatory work is of that nature that grace must necessarily follow it.

But yet, on the other hand, we say, speaking of the Lord's bringing home of his chosen ones who are come to age (for as to his children we are strangers thereunto, and cannot understand that) that,

1. A man in nature is not only indisposed, but unwilling to receive Christ and his righteousness. . . .

2. That therefore the Lord must prepare them, and bring them off their quiet rest and sleep in a state of sin and unworthiness, to accept of the gospel way of salvation, by discovering their lost condition by nature. . . .

3. And so we say, that this is God's usual method of bringing home his own, rationally working upon them, causing them to see their own misery, that they may cry for mercy . . .

OBJECTION 1. But cannot God do this without these preparations? I answer, What God may do is needless for us to enquire; it is enough for us to know that thus he doth ordinarily with adult persons . . .

OBJECTION 2. Are not sinners, as sinners, called to accept and lay hold on Christ in the gospel? It is true that Christ is offered to sinners as such. But though the deadest sinner, the proudest Pharisee, the greatest justiciary, or self-righteous legalist, is under obligation to accept of Christ, yet remaining such, will not accept of Christ and his righteousness, but must first be brought off the false selfish ground they now stand upon, and quit grips of their own righteousness.

OBJECTION 3. Can a soul come too soon to Christ? Answer: a soul can never too soon come to Christ, if you speak of time; but a soul can too soon think that they are allowed to lay hold of the comforts of Christ, and so deceive themselves. We can give no allowances to hold back any from coming to Christ that are willing; but only hereby shew what is the Lord's ordinary method, and what must precede a soul's closing with Christ, according to the terms of the gospel . . .

OBJECTION 5. It would seem that one is warranted to believe, because he is so and so humbled and convinced, not before he hath such preparatory works in himself. I answer, to speak properly, seeing necessity giveth not a warrant, but hath the force of a strong motive, to exert and press the soul to seek help and relief.

QUESTION. Doth the Lord take this course with all whom he takes by the heart this way? I answer, we dare not set limits to the Holy One of Israel: for,

1. Some are wrought upon when young, in whom this work cannot much be observed . . .

2. Some of riper age may be brought in without feeling much of the terrors of the law; the Lord thinketh good to deal with them in a sweeter, milder way, overpowering their heart with love, and quickly persuading them.

3. Yet all are, in some competent measure, brought to a conviction of their sin and misery, that they see Christ must help them or they are gone irrecoverably . . . I grant that this work be greater in some than in others; but as to those whom the Lord intendeth to save, whatever method or way he follow, the effect and result is the same: a conviction of the impossibility of life by the law, and a fixed quitting and renouncing of it, and a rational and resolute fleeing unto Christ, and resting in him for life and salvation.'[52]

THOMAS SCOTT, 1747-1821: THE OFFENCE OF THE CROSS CEASING

'Leave out the holy character of God, the holy excellence of his law, the holy condemnation to which transgressors are doomed, the holy loveliness of the Saviour's character, the holy nature of redemption, the holy tendency of Christ's doctrine, and the holy tempers and conduct of all true believers: then dress up a scheme of religion of this unholy sort: represent mankind in a pitiable condition, rather through misfortune than crime: speak much of Christ's bleeding love to them, of his agonies in the garden and on the cross; without showing the need or the nature of satisfaction for sin: speak of his present glory, and of his compassion for poor sinners; of the freeness with which he dispenses pardons; of the privileges which believers enjoy here, and of the happiness and glory reserved for them hereafter: clog this with nothing about regeneration and sanctification, or represent holiness as somewhat else than conformity to the holy character and law of God: and

---

[52] Abbreviated from John Brown, *A Mirror or Looking Glass for Saint and Sinner: The Important Doctrines of the Law and Gospel Opened* (Glasgow: M'Arthur, 1793), pp. 154–64.

you make up a plausible gospel, calculated to humour the pride, soothe the consciences, engage the hearts, and raise the affections of natural men, who love nobody but themselves.'[53]

ALEXANDER WHYTE, 1836-1921: PREACHING TO THE CONSCIENCE

'Spiritual preaching; real face to face, inward, verifiable, experimental, spiritual preaching – that kind of preaching is scarcely ever heard in our day. There is great intellectual ability in the pulpit of our day, great scholarship, great eloquence, and great earnestness, but spiritual preaching, preaching to the spirit – 'wet-eyed' preaching – is a lost art. At the same time, if that living art is for the present overlaid and lost, the literature of a deeper spiritual day abides to us, and our spiritually minded people are not confined to us, they are not dependent upon us. I cannot preach to you as I would like on such subjects, but I can tell you who could, and who, though dead, yet speak by their immortal books . . .

'Rather remain ten years vacant than call a minister that has no conscience. The parish minister of Mansoul sometimes seemed to be all conscience, and it was this that made his head so full of judgment, his tongue so full of brave boldness, and his heart so full of holy love. Your minister may be an anointed bishop, he may be a gowned and hooded doctor, he may be a king's chaplain, he may be the minister of the largest and the richest and the most learned parish in the city, but, unless he strikes terror and pain into your conscience every Sabbath, unless he makes you tremble every Sabbath under the eye and hand of God, he is no true minister to you. As Goodwin says, he is a wooden cannon.'[54]

[53] *Letters and Papers of Thomas Scott*, ed. John Scott (London: Seeley, 1824), pp. 441–2.

[54] Alexander Whyte, *Bunyan Characters, Third Series: The Holy War* (Edinburgh: Oliphant, Anderson & Ferrier, 1902), p. 202, 243. The testimony of Whyte's books entered into the recovery of the reading and publishing of the Puritans fifty years later.

Preaching and Awakening

D. M. LLOYD-JONES, 1899–1981: THE LAW

'It is the law of God alone that really gives us a right conception of the true character and nature of sin. This is a tremendous proposition. The real trouble with the unregenerate is that they do not know and understand the truth about sin. They have their moral code, they believe that certain things are right and certain things are wrong; but that is not to understand sin. The moment a man understands the true nature and character of sin he becomes troubled about his soul and seeks for a Saviour. It is the peculiar function of the law to bring such an understanding to a man's mind and conscience. That is why great evangelical preachers three hundred years ago in the time of the Puritans, and two hundred years ago in the time of Whitefield and others, always engaged in what they called a preliminary "law work". In their preaching of the Gospel they generally started with a presentation of the Law. They knew that a man would not understand salvation unless he understood the nature of sin.'[55]

[55] D. M. Lloyd-Jones, *Exposition of Romans, Chapters 7:1–8:4, The Law: Its Functions and Limits* (Edinburgh: Banner of Truth, 1973), p. 114.

2

SPURGEON AND
TRUE CONVERSION

'How are we to expect the gospel to be kept alive in the world if we do not hand it on to the next generation as the former generation handed it down to us. Oh, shall it ever be said a century hence, "The people of 1880 never thought of us of 1980, they let the gospel go: they allowed the doctrines to be denied one after another"?'

C. H. Spurgeon, *Metropolitan Tabernacle Pulpit,*
vol. 26, 1880, p. 619.

'Very great mistakes have been made about the law. . . . We are not under the law as the method of salvation, but we delight to see the law in the hand of Christ, and desire to obey the Lord in all things.'

'The Perpetuity of the Law of God',
Metropolitan Tabernacle Pulpit, vol. 28, p. 277.

On Sunday morning, January 6, 1850, after a night of snow, Spurgeon as a boy of fifteen went into a Primitive Methodist Chapel in Colchester, and through the message of an unknown preacher came to faith in Christ. 'Young man,' said the preacher pointedly, 'look to Jesus Christ. Look! Look! Look! You have nothin' to do but to look and live.' 'I saw at once,' said Spurgeon, 'the way of salvation.'[1]

Conversion is thus wonderfully simple. Spurgeon summarizes what it means in these words: 'In all true conversions there are points of essential agreement: there must be in all a penitent confession of sin, and a looking to Jesus for forgiveness of it, and there must also be a real change of heart, such as shall affect the entire after life, and where these essential points are not to be found there is no genuine conversion.'[2]

But simple although this sounds, all that is involved is more profound than we can attain to in our present understanding. Spurgeon was to study the subject of conversion, preach on it, and see many converted during forty years, and yet he never got to the bottom of it. Our danger today is to suppose that the truth about conversion is only a preliminary to the Christian faith, something like the two-times table is for mathematics, and therefore that it need not detain our attention for long. If this opinion is doubted, consider the content of the vast number of books now available from Christian publishers. There is a multiplicity of titles on almost all aspects

[1] C. H. Spurgeon, *Autobiography: Vol. 1, The Early Years 1834–1859* (1897–1900; revised ed., Edinburgh: Banner of Truth, 1976), p. 88.

[2] *Metropolitan Tabernacle Pulpit,* vol. 20 (London: Passmore & Alabaster, 1875) p. 398. Hereafter *MTP.*

of Christian belief, and yet few on the biblical teaching of conversion. As far as our contemporary evangelical literature is concerned, what is central in the New Testament has been moved to the periphery, and this reflects a general situation in our churches.

There is in this regard a pattern in church history. At various periods in Christian history the subject of conversion has ceased to be in the foreground of Christian attention, and when that happens the consequence is always the same, convincing evangelistic preaching declines and sometimes almost disappears. An evangelist is a person for whom conversion is of supreme concern. He lives to see conversions. But when the subject ceases to be paramount it ought to be no surprise that evangelistic endeavour falters.

Dr Robertson Nicoll has written of the benefit he once found in being shut up in a Highland manse in Scotland with scarcely any company apart from volumes of Spurgeon's sermons. I am certain that if that could happen to many preachers today it would be greatly to the benefit of the churches. In particular, if we think of what percentage of our preaching is concerned with conversion, and compare it with Spurgeon's percentage, I think the difference would be striking. If our practice was closer to Spurgeon's who can doubt that true conversions would be more common among us. I propose, then, in this address to take up Spurgeon's thought as a stimulus for us on this great issue.

CONVERSION, PROFOUND AND MYSTERIOUS

Because conversion is both a gift and a duty, it has two sides to it, the divine and the human. The human side has to do with our obedience and responsibility: it is referred to in a multitude of texts, such as: 'If you seek him, he will be found by you, but if you forsake him he will forsake you'; 'Repent and be baptized every one of you in the name of Jesus Christ for the forgiveness of your sins'; 'Whosoever shall call on the name of the Lord shall be saved'; 'And this is his commandment, That we should believe on the name of his Son Jesus Christ' (*2 Chron.* 15:2; *Acts* 2:38; *Rom.* 10:13; *1 John* 3:23).

These duties may appear to be simple, and in one respect they are, but the New Testament shows that there is an ever-present danger that people may sincerely suppose they have obeyed these commands when they have not done so. 'Not everyone that says unto me, Lord, Lord, shall enter the kingdom of heaven.' There is a genuine faith, and there is a faith that does *not* save, and the Scriptures do not teach that it is always easy to tell the difference. Even those belonging to the church need the exhortation, 'Examine yourselves, whether you be in the faith' (*2 Cor.* 11:5).

The Scripture also says much on the Godward side of conversion. Man is active in conversion, as many Scriptures prove, but a conversion which is only man's is no conversion at all. Conversion involves a new birth – a new nature, a resurrection from death, the infusion of a new life. Christians are 'born, not of blood, nor of the will of man, but of God'. This is an act of God in which man is passive, not active. 'No man can come unto me, except the Father which hath sent me draw him.' 'It is the Spirit that makes alive, the flesh profits nothing.' 'For by grace are you saved through faith; and that not of yourselves: it is the gift of God' (*John* 1:13; 6:44, 63; *Eph.* 2:8).

The particular word most commonly used to describe the work of God in conversion is 'regeneration'.[3] In speaking of this, Spurgeon says:

[3] While conversion and sanctification are gradual processes, the work of God implanting new life in a sinner is an instantaneous act in which man plays no part. Spurgeon followed Reformed theology in denoting that act as regeneration. See Thomas Goodwin, *Works,* vol. 6 (reprint, Edinburgh: Banner of Truth, 1979), pp. 407–9; John Owen, *Works*, vol. 3, p. 336; or, for wider evidence on usage, Heinrich Heppe, *Reformed Dogmatics*, trans. G. T. Thomson (Grand Rapids: Baker, 1978), p. 519. For full exposition of regeneration, thus understood, see C. Hodge, *Systematic Theology* (London: Nelson, 1873), and W. G. T. Shedd, *Dogmatic Theology*. A recent writer refers to what he calls the 'all-at-once' view of

It is a great mystery. Certainly it is entirely *superhuman*. We cannot contribute to it. Man cannot make himself to be born again. His first birth is not of himself, and his second birth is not one jot more so. It is a work of the Holy Ghost, a work of God. It is a new creation; it is a quickening; it is a miracle from beginning to end.[4]

Mystery although this certainly is, and recognizing that the full comprehension of this subject is beyond us, Scripture nevertheless reveals vital truth about the relationship between the divine and the human in conversion. When that truth is not understood then belief about conversion will necessarily be wrong and the presentation of the gospel adversely affected.

One common and still popular explanation of the relationship between the divine and the human is that the decision of the human will is the occasion for the regenerating work of God to come into operation: 'We believe and so we are born again.' The fallacy of this view lies in its failure to take account of the condition of man in sin. As the result of the Fall, the human heart is at enmity to God and the things of

---

regeneration as 'a novelty': Peter Masters, *Physicians of Souls* (London: Wakeman Trust, 2002), p. 104. Masters instances John Flavel as not holding the 'all-at-once' belief, but Flavel says, 'When the Spirit comes once to quicken the soul, it is done in a moment.' *Works*, vol. 2 (Edinburgh: Banner of Truth, 1968), p. 93. Stephen Charnock likewise say, 'Grace is sown in an instant . . . At the first regeneration there is the forming of all the essential parts of grace, yet afterwards there is a daily augmentation.' *Works of Charnock*, vol. 3 (Banner of Truth, 1986), pp. 143,155. Dr Masters wants to treat regeneration not as an act but as a process in order to leave room for human participation, but to look for participation in the rebirth is to change its meaning. This discussion can, of course, only be settled by the terminology of the New Testament itself, and a helpful starting point can be found in B. B. Warfield, 'On the Biblical Notion of "Renewal" in his *Biblical Doctrines* (1929; reprint, Edinburgh: Banner of Truth, 1988).

[4]*MTP*, vol. 38, p. 271.

God. It knows no attraction to God, and the idea of friendship with God through Jesus Christ is totally without appeal. According to Scripture there are only two types of men. Of the natural man, man in 'the flesh', it is said that he is 'dead in trespasses and sins'.

He must therefore have *a change of nature* before he can repent of what he loves, and before he can believe what he hates. 'For the natural man receives not the things of the Spirit of God: for they are foolishness unto him: neither can he know them, because they are spiritually discerned' (*1 Cor.* 2:14). This being true, repentance and faith have to be understood not as the *cause* of new life but as the actions of one who has been renewed:

> There is one turning point, and one only, which will secure salvation and eternal life; and that is what we call conversion, which is the first apparent result of regeneration, or the new birth. The man being renewed, the current of his life is turned: he is converted.[5]

> To receive Christ, a man must be born of God. It is the simplest thing in all the world, one would think, to open the door of the heart, and let him in; but no man lets Christ into his heart till first God has made him to be born again, born from above.[6]

> What is primary, then, in anyone becoming a Christian is the act of God in regeneration, but regeneration is never without conversion and the latter is a process rather than any single act. There is no need to labour this point.[7]

---

[5] *MTP,* vol. 35, p. 494. 'Regeneration and conversion, the one the secret cause, the other the first overt effect, produce a great change in the character.' *MTP,* vol. 20, p. 401.

[6] *MTP*, vol. 38, p. 274. For full Puritan treatment of regeneration see Charnock's *Works*, vol. 3.

[7] I deal with it more fully in *The Forgotten Spurgeon* (London: Banner of Truth, 1966).

WHERE CONVERSION HAS TO BEGIN

We proceed to the question how understanding regeneration as the work of God affects the presentation of the gospel.

There are false deductions that can be drawn. Some preachers, believing firmly in the divine side of salvation, have given little place to human obligation and duty. They fail to urge their hearers to repentance and faith because they fear it would mislead people into thinking they have the ability to change themselves. This is a serious error and thankfully its advocates are not many today.

But there is another error, perhaps closer to us, and that is of supposing that because conversion depends on God, there is nothing particularly important or effective that can be said to the unconverted, nothing that can bring them nearer the kingdom of God. It is thought that whatever subject we address to the unconverted, it will make no difference until God intervenes and gives regeneration. So, it is deduced, provided our material is scriptural, it matters little what we are preaching on. It may be because of such reasoning, perhaps unconsciously adopted, that a number of preachers today have abandoned what used to be called 'evangelistic preaching'. Instead of what were called 'gospel sermons', they see the work of preaching as simply 'teaching the Bible' in a consecutive manner. They say, 'All the Bible is the sword of the Spirit, and we can leave it to God to use whatever truths he pleases.'

What is wrong with this thinking? It is that, while God keeps the gift of new life in his own hands, he has made it very clear in his Word that those to whom this gift is given are first made aware of their need. There is an order and sequence that God follows. In the words of Jesus, 'I came not to call the righteous but sinners to repentance' (*Mark* 2:17). In other words, he saves the sick, the lost, the prodigal sons who have gone into a far country. He has come for the blind and the captives. Now not all Scripture is equally adapted to reveal to men their real condition. There are particular truths that need to be heard if man's natural high estimate of himself is to be changed. Conviction of sin does not by-pass the mind. A man has to despair of himself before he will think anything of Christ. Once that is understood, the order in which Scripture directs us to address the unconverted is meaningful. 'God the Holy Spirit can convert a soul by any text of Scripture,' says Spurgeon, 'but there are certain Scripture passages, as you know, that are the best to bring before the minds of sinners.'[8]

Among truths *intended* for conviction of sin, Scripture gives first place to the 'law of God': 'Now we know that whatever the law says, it says to those who are under the law, that every mouth may be stopped, and all the world may become guilty before God' (*Rom.* 3:19). 'Where no law is there is no transgression' (*Rom.* 4:15).

If Paul's own conversion is looked at solely in terms of the event on the Damascus Road it might seem to contradict his words just quoted. We might suppose he knew no preparatory work of the law. Yet he expressly affirms it in his own case: 'I had not known sin but by the law . . . I was alive without the law once: but when the commandment came, sin revived, and I died' (*Rom.* 7:7,9). Similarly with Spurgeon's experience. If we took that one Sunday in January 1850 as a complete description of how he became a Christian we would be mistaken, for his testimony included much more:

> My heart was fallow, and covered with weeds; but on a certain day, the Great Husbandman came, and began to plough my soul. Ten black horses were His team, and it was a sharp ploughshare that He used, and the ploughers made deep furrows. The ten commandments were these black horses, and the justice of God, like a ploughshare, tore my spirit. I was condemned, undone, destroyed – lost, helpless, hopeless – I thought hell was before me

[8] *The Soul-Winner*, p. 92.

. . . I prayed but found no answer of peace. It was long with me thus.[9]

Elsewhere he speaks of being under conviction of sin for several years (and that in an upbringing in which he was surrounded with gospel light and exhortation).[10] But the important thing for him was not the length of time, it was the scriptural principle that law is necessary before gospel:

The Christian minister should declare very pointedly *the evil of sin* . . . Open up the spirituality of the law as our Lord did and show how it is broken by evil thoughts, intents and inclinations. By this means many sinners will be pricked in their hearts. Robert Flockhart used to say, 'It is no use trying to sew with the silken thread of the

---

[9] *Autobiography, Vol. 1*, p. 53. Spurgeon gives a whole chapter of his autobiography to this subject, before coming to the account of his conversion. Spurgeon's length of time under conviction has been, by some, blamed on defective teaching and books – particularly Alleine's *Alarm to the Unconverted*, ignoring the fact that Spurgeon could, in later years, write: 'I have to bless God for many good books; I thank him for . . . Alleine's *Alarm to Unconverted Sinners*.' *Autobiography*, vol. 1, p. 86.

[10] 'I had heard of the plan of salvation by the sacrifice of Jesus from my youth up: but I did not know any more about it in my innermost soul than if I had been born and bred a Hottentot.' *Autobiography*, vol. 1, p. 80. Lest what he had suffered under conviction should be regarded as a needless mistake, he tells us: 'A spiritual experience which is thoroughly flavoured with a deep and bitter sense of sin is of great value to him that hath it . . . Possibly much of the flimsy piety of the present day arises from the ease with which men attain to peace and joy in these evangelistic days. We would not judge modern converts, but we certainly prefer that form of spiritual exercise that leads the soul by the way of Weeping-cross, and makes it see its blackness before assuring it is "clean every whit". Too many think lightly of sin, and therefore think lightly of the Saviour.' Ibid., p. 54. But Spurgeon did not think that all Christians should pass through the degree of conviction that he experienced: 'Be thankful that you are spared the ordeal. Those who have to be champions must be trained for war after a sterner sort than those who only make up the rank and file of the army.' *MTP*, vol. 34, p. 251.

gospel unless we pierce a way for it with the sharp needle of the law.' The law goes first like the needle and draws the gospel thread after it.[11]

In the course of his ministry Spurgeon became deeply concerned at the way in which it had come to be thought that evangelism could proceed without any law-work. 'Many preachers of God's gospel have forgotten that the law is the schoolmaster to bring us to Christ . . . We have seen too much of trying to sew without the sharp needle of the Spirit's convicting power.'[12]

How the Law Came to Be Put Aside

Why did this omission of the moral law take place in evangelism?

1. The teaching was rapidly gaining ground that the ethic taught by Christ presents a higher standard than that of the ten commandments. Therefore, it was said, all we need to do is to 'preach Christ'. Accordingly, John 1:17 came to be quoted as though it meant that the gospel is intended to displace the law: 'For the law was given by Moses, but grace and truth came by Jesus Christ.' But the New Testament explicitly denies such an interpretation. It says, not that 'the law *was* holy, just and good,' but that it '*is* holy, just and good' (*Rom.* 7:12). It remains the perfect expression of the character of God, it calls us to be holy as God is holy. Christ presents us with no higher standard, and his whole work of obedience and suffering under the law was in order to raise us to that standard: 'that the righteousness of the law might be fulfilled

---

[11] *MTP,* vol. 20, p. 181.

[12] *MTP*, vol. 17, p. 376. On the basis of one critical reference to some Puritans in an early sermon (*MTP* vol. 9, 1863), some have supposed Spurgeon rejected their understanding of the place of the law in conviction. But explicit statements as well as the whole tenor of his ministry deny any such supposition. For his mature judgment see his sermons on the law in *MTP*, vol. 28, pp. 277–88, and vol. 37, pp. 553–64. 'By lowering the law you weaken its power in the hands of God as a convincer of sin.'

in us' (*Rom.* 8:4). 'Do we make void the law through faith? God forbid: yea, we establish the law' (*Rom.* 3:31).[13]

So to preach the ten commandments is not simply to preach the Old Testament. It is Christ who expounds their full significance (*Mark* 12: 28–31) and at the cross, as nowhere else, the law is magnified. But the law of Old and New Testaments is one. Thus Spurgeon can say:

> Brethren, read the ten commands, and study each separate precept, and you will find in these ten short precepts you have all the moral virtues, the full compass of your accountability to God, and of your relationship to your fellow men. It is a wonderful condensation of morals . . . Perfection is there photographed and holiness is mapped out.[14]

2. But there is another objection to preaching the law. It is said that if we preach the law to the unconverted we are going back to preaching salvation by works, for surely salvation is by Christ's obedience, not our own.

This argument overlooks vital scriptural information on the place of the law. First, the moral law does not come to sinners as something unknown to them. The apostle says of pagan Gentiles that they 'shew the work of the law written in their hearts, their conscience also bearing witness' (*Rom.* 2:15). So even while the unconverted are dead to God, there is a witness within them that authenticates the justice of the obedience that the law of God demands. The law has an ally in the heart of every sinner and preaching has to address that ally – in Paul's words, 'commending ourselves to every man's conscience in the sight of God'(*2 Cor.* 4:2).

---

[13] Confusion has often arisen by the failure to note that the Christian's status as 'dead to the law' (*Gal* 2:19), and his being 'not under law but under grace' (*Rom.* 6:15), refer to Christ ending the law's condemning power. For the forgiven, the law's precepts are all a blessing; it is 'the perfect law of liberty' which, in sanctification, love finds pleasure in fulfilling (*James* 1:25; *Rom.* 13:10). See *MTP,* vol. 28, p. 280.

[14] *MTP,* vol. 20, p. 554.

Scriptural examples ought to settle the point. John the Baptist had not forgotten the message of 'Behold the Lamb of God' when he preached to Herod, 'It is not lawful for you to have your brother's wife' (*Mark* 6:18). Jesus did not go aside from his mission when, after the quotation of the ten commandments, he told a lawyer, 'This do and you will live' (*Luke* 10:28). Paul had not forgotten that he was a gospel preacher when, before Felix, 'he reasoned of righteousness, temperance and judgment to come' (*Acts* 24:25).

Such preaching was not pointless: 'Felix trembled,' and he did so because, as with all men, he had a conscience that is an ally to the truth. He trembled also because the Holy Spirit himself works upon unconverted men, convicting them by the truth. God is said to 'strive with men' (*Gen.* 6:3). For a while the unregenerate may be 'made partakers of the Holy Spirit,' 'taste' the word of God, and feel 'the powers of the world to come' (*Heb.* 6: 4,5), and yet, in the end, harden their hearts and 'resist the Holy Spirit' (*Acts* 7:51). With the preaching of the truth there is this 'common work of the Spirit,' a divine witness that may come to those that are finally lost as well as to those who are saved.

This fact is important for the understanding of temporary conversions. It enables us to see that those who 'receive the word with joy' but afterwards fall away (*Luke* 8:13) are not to be seen as hypocrites, merely acting a part. No, they were temporarily awakened and moved by the power of the truth. Similarly, men may be greatly distressed on account of their sins, and yet never be regenerate. Sometimes whole congregations have been moved under powerful preaching yet time has revealed that many remained unsaved.[15]

---

[15] 'I know of no truth that ever causes me so much pain to preach as this, not that sinners will be damned, awful though the truth of that is, but that *awakened* sinners will be damned unless they believe in Jesus. You must not make a Christ out of your tears, you must not hope to find safety in your bitter thoughts and cruel despair. Unless you believe you will never be established.' Spurgeon, *Advice for Seekers* (reprint, Edinburgh: Banner of Truth, 1993), pp. 37–8.

So grief is no sure sign of conversion, and in words such as the following Spurgeon would warn against thinking that it is: 'A young preacher once remarked, "Were you not greatly struck to see so large a congregation weeping?" "Yes," said his judicious friend, "but I was more struck with the reflection that they would probably have wept more at a play".'[16]

WHY LAW PREACHING?

If men may experience conviction and only a temporary conversion under the preaching of the law, it might be thought that the whole process is needless. After all, the law cannot change the heart. But this reasoning is wrong. Those whom God is bringing to salvation he first humbles by the same truths as are addressed to others. The law dispels their ignorance and shows that God justly requires their obedience: sin is pin-pointed, consciences aroused and self condemned. Now the individual begins to understand that he is really lost, and alienated from God. Let the duties of the law be pressed home on this awakened person and he will try to obey. And when he hears of the duties of repentance and faith he may try to perform them, but it is only to find that sin is stronger than all his endeavours and resolutions.[17]

Why preach the law to the unregenerate? Because it teaches them not what they *can do*, but what they *ought to do*. Far from encouraging salvation by works, it demonstrates the impossibility of rendering the obedience that God requires. It brings home to the non-Christian that he cannot change his own nature, he cannot save himself. It was of conversion that

[16] *The Soul-Winner,* p. 23.

[17] 'The awakened sinner always, at first, struggles resolutely to comply with the terms of the gospel, repentance and faith; but as he proceeds with the effort to save himself, the blindness and hardness prove too much for him, and at last he realizes it is true as the Bible said, he is a helpless sinner.' C. R. Vaughan, *The Gifts of the Holy Spirit, To Unbelievers and Believers* (1894; reprint, Edinburgh: Banner of Truth, 1975), p. 172.

Jesus was speaking when he said, 'With men this is impossible' (*Matt.* 19:26). Spurgeon, far from thinking that the
recognition of this truth discourages evangelism, believed it
to be an important part of it. He told his hearers:

> When I was seeking the Lord, I not only believed that I
> could not pray without divine help, but I felt in my very
> soul that I could not . . . I felt bound, hampered, and
> paralysed. This is a humbling revelation of God's Holy
> Spirit, but a needful one; for the faith of the flesh is not
> the faith of God's elect.[18]

Preaching on the inability of the natural man on another
occasion, he said:

> Now, I think I hear passing through the congregation at
> this moment the whisper of many hearts who are saying,
> 'This is very discouraging. We like to hear "Only
> believe, and you shall be saved".' . . . Would to God we
> could bring you, not only to discouragement, but to
> despair of yourselves. When you shall feel you are pow-
> erless we shall have hope for you, for then you will leave
> yourselves in the hands of him who can do all things.
> When self's strength is gone, God's strength will come
> in . . . I do not want to rouse your activity, you un-
> converted people: I want to rouse you to the conviction
> that you are lost, and I pray God the Holy Spirit may
> convince you.[19]

---

[18] *MTP,* vol. 20, p. 380.

[19] *MTP*, vol. 25, pp. 58-9. This note is not rare in Spurgeon's preaching. See it again, for instance, in his sermon, 'The Necessity of
Regeneration', preached in 1874 and in *MTP,* vol. 54, pp. 585–6. Whitefield, whom Spurgeon early took as a model, spoke similarly: 'We call to
you to believe, on the same account as Jesus said unto the lawyers, "Do
this and thou shalt live;" that you seeing your utter inability to come,
might thereby be convinced of your unbelief, and be led to ask faith of
him whose gift it is.' G. Whitefield, *Sermons on Important Subjects* (London:
William Baynes, 1825), pp. 281–2.

The law, then, is to be preached for conviction, yet it is not conviction but regeneration, introducing a change of nature, that brings 'repentance unto life'.

WHAT IS REGENERATION?

1. *Regeneration is hidden.* We have noted Spurgeon calling it 'a great mystery'. Part of that mystery is the inscrutable manner in which it occurs. It is a work at the inner springs of our being, below the level of our consciousness, a birth in which we do not consciously co-operate. 'The wind blows where it wishes, and you hear the sound of it, but cannot tell where it comes from and where it goes. So is everyone who is born of the Spirit' (*John* 3:8).

Scripture does not teach that Christians know the moment of their rebirth.

> No man can describe his first birth; it remains a mystery. Neither can he describe his new birth; that is a still greater mystery, for it is a secret inward work of the Holy Ghost, of which we feel the effect, but we cannot tell how it is wrought.[20]

> I do not think you can tell, with regard to yourself, when the first gracious thought was sown in you, when first you lived towards God. You can tell when you first perceived that you believed in God; but there was an experience before that. You cannot put your finger on such and such a place and say, 'Here the east wind began,' nor canst thou say, 'Here the Spirit of God began to work in me.'[21]

This truth has an important practical lesson: an individual may have passed from death to life in regeneration and yet not recognize it at first. This explains how a person can be truly 'willing to believe' and yet uncertain if Christ will accept him. To such a person Spurgeon could say, 'If the

[20] *MTP*, vol. 38, p. 362.
[21] *MTP*, vol. 35, p. 56.

power of God has made a man will to believe, the greater work has been done, and his actual believing will follow in due course . . . Rising from the dead is a greater thing than the performance of an act of life.'[22]

Similarly the truth that the saving operation of the Spirit is hidden can be used to help the humbled individual who struggles with doubt. Spurgeon expressed the thoughts of another such a person in the words: 'I feel I must believe, I must trust him; but suppose that trust of mine should not be of the right kind? Suppose it should be a natural trust?' His response was:

> Ah, my friend, a humble trust in Jesus is a thing that never grew in natural ground. For a poor soul to come and trust in Christ is always the fruit of the Spirit . . . 'But,' says one, 'the Spirit must lead me to believe him!' Yes, but you cannot see the Spirit; his work is a secret and a mystery. What you have to do is to believe in Jesus.[23]

2. Regeneration is instantaneous and once-for-all. It may be asked, how can regeneration be asserted to be instantaneous if we are not aware when it takes place? The answer lies in what Scripture teaches about its nature. It is not a gradual moral change but the communication of a new, spiritual and heavenly life. All the New Testament evidence shows that there is no intermediate state between this life and the un-regenerate state, rather, in an instant the old man is dead and the new man lives. Regeneration is an event, not a process. It is the entrance of the resurrection life of Christ (*Col.* 3:1), and parallel to Christ's resurrection in its finality. One moment Jesus was dead in the tomb, another he lives forever. Even so it is with the sinner when Christ comes to live in

---

[22] *Advice for Seekers,* p. 82. This statement depends on a distinction that has to be made between the 'habit' of faith (introduced at regeneration) and the conscious 'exercise' of faith.

[23] *Advice for Seekers*, p. 40.

him (*Gal.* 2:20). Risen with Christ, he is made 'free from sin'. Such is the argument of Romans chapter 6. Suddenly the natural man has become a spiritual man, and is hence-forth indwelt by the Spirit of God. 'It is called a creation. Now creation is necessarily a work which happens in an instant, for either a thing is or is not. There is no intervening space between non-existence and existence.'[24]

That regeneration is unrepeatable follows from its nature.

> Some seem to believe in a new birth once a week. A Methodist once said to me, 'See this man coming down the street? Now he has been born again five times. It is no use his being converted unless he is a teetotaller.' But the Bible knows nothing of such a doctrine. Christians are born again once, but never again and again. We believe in regeneration, but not in *re-re*-regeneration.[25]

3.   *When does regeneration take place?* This is an all-important question. One of the most dangerous errors ever to be made in the churches has been to think men can arrange the time of regeneration. This has been done both in the Roman Catholic tradition that identifies the rebirth with baptism, and in forms of evangelicalism that treat a decision for Christ as necessarily securing a changed heart. But if what has been said above is true, then neither church, evangelist nor convert has control in this matter. The time of rebirth belongs to God. The one thing that is certain is that God brings men low before he raises them up.[26] Before the Prodi-gal Son 'came to himself' and remembered his father's house, he knew something of the pain of being in a far country.

Yet to assert that the law comes before gospel is not to be understood as meaning that conviction of sin makes men 'fit'

[24] *MTP,* vol. 20, p. 404.

[25] W. Williams, *Personal Reminiscences of Charles Haddon Spurgeon* (London: Religious Tract Society, 1895), p. 167.

[26] I am not, of course, excluding the possibility of regeneration in infancy, or in the case of the mentally defective.

to be born of the Spirit, as though regeneration follows conviction as a necessary sequence. There is no *causal* connection
between conviction and rebirth. Nor does conviction have to
reach a certain measure before there can be regeneration.
Some, like Spurgeon, may know conviction for a long time,
before the great change comes; others may know little of
strong conviction and yet pass quickly from death to life.
There is no stereotype pattern. God deals with each of us
personally and no two conversions are identical.[27] The common factor is that all true converts are penitent. Conviction
does not save anyone but no one is saved without conviction.

It is also essential to assert that the experience of conviction does not provide the warrant for believing. The sinner is
not first to look within to be sure God is speaking to him.
The warrant lies wholly in the promises and invitations of the
gospel. As has been rightly said, *the way* to faith is not the
same as the warrant for faith.

4. *Regeneration is known by its effects.* Here the Scripture
shows us that there is a definite pattern. The two invariable
effects of the new birth are repentance and faith. A person
born of the Spirit has a different view of sin and a different
view of Christ.[28]

A person may 'repent' of sin while they are still unregenerate, but it is not evangelical repentance. It is only sorrow for
the consequences of sin, for its shame and unhappiness, while
a true love for God, and a change of nature are still absent. It
is 'the sorrow of the world' that 'works death' (*2 Cor.* 10).
Likewise a person may 'believe' while still unregenerate, that

---

[27] Therefore it is foolish, Spurgeon points out, for anyone to read
Christian biography and to conclude that a true conversion experience
must match what they read in others.

[28] 'The character of God, instead of appearing offensive, begins to
reveal its intrinsic beauty. The law of God, instead of appearing harsh,
overstrained, an object of disgust and terror, begins to appear as the ven-
erable bond of all justice, wisdom, and goodness.' Vaughan, *Gifts of the
Spirit*, p. 183.

is to say, give their assent to the truth, yet there is no surrender of the whole life to Christ and holiness.[29] The saving repentance and saving faith of a regenerate person are very different things. Now there is grief for having offended a loving and gracious God. Now sin *as such* is hated and condemned. Now faith in Christ involves a supreme attraction to his Person, a trust in him alone, and a commitment of the whole life to him.

Spurgeon believed that this was the invariable scriptural pattern. 'In regeneration it is the Spirit who begins by infusing the life, and then the new nature begins to pray and repent.'[30] Nevertheless, he knew that there is much variation within the pattern. The speed with which the effects of the new birth show themselves are not the same in all. For some conversion may appear a sudden thing, for others the consciousness of change is much more gradual. In the words of John Duncan, 'I believe that the act of "renewal" is instantaneous; but there is a power as well as an act, and in its development to the observation of others, or even to a man's own consciousness, it may be slowly progressive.'[31]

[29] 'Men labour to fortify their actual persuasion of the mercies of Christ before the carnal life be renounced. It is a mistake to look to faith first, and the settling our particular assurance, as if that were the difficultest thing in religion. The great difficulty lies in self-denial. As Christ put the young man in *Matt.* 19:26 upon the trial, Canst thou leave all and follow me? so we are to put ourselves upon the trial, otherwise our application to God's mercy, and settling our particular persuasion, will be but a rash confidence.' *Works of Thomas Manton*, vol. 15 (London: Nisbet, 1873), pp. 192–3.

[30] *MTP*, vol. 25, p. 53.

[31] *'Just a Talker': Sayings of John Duncan*, p. 214. Older writers made the same point: '*Repentance is a gradual thing in working*. Though the habitual implantation of it be instantaneous (for it is a grace infused, and therefore admits not of space or leisure), yet the actual operation of it is successive and by degrees.' Obadiah Sedgwick, *The Parable of the Prodigal* (London: Gellibrand, 1660), p. 88. The same is true of faith. As a 'habit', faith's origin is instantaneous in regeneration, although its exercise is gradual and marked by degrees of strength and weakness.

Again, in the conversion experience of some, at first what they are most aware of is their repentance, with others it is the reality of faith. This has sometimes led to discussion about which comes first, repentance or faith.

For Spurgeon the question is needless, because the new life necessarily contains both – like the spokes on a wheel, they move at the same time. Yet this is not always apparent to the individual who is converted. An individual may be so downcast in true repentance that he is not even conscious that he has faith. Spurgeon, preaching on saving repentance, can tell his hearers:

> *Repentance is the result of an unperceived faith.* When a man repents of sin he does inwardly believe, in a measure, although he may not think so. There is such a thing as latent faith: although it yields a man no conscious comfort, it may be doing something even better for him; for it may be working in him truthfulness of heart, purity of spirit, and abhorrence of evil. No true repentance is quite apart from faith . . . It is clear that no man can repent towards God unless he believes in God. He could never feel grief at having offended God, if he did not believe that God is good. To the dark cloud of repentance there is a silver lining of faith; yet at first, the awakened soul does not know this, and therefore laments that he cannot believe; whereas his very repentance is grounded on a measure of faith.[32]

But Spurgeon is equally clear in saying that this experience is not universal in true converts. For some their faith in Christ is so real that they seem to be immediately lifted up rather than remaining cast down. Joy predominates over sorrow. Yet he is careful to insist that if this faith is real – the result of new divine life – it will always be accompanied by humility. 'I will not believe in that faith which has no repentance with it, any more than I would believe in that

[32] *MTP,* vol. 35, p.130.

repentance which left a man without faith in Jesus.'[33] Real faith in Christ is always accompanied by a sense of personal unworthiness. Joy that lacks that element is only presumption.[34]

> No man, rest assured, ever found peace with God without first repenting of sin, and knowing it to be an evil thing . . . True conversion always has in it a humbling sense of divine grace.[35]

> I am still a believer in the old-fashioned type of conversion . . . I think I have seldom seen a conversion turn out well that had not the foundations of it laid in some measure of abhorrence of sin, and loathing of self.[36]

PREACHING FOR CONVERSION

If a change of heart, beyond the powers of man, is necessary for there to be repentance and faith, how can these duties be pressed upon individuals as the way of salvation?

This question is in essence the same as the objection which says that human responsibility cannot be upheld if divine grace is made the cause of conversion. The answer of Scripture is not to give us a full explanation of the relationship between responsibility and the work of God; it is rather to insist that faith and repentance are to be presented to men as the *only way* to salvation. 'Be converted,' is a command. Man is active in conversion. In the words of John Murray:

---

[33] *MTP*, vol. 35, p.131. As C. R. Vaughan points out, faith is the opposite of self-sufficiency: 'It appeals to a power outside of itself, and thus confesses its own weakness. It appeals to the righteousness of Christ, and thus confesses the want of it in itself. It appeals for all things to an outward source, and thus confesses its own barrenness.' *Gifts of the Spirit,* p. 127. In this way the words are true, 'It is of faith, that it might be of grace' (*Rom.* 4:16).

[34] 'He who is a merry penitent, proves an easy delinquent; if former sinning be no grief, future sinning will be no fear.' Sedgwick, *Prodigal*, p. 44.

[35] *MTP*, vol. 20, p. 406.   [36] *MTP*, vol. 54, p. 586.

The fact that regeneration is the prerequisite of faith in no way relieves us of the responsibility to believe nor does it eliminate the priceless privilege that is ours as Christ and his claims are pressed upon us in full and free overtures of his grace. Our inability is no excuse for our unbelief nor does it provide us with any reason for not believing.[37]

The inscrutable operations of God are not the rule of our conduct nor the grounds of our action.[38]

There is nothing in this standpoint, rightly understood, that militates against a full and persuasive preaching of the gospel. Spurgeon could say, 'There is not a sinner in the world who is to be told that he may not come to Jesus, and receive the whole of the blessings of the gospel.'[39] Nothing in his theology prevented him calling upon sinners to cast themselves in the Saviour's arms, and saying, 'The moment a sinner does that he is born of God.' He did not preach regeneration as a gospel *duty*, for it lies outside the sphere of human obligation (just as election lies outside that sphere), yet he ever insisted that faith in Christ *is* the sinner's duty – faith that 'comes by hearing, and hearing by the word of God' (*Rom.* 10:17). The gospel message is therefore essential to the response of faith, and faith is the instrumental cause of salvation. Yet behind saving faith there is ever *the capacity* to believe that is the result of a God-given change of nature: 'By grace are you saved through faith, and that not of yourselves, it is the gift of God' (*Eph.* 2:8). While from the divine side,

---

[37] John Murray, *Redemption – Accomplished and Applied* (1955; reprint, London: Banner of Truth, 1961), p. 113. Yet Professor Murray's teaching in this book is criticized by Peter Masters on the grounds that it 'destroys at a stroke the kind of persuasive evangelism which we seek to defend.' *Physicians of Souls*, p. 107.

[38] John Murray, *Collected Writings*, vol. 2 (Edinburgh: Banner of Truth, 1977), p. 199.

[39] 'Preaching to Sinners,' in *Only a Prayer Meeting* (London: Passmore and Alabaster, 1901), p. 303.

regeneration may therefore be said to be the turning-point from death to life, from the standpoint of human conscious-ness it is the exercise of repentance and faith. The two sides have to be understood as components of *one* salvation. In the words of B. B. Warfield:

> At the root of all lies an act seen by God alone, and mediated by nothing, a direct creative act of the Spirit, the new birth. This new birth pushes itself into man's own consciousness through the call of the Word, res-ponded to under the persuasive movements of the Spirit; his conscious possession of it is thus mediated by the Word. It becomes visible to his fellow-men only in a turning to God in external obedience.[40]

Some argue that there must be an artificiality in the preacher urging repentance and faith unless the word spoken is somehow able to *effect* in hearers an ability to obey. They therefore want to say that it is the truth *spoken* that gives the ability to respond. But while the truth spoken is essential to faith, it is not the truth *of itself* that is saving, no matter how earnestly it is presented. The effectiveness of the presentation of Christ depends on the existence of an inward call [regen-eration] that man cannot give. All who are thus 'called' believe (*Acts* 13:48; *Rom.* 8:30). To say this is no disincentive to earnest preaching. There are truths necessary to be believed in order to salvation; our business is to make them known, while possessed with the confidence that it is God who gives the grace necessary to faith. Confidence placed anywhere else is not the confidence of the New Testament preacher.

For Spurgeon there was no way at all in which the neces-sity of the supernatural intervention of God lessens the urgency of human instrumentality. The work of the Spirit in regeneration, he writes, 'might seem at first sight to put human instrumentality altogether out of the field; but on

[40] B. B. Warfield, *Biblical Doctrines,* p. 457.

turning to Scripture we find nothing to justify such an inference.'[41] In speaking to pastors and students for the ministry
he never failed to press this point:

> Impressed with a sense of their danger, give the ungodly
> no rest in their sins; knock again and again at the door
> of their hearts, and knock as for life and death. Your
> solicitude, your earnestness, your anxiety, your travailing
> in birth for them God will bless to their arousing. God
> works mightily by this instrumentality. But our agony
> of soul must be real and not feigned, and therefore our
> hearts must be brought into true sympathy with God.
> Low piety means low spiritual power.[42]

Given such words as the above, some Southern Baptists
today are incredulous at the statement that Spurgeon never
added to his preaching an 'appeal' or 'altar call' for an immediate *public* decision on the part of individuals who wished to
become Christians. Why he did not do so should be clear
from what he believed on regeneration. He did not regard
the practice as an evangelistic aid, but rather as calculated to
confuse the meaning of conversion. He knew that receiving
Christ is never without a change of nature (regeneration) and
such a change cannot be effected by any *physical* action such
as asking a person to come to the front. 'You must never divide the renewing of the Holy Ghost from the pardon of sin
. . . The work of regeneration and the act of faith which
brings justification to the sinner are simultaneous, and must
in the nature of the case always be so.'[43] If it be said that the
purpose of the public invitation is only to allow individuals to
confess that they *have* received Christ, that is to concede that
it is no part of *becoming* a Christian and it should not be
treated as though it were. The public witness that marks a
Christian is better in another context. The 'public decision' as

---

[41] *The Soul-Winner*, p. 25.
[42] *Lectures to My Students*, second series, pp. 189–90.
[43] *MTP*, vol. 37, p. 561.

a means to number converts Spurgeon regarded as utterly untrustworthy.[44]

CONCLUSIONS

1. *This subject surely shows how the right preaching of the gospel is the most demanding of all duties.* Not one truth but many are bound up with a right understanding of conversion. Law and gospel, inability and responsibility, must all be present. If any one truth is exaggerated, being emphasized for too long while other truth is ignored or neglected, then lives will suffer. All the relevant truths have to be presented in scriptural proportion, and with an appreciation of the particular condition of those to whom we speak. Sometimes it is the indifference or the presumption of listeners that most needs to be addressed, at other times it may be the freeness of the gospel to those labouring under their unworthiness.

---

[44] 'Some of the most glaring sinners known to me were once members of a church; and were, as I believe, led to make a profession by undue pressure. . . . I am weary of this public bragging, this counting of unhatched chickens, this exhibition of doubtful spoils.' *The Soul-Winner,* p. 15. Further on this subject, see D. M. Lloyd-Jones, *Preaching and Preachers* (London: Hodder and Stoughton, 1971), 'Calling for Decisions', pp. 265–82. On the basis of one statement, it is alleged that Spurgeon did encourage the altar call, but the claim clearly rests on a misinterpretation of the words. It was reported (*Sword and the Trowel*,1865, p. 70): 'Spurgeon earnestly exhorted those who had accepted Christ as their Saviour to come forward amongst his people.' This refers not to walking the aisle but to those who were already believers and not yet committed to churches.

It has also been argued that the reason Spurgeon did not give a 'public appeal' was that the architecture of the Metropolitan Tabernacle 'did not lend itself to hundreds coming forward to an invitation to receive Christ'. But it was Spurgeon principally who determined the shape of his building, not to speak of the multitudes of other places where he preached, including the open-air, where no such appeal was ever given! Dealing with enquirers was a different matter, which he encouraged, although he opposed making the 'enquiry room' an integral part of evangelism.

Repentance has ever to be preached and Spurgeon at times urged it so strongly that he could say 'Are you willing to give sin up? If not, it is all lost time to preach Christ to you.' [45] Yet he never ceased to present Christ as the Saviour ready to receive all who will come to him. He would not hesitate to say, 'Jesus is yours now if you will have him.'[46] He never erred in supposing that the promises and invitations of Christ are to be held back until there is some personal evidence of conviction. Faith is the immediate duty of all and it was at the very heart of his preaching to urge that the way to life and peace lies solely in believing.

In some sermons, as we have seen, Spurgeon made clear the relationship between regeneration and faith, while in others he did not. He knew that inquirers do not need to be theologians. He was often content to say that faith 'occurs at the same time as the new birth.' What he ever regarded as supremely important was that no truth should ever be preached harshly. He counselled students for the ministry: 'More flies are caught with honey than with vinegar. Preach much on the love of God.'[47]

Spurgeon's example surely gives us one of the best guides to true evangelistic preaching in the English language.

2. *When a wrong model of conversion becomes widely adopted the implications are vast and tragic.* In the later nineteenth century the idea became very popular among preachers that if conversion could be 'simplified' into a once-done act, performed at a given point by any person, then evangelism would be more successful. 'Success' came to displace every other priority. Spurgeon, and a few others, were in a minority in warning that the gospel wrongly presented was doing injury and could bring calamity to the churches.

[45] *Advice for Seekers*, p. 42.

[46] *Cheque Book of the Bank of Faith* (Fearn, Ross-shire: Christian Focus, 1996), entry for Jan. 23.

[47] Williams, *Personal Reminiscences*, p. 172.

In particular, what he came to miss in the wider evangelical scene was the absence of conviction of sin and of the fear of God. What the Bible calls 'the beginning of wisdom' (*Psa.* 111:10; *Prov.* 1:7) was disappearing in the churches, and with this came a loss of reverence and awe. The description of Christians as 'God-fearing people' passed out of fashion. Happiness, not fear, was the one theme, but Spurgeon argued that the two are not to be separated. The happy Christian

> feels a jealous fear of doing wrong. Holy fear looks not only before it leaps, but even before it moves. It is afraid of error, afraid of neglecting duty, afraid of committing sin. It fears ill company, loose talk, and questionable policy. This does not make a man wretched, but it brings him happiness.[48]

Spurgeon had no doubt that superficial evangelism was a major contributing cause for the absence of converts of this type. Far too many 'results' were impermanent:

> We have had plenty of revivals of the human sort, and their results have been sadly disappointing. Under excitement nominal converts have been multiplied: but where are they after a little testing? I am sadly compelled to own, so far as I can observe, there has been much sown, and very little reaped that was worth reaping. Our hopes were a flattering dream; but the apparent result has vanished like a vision of the night. But where the Spirit of God is really at work the converts stand.'[49]

> The Holy Ghost is come to convince of sin. It is absolutely necessary that men should be convinced of sin. The fashionable theology is – 'Convince men of the goodness of God: show them the universal fatherhood and assure them of unlimited mercy. Win them by God's love, but never mention his wrath against sin, or the

[48] *Cheque Book of the Bank of Faith*, entry for Sept. 9.
[49] *MTP*, vol. 27, p. 531.

need of an atonement, or the possibility of there being a place of punishment. Do not censure poor creatures for their failings. Do not judge and condemn. Do not search the heart or lead men to be low-spirited and sorrowful. Comfort and encourage, but never accuse and threaten. Yes, that is the way of man; but the way of the Spirit is very different. He comes on purpose to convince of sin, to make men feel that they are guilty, greatly guilty – so guilty that they are lost, ruined and undone. He comes to make sin appear sin, and to let us see its fearful consequences. He comes to wound so that no human balm can heal; to kill so that no earthly power can make us live. What is it that makes the beauty and excellence of human righteousness to wither as the green herb? Isaiah says it is 'because the Spirit of the Lord bloweth upon it'. There is a withering work of the Holy Spirit which we must experience, or we shall never know his quickening and restoring power. This withering is a most needful experience, and just now needs much to be insisted on. Today we have so many built up who were never pulled down; so many filled who were never emptied; so many exalted who were never humbled; that I the more earnestly remind you that the Holy Ghost must convince us of sin, or we cannot be saved.

This work is most necessary, because without it there is no leading men to receive the gospel of the grace of God. We cannot make any headway with certain people because they profess faith very readily, but they are not convinced of anything. 'Oh, yes, we are sinners, no doubt, and Christ died for sinners': that is the free-and-easy way with which they handle heavenly mysteries, as if they were the nonsense verses of a boy's exercise, or the stories of Mother Goose. This is all mockery, and we are weary of it. But get near a real sinner, and you have found a man you can deal with: I mean the man who is

a sinner, and no mistake, and mourns in his inmost soul
that he is so. In such a man you will find one who will
welcome the gospel, welcome grace, and welcome a
Saviour.[50]

There is urgent need today for the recovery of the truth
about conversion. A widespread controversy on this subject
would be a healthy wind to blow away a thousand lesser
things. A renewed fear of God would end much worldly
thinking and silence a multitude of raucous services. There
has been much talk of more evangelism, and many hopes of
revival, but Spurgeon would teach us that the need is to go
back to first things.

[50] *MTP*, vol. 29, pp. 125–6.

ADDITIONAL NOTES

D. M. LLOYD-JONES, 1899–1981:
EVANGELISM AND CONVICTION OF SIN

'There is no true evangelism without the doctrine of sin, and without an understanding of what sin is. I do not want to be unfair, but I say that a gospel which merely says "Come to Jesus", and offers Him as a Friend, and offers a marvellous new life, without convicting of sin, is not New Testament evangelism. The essence of evangelism is to start by preaching the law; and it is because the law has not been preached that we have so much superficial evangelism . . . evangelism must start with the holiness of God, the sinfulness of man and the eternal consequences of evil and wrong-doing. It is only the man who has been brought to see his guilt in this way who flies to Christ for deliverance and redemption.'[51]

'[False teaching] does not emphasize repentance in any real sense. It has a very wide gate leading to salvation and a very broad way leading to heaven. You need not feel much of your sinfulness; you need not be aware of the blackness of your own heart. You just "decide for Christ" and you rush in with the crowd, and your name is put down, and is one of the large number of "decisions" reported by the press. It is entirely unlike the evangelism of the Puritans and of John Wesley, George Whitefield and others, which led men to be terrified of the judgment of God, and to have an agony of soul sometimes for days and weeks and months.'[51]

[51] D. M. Lloyd-Jones, *Studies in the Sermon on the Mount*, vol. 1 (London: IVF, 1959), p. 235.
[51] D. M. Lloyd-Jones, *Studies in the Sermon on the Mount*, vol. 2 (London: IVF, 1960), p. 247. These two volumes remain among the most significant books to have been published in the twentieth or indeed any century.

A. W. TOZER, 1897–1963:
'CONVERSION' WITHOUT REGENERATION

'The doctrine of justification by faith – a biblical truth, and a blessed relief from the sterile legalism and unavailing self-effort – has in our time fallen into evil company and been interpreted by many in such a manner as actually to bar men and women from the knowledge of God.

'The whole transaction of religious conversion has been made mechanical and spiritless. Faith may now be exercised without a jar to the moral life and without embarrassment to the Adamic ego. Christ may be "received" without creating any special love for him in the soul of the receiver. The man is "saved" but he is not hungry or thirsty after God!'[52]

---

[52] A. W. Tozer, *Renewed Day by Day: A Daily Devotional* (Camp Hill, PA: Christian Publications, 1980), entry for Dec. 12.

3

'CHRIST OUR RIGHTEOUSNESS'
– GOD'S WAY OF SALVATION

'The Lord our Righteousness'
(*Jehovah Tsidkenu*)

I ONCE was a stranger to grace and to God,
I knew not my danger, and felt not my load;
Though friends spoke in rapture of Christ on the tree,
Jehovah Tsidkenu was nothing to me.

When free grace awoke me, by light from on high,
Then legal fears shook me, I trembled to die;
No refuge, no safety in self could I see –
Jehovah Tsidkenu my Saviour must be.

My terrors all vanished before the sweet name;
My guilty fears banished, with boldness I came
To drink at the fountain, life-giving and free –
Jehovah Tsidkenu is all things to me.

Even treading the valley, the shadow of death,
This 'watchword' shall rally my faltering breath;
For when from life's fever my God sets me free,
Jehovah Tsidkenu my death-song shall be.

ROBERT MURRAY M'CHEYNE

Memoir and Remains of R. M. M'Cheyne,
Andrew Bonar (1892; reprint, London:
Banner of Truth, 1966), pp. 632–3.

About a hundred years ago Alexander Whyte, as a pastor in Edinburgh, visited one of his elders who was dying. A book was close to the man's hand and, recognizing that it was not the Bible, Whyte looked on the open page to see what it might be. There his eyes fell on the words, 'Chapter 11 – Of Justification':

> Those whom God effectually calleth he also freely justifieth; not by infusing righteousness into them, but by pardoning their sins, and by accounting and accepting their persons as righteous; not for anything wrought in them, or done by them, but for Christ's sake alone; not by imputing faith itself, to them as their righteousness; but by imputing the obedience and satisfaction of Christ unto them, they receiving and resting on him and his righteousness by faith; which faith they have not of themselves, it is the gift of God.

We too will die, and when that day comes there will be no truth we shall value more than the doctrine thus stated in the *Westminster Confession of Faith*. We know what it meant to David Sandeman, a Scottish missionary who ended his work in China at the age of thirty-two. As he lay dying in the midst of an epidemic of cholera, a friend asked how he was. He answered, 'I am head-to-foot righteousness.' Our responsibility is both to be able to say that of ourselves and so to aid our hearers that they will bear the same testimony.

THE IMPORTANCE OF THE DOCTRINE

1. It is the truth of imputed righteousness that shows how *all religions can be classified in only two groups*. There are only

two systems of belief. The Jews, who rejected Christ, are the permanent representatives of one. Their position is characterized by the Apostle Paul in the words, 'seeking to establish their own righteousness' (*Rom.*10:3). That is to say, they looked for acceptance with God on the basis of their own personal lives and characters. They answered the question, 'How can men be right with God?' by saying, 'It is by what we do and by what we are.' In contrast with that belief, the New Testament represents the Christian way of entrance into God's favour as having no dependence at all on man's doing. Our acceptance with God, it teaches, is not by any moral or religious efforts of our own; it is due solely to 'the righteousness of God' – that is to say, righteousness provided by God, 'the gift of righteousness' (*Rom.* 5:17) – righteousness not performed by us but received freely from God through faith in Jesus Christ. What makes these two classifications of belief so significant is that there is no other alternative. There is no third system.

Unbelieving Judaism had fallen into the type of belief which marks all the religions ever invented by fallen men.[1] In varying degrees every form of false religion places its emphasis on man's actions and on the duties or ceremonies he may perform. Christianity alone effectively denies any acceptance with God on the basis of our works. It teaches that men can never be saved from condemnation by what they are or by what they do. The gospel is that sinners have peace with God

---

[1] In the words of Stephen Charnock, 'It is the disease of human nature, since its corruption, to hope for eternal life by the tenor of the covenant of works . . . The heathens thought God should treat men according to the merit of their services, and it is no wonder that they should have this sentiment, when the Jews, educated by God in a wiser school, were wedded to that notion.' *Works*, vol. 2 (Edinburgh: Nichol, 1864), p. 32. It has been argued in recent times that Protestant expositors have all erred in supposing that the Jews of the first century held to a 'salvation by works' religion. But the evidence in the New Testament itself is surely clear (*Matt.* 19:16–20; *Luke* 18:9–14; *John* 6:28 etc.) and it is with that evidence that Paul's polemic against Judaism concurs.

only when they have received Christ's righteousness, which is the same as saying when they have 'submitted themselves unto the righteousness of God' (*Rom*.10:3). So although the world in the time of the apostles was full of all kinds of religious ideas, just as the world is in our times, the truth is that men and women are faced with only two real alternatives: they will act either according to what Paul calls 'the righteousness of the law', or they will depend on 'the righteousness which is of faith' (*Rom*.10:5–6).

This brings us to a second reason why this doctrine is so critically important.

2. One of the most prevalent ideas today in what professes to be Christianity is that *salvation does not rest on matters of belief.* Questions and controversies over creeds and beliefs are said to be matters of opinion and very secondary things. It is supposed that all differences are to be tolerated because in the end it is only our conduct that will count with God. If men and women do their best to live upright lives, and if they are sincere in their religious practice, we must surely believe that they will be accepted. To divide people in terms of differences of belief is therefore commonly regarded as the worst form of prejudice and bigotry. The problem with this outlook is that, if Christianity is to be decided by Scripture, then this is not Christianity at all.

According to the New Testament the Jewish people who did not believe the Christian revelation were outside the kingdom of God, and were under God's condemnation despite their high moral aspirations. On this point nothing could be more plain than the history of Saul of Tarsus. In external righteousness Saul, the Jew *par excellence,* was 'blameless' (*Phil.* 3:6), yet he remained an enemy of God. Of his fellow kinsmen, the converted Saul does not hesitate to say that they 'followed after the law of righteousness' (*Rom.* 9:31); more than that, they had 'a zeal for God' (*Rom.* 10:2). The Jewish religion in the apostolic era was a matter of earnest and sincere practice and yet they knew not God. In anguish of heart Paul wrote: 'Brethren, my heart's desire and prayer to God for Israel is, that they might be saved' (10:1). In not 'submitting themselves unto the righteousness of God', the Jews gave proof that they were lost.

The testimony of Scripture is that where there is no faith in Christ and his righteousness there is no salvation. There is no other way to everlasting life. 'No one comes to the Father but through me' (*John* 14:6). So here is a clarifying principle. In a world of multiple faiths only one is true. And all the remainder, whatever form they take, are owned by people who are 'seeking to establish their own righteousness'. The one alternative is faith in 'the righteousness of God'. Here then are two systems of belief which are directly and permanently opposed. They can never be adjusted or accommodated to each other. As has been said, salvation by faith is self-renouncing, salvation by works is self-congratulatory. To believe the one is necessarily to contradict the other.

ALL MANKIND IN DARKNESS

Coming directly to our subject, let us, in the first place, *consider why all men by nature are blind to salvation through faith in Christ's righteousness.* The reason is that the Fall has put men in a position where they depend upon themselves, and therefore they will ever choose to seek acceptance with God by their own actions. This is as true of humanity today as it was of the Jews of the first century, men will not submit themselves to the righteousness of God. The religion of the natural man is always a religion of self-righteousness.

The reason why people can remain satisfied with this religion is also the same today as it was in the first century. It is because they are ignorant of God. 'You know neither me nor my Father,' Jesus said to the Jews (*John* 8:19). Here is a spiritual darkness concerning God which affects Jew and Gentile alike: 'There is no one who understands; there is no one who seeks after God' (*Rom.* 3:11). It was not so at man's first creation. God made man perfect and in his own likeness.

At the creation the very character of God was imprinted on man's own nature and life. 'God is light and in him is no darkness at all' (*1 John* 1:5), and man was at home in the purity of that light. But it was revealed to man in the Garden of Eden that the preservation of his happiness depended upon his obedience to the holy law of God that was written upon his heart. The requirements of that law were no burden to sinless man and obedience would have confirmed him in the favour and presence of God forever. This is what Scripture means when it says that the law was 'ordained to life' – life was the promise it carried with it (*Rom.* 7:10); the law is 'holy, just and good'.

Speaking of the blessing which the law was originally able to secure, Paul writes in Romans 10:5, 'Moses writes about the righteousness which is of the law, "The man who does those things shall live by them."' When Adam sinned, his position and that of his posterity was entirely changed. God continued to require perfect obedience. Man was still obligated to the holiness that God demands in thought, word and deed, but man is no longer in the light. His knowledge and fellowship with God are gone. He has lost the very conception of the divine purity he once knew, and his moral nature is so changed that now he loves darkness rather than light (*John* 3:19).

This ignorance of God which is the universal characteristic of fallen man shows itself in two ways: First, in his darkness man now supposes that he can satisfy God with something less than perfect obedience. In his low views of God, he hopes that the debt he owes is small enough for him to repay it himself. No longer knowing the infinite holiness of God, he is blind to the magnitude of the spiritual obedience for which he is responsible. But God has not changed the standard first given to man before his fall: 'You shall love the Lord your God with all your heart and with all your soul and with all your strength and with all your mind, and your neighbour as yourself' (*Luke* 10:27).

It was to deliver a man from the delusion of seeking acceptance with God by his own efforts that Jesus said, 'If you want to enter into life, keep the commandments' (*Matt.* 19:17). When that is attempted in sincerity it must lead to self-despair, for the obedience required is not in our power to perform. Paul's testimony was, 'When the commandment came, sin became alive and I died' (*Rom.* 7:9). Men awakened to the obedience God demands all begin to say:

> O how shall I, whose native sphere
> Is dark, whose mind is dim
> Before the Ineffable appear,
> And on my naked spirit bear
> The uncreated beam?

Man's ignorance of God has a second consequence. It leads him to minimize the penalty which is due to sin. He hears that death is the wages of sin but he thinks that he is able to make amends for sins past and does not believe that his guilt merits an eternal judgment. He refuses to see physical death as evidence of a present condemnation. In so thinking man is proving how far removed he is from the truth.

There is a moral necessity in the very nature of God that makes it certain that sin will be punished. Yet for us the defilement of sin is so ordinary and commonplace – we who 'drink iniquity like water' (*Job* 15:16) – that we are incapable of seeing its consequences. The repeated warnings of Scripture that God will overlook no sin are lost on us. He 'will in no wise clear the guilty' (*Exod.* 34:7). 'Every transgression and disobedience received a just recompense of reward' (*Heb.* 2:2). Upon the disobedient 'he shall rain snares, fire and brimstone, and an horrible tempest: this shall be the portion of their cup.' And far from this being unjust, the same text tells us that it is God's very holiness which requires such actions, 'For the righteous LORD loves righteousness' (*Psa.* 11:6,7).

In their blindness men cannot see that the anger of God is already present against sin: 'The wrath of God is revealed from heaven against all ungodliness and unrighteousness of men' (*Rom.* 1:18). But we are warned that what our sin deserves will not appear fully until God's present long-suffering with sinners come to an end: 'He has appointed a day on which he will judge the world in righteousness' (*Acts* 17:31). It will be 'the day of wrath and revelation of the righteous judgment of God; who will render to every man according to his deeds' (*Rom.* 2:5,6).

This is a refrain which runs throughout the Word of God, and yet an attempt is often made to say that it is not in harmony with Christ's gospel of God's love. The truth is that no one in Scripture speaks more repeatedly and definitely about the terror of future judgment than the Lord Jesus Christ. It is he who speaks of the duty to fear 'him who is able to destroy both soul and body in hell' (*Matt.* 10:28). He affirms that God's judgment will be so exact 'that every idle word men may speak, they will give account of it in the day of judgment' (*Matt.* 12:36); at that day holy angels 'will gather out of his kingdom all things that offend, and practise lawless-ness, and will cast them into the furnace of fire. There will be wailing and gnashing of teeth' (*Matt.* 13:41–42). He affirms that the division then made for ever will be a division in terms of strict righteousness: 'And these shall go away into everlasting punishment: but the righteous into life eternal' (*Matt.* 25:46). It is Jesus who says that for all their religious duties, and their 'zeal for God', the scribes and Pharisees would be found without the righteousness that men must have to enter heaven: 'For I say unto you, that unless your righteousness exceeds the righteousness of the scribes and Pharisees, you will by no means enter the kingdom of heaven' (*Matt.* 5:17).

Here then is the explanation for the natural man's religion of self-righteousness. He neither knows God nor himself. That is why the first need of every individual is to learn the truth. Yet we cannot learn it as we may learn other things. We are so addicted to pride that it takes the action of God to enlighten us and humble us. The only One who can 'convict of sin, and of righteousness, and of judgment' (*John* 16:8) is a divine Person; the Holy Spirit of God has been sent for that purpose. He alone can change our good opinion of ourselves: 'When with rebukes you correct man for iniquity, You make his beauty melt away like a moth' (*Psa.* 39:11).

> But though it needs the power of the divine Spirit to make us believing men, this is not because faith is a mysterious thing, a great exercise or effort of soul which must be very accurately gone through, in order to make it, and us, acceptable; but because of our dislike to the truth believed, and our enmity to the Being in whom we are asked to confide. Believing is the simplest of all mental processes; yet not the less is the power of God needed.[2]

Here is the reason why two things are invariably true of the non-Christian. He has not seen his own depravity and he has never experienced the convicting work of the Holy Spirit. The conversion of Merle d'Aubigné illustrates this exactly. When d'Aubigné first heard a stranger called Robert Haldane speaking in Geneva in 1816, although he was a divinity student, he could not understand what he was talking about and certainly did not agree with it. 'The natural corruption of man', he later acknowledged, was 'a doctrine of which I had never heard. In fact I was quite astonished to hear of men being corrupt by nature.' Then the day came when the visitor read and taught from Romans 3, with its words, 'We have before proved both Jews and Gentiles, that they are all under sin; as it is written, There is none righteous, no, not one' (*Rom.* 3:9). 'It was', Merle d'Aubigné said, 'the sword of the Spirit; and from that time I saw that my heart was corrupt.'[3]

---

[2] Horatius Bonar, *God's Way of Peace* (London: Nisbet, 1879), p. 124.
[3] Alexander Haldane, *The Lives of Robert and James Haldane* (1852; reprint, Edinburgh: Banner of Truth, 1990), p. 431.

Nothing could be more important than the principle involved here: where the Fall of man is unrecognized God's way of salvation will never be received. Conversely, where human nature is seen for what it is, the gospel becomes the most desirable message in all the world. There is therefore nothing more adverse to man's highest interests than to hide from him his true condition and the wrath of God which he deserves. 'It is not possible to speak too much about Jesus,' said J. C. Ryle, 'but it is possible to speak too little about hell.' All the preachers greatly used of God have understood this well.

It is written of the preaching of John Elias in nineteenth-century Wales that on one occasion he was so helped by the Spirit of God in speaking of man's fallen condition and of the coming judgment that people trembled, and from their midst a man cried out, 'O that I could hear Richardson of Caernarvon but for five minutes.'[4] Evan Richardson, it needs to be explained, was one of the most tender gospel preachers of the day, and what the man who interrupted was really saying was, 'Oh! let us hear the gospel!'

John Elias had not made a mistake. A cry for the gospel was exactly what he had in view. The reason there is so little of such crying is that people are at peace in a delusion. By nature we are all asleep in a hiding place of self-righteousness and self-sufficiency, and we will never leave it unless we are driven out. We ought not to be the least surprised that there is no relish for justification by faith today. No man is ever ready to hear that truth until he is awakened to his ignorance of the true character of God. So when God promises Christ as a foundation for sinners, a sure corner stone, he also says, 'I will make justice the measuring line, and righteousness the plummet; the hail will sweep away the refuge of lies, and the waters will overflow the hiding place' (*Isa.* 28:17). Conviction must go before conversion. The first question is not,

---

[4] *John Elias, Life, Letters and Essays*, ed. Edward Morgan (1844–7; reprint, Edinburgh: Banner of Truth, 1973), p. 104.

'What must I do to be saved?' It is, 'Who among us shall dwell with the devouring fire? who among us shall dwell with everlasting burnings?' (*Isa*. 33:14)

WHY 'THE RIGHTEOUSNESS OF GOD' IS GOOD NEWS

We turn now to the message which the man who interrupted John Elias was so anxious to hear. There is a way open to heaven. It is by receiving 'the gift of righteousness', the action, as already noted, which is the opposite of what Paul describes when he says of the Jews, 'they have not submitted themselves to the righteousness of God' (*Rom.*10:3). What does Paul mean by charging the Jews with this sin? What is 'submitting to the righteousness of God'? It cannot mean an acceptance of God's holy character for it is the recognition of God's holiness which makes the condemnation of sinners certain. But Paul is speaking of a righteousness which secures the very opposite of condemnation: it is the good news of the 'righteousness of God revealed from heaven' as a gift which is the sure provision against the wrath of God (*Rom.* 1:17–18). The gift is none other than Christ himself, both his Person and his work.

The doctrine of justification is all about Christ. God does not save sinners by overlooking their sin, or by lowering the demands of his righteousness. It is not love at the expense of justice. It is not mercy overriding law and setting it aside. Such a procedure would be a denial of the character of God. When we set justification by faith against justification by works we have to remember that in one sense the words can be misleading. 'To justify' means to pronounce – to reckon and count – righteous,[5] and that pronouncement cannot be

---

[5] Everything turns on this being understood. The verb 'to justify' (*dikaioo*) has the same root meaning as the noun that is translated 'righteousness' (*dikaiosune*). For God 'to justify' is one and the same thing as 'to pronounce righteous'. For full technical discussion, see John Murray, *Epistle to the Romans* (Grand Rapids: Eerdmans, 1980), pp. 336–62, or for a very influential and more popular exposition, D. M. Lloyd-Jones,

made except on the basis of an existing righteousness. That basis is Christ's doing and dying in our place. Far from the gospel dispensing with the holy law of God, the New Testament shows that the work of Christ cannot be understood apart from the demands of that law (*Rom.* 3:31; 8:1–4). The law is the key to the death of Christ for it is the law which tells us that sin deserves condemnation and death. 'The soul that sins, it shall die' (*Ezek.* 18:20). 'Cursed is everyone who does not continue in all things which are written in the book of the law, to do them' (*Gal.* 3:10). 'The sting of death is sin; and the strength of sin is the law' (*1 Cor.* 15:56).

For this reason Scripture tells us that 'Christ had to suffer' (*Acts* 17:3); had to because he is the Substitute who met the full penalty of the divine law on behalf of others. 'The LORD has laid on him the iniquity of us all . . . By his knowledge my righteous Servant shall justify many, for he shall bear their iniquities' (*Isa.* 53: 6,11). 'For this is my blood of the new covenant, which is shed for many for the remission of sins' (*Matt.* 26:28). Justification thus proceeds on the basis of judgment being satisfied – of wrath being turned aside – so that we read of sinners being 'justified by his blood' (*Rom.* 5:9); 'justified freely by his grace through the redemption that is in Christ Jesus, whom God set forth to be a propitiation by his blood' (*Rom.* 3:24–25). 'Christ has redeemed us from the curse of the law, being made a curse for us' (*Gal.* 3:13).

Thus the gospel message is that sinners who believe in Christ are treated and regarded by God as possessing what belongs to Christ. His obedience and death is *their* righteousness. Before the law of God, Christ and those for whom he died stand as one single person, and therefore the believer shares fully in all that Christ did for him (*Rom.* 5:18). Christ's

---

Romans: Exposition of Chapters 3:20–4:25, Atonement and Justification (London: Banner of Truth, 1970). More recently the same truth is defended in John Piper, *Counted Righteous in Christ: Should We Abandon the Imputation of Christ's Righteousness?* (Wheaton: Crossway, 2002).

work is as truly ours as if we had accomplished it ourselves (*Gal.* 2:20).

But Christ's bearing the penalty of sin is not the whole of his work. Man at creation was put under a law which made life dependent upon obedience. God still holds fallen man to that obedience and, if Jesus was acting for sinners, then obedience was also essential to his work. Thus we read: 'When the fullness of the time was come, God sent forth his Son, born of a woman, born under the law' to redeem us from the law's demands (*Matt.* 3:13; *Gal.* 4:4). The sufferings of Calvary were not the beginning of his obedience but its climax: 'He became obedient to death, even the death of the cross' (*Phil.* 2:8). Christ's obedience is as much related to our justification as is the penalty he bore: 'By the obedience of one shall many be made righteous' (*Rom.* 5:19).

When the connection between Christ's work and the law of God is broken the meaning of justification is lost. This is the case with the teaching which says that when God justifies a believing sinner he does so by accepting his faith *in place of* righteousness. On this understanding it is the act of faith that God reckons to an individual for his righteousness. But this is to misconceive entirely the true role of faith. It is not faith instead of righteousness that saves us, it is what faith *receives*, that is Christ and his righteousness. We are saved not *because of* faith but *through* faith. It is Christ not faith that saves us: 'His blood, not our faith; his satisfaction, not our believing it, is the matter of our justification before God.'[6]

---

[6] *Works of John Flavel*, vol. 2, p. 119. The teaching here criticized interprets 'for' (*eis*) in the words, 'his faith is counted for righteousness' (*Rom.* 4:5, KJV), as meaning 'instead of,' or, 'in place of'. Many modern versions of Scripture would seem to give countenance to the error by translating, 'his faith is credited as righteousness'. But *eis* here, as elsewhere, means 'in order to,' expressing result. 'We are saved by, or through faith, but never on account of our faith, or on the ground of it.' Charles Hodge, *Romans* (1864; reprint, Edinburgh: Banner of Truth, 1975), on *Rom.* 4:3, p. 109. After full comment on the meaning of 'for righteousness,' Haldane

The consistent language of Scripture demands nothing less: 'Christ is made unto us righteousness' (*1 Cor.* 1:30). 'For if by one man's offence death reigned through one; much more those who receive abundance of grace and of the gift of righteousness shall reign in life through the One, Jesus Christ. Therefore, as through one man's offence judgment came to all men, resulting in condemnation; even so by the righteousness of the One the free gift came upon all men resulting in justification of life' (*Rom.* 5:17–18).

On the subject of Christ's relation to the law perhaps no text is more clear than Romans 10:4. The words can be literally translated, 'For an end of law [is] Christ for righteousness, to everyone believing.' The assertion is that for all united to Christ the demands of the law, in respect to their acceptance with God, are ended by Christ's obedience. Law has been terminated – abolished – by Christ as a means to attaining righteousness. For Christ himself has satisfied law once and forever on behalf of believers – 'An end of law is Christ for righteousness'! We are thus to see the completeness of Christ's work by the way it answers the two parts of the law, both the penalty it threatens and the obedience it requires. The sinner who receives Christ is at that moment entirely acquitted of the guilt of sin: 'There is therefore now no condemnation to those who are in Christ Jesus . . . Who shall bring a charge against God's elect? It is God who justifies' (*Rom.* 8:1,33). For the believer the threat of the law is forever silenced. But Christ's justifying righteousness does more than secure forgiveness; his obedience is counted – imputed – to us, ensuring for all time our standing as righteous in the sight of God. Justification means nothing less than that. The justified have therefore a sure title to eternal life and glory. Faith in Christ secures both deliverance from perishing *and* everlasting life (*John* 3:16; 5:24).

---

concluded: 'Nothing, then, can be a greater corruption of the truth than to represent faith itself as accepted instead of righteousness.' *Exposition of Romans* (1874; reprint, London: Banner of Truth, 1958), p. 163.

To summarize, then, the good news is not, 'Do this and live', but, 'Receive Christ and his righteousness.' It is salvation for believers, not workers; for the ungodly, not the righteous; and by Christ's obedience, not our own: 'Not by works of righteousness which we have done, but according to his mercy he saved us' (*Titus* 3:5). The statement of the *Shorter Catechism* can scarcely be improved: 'Justification is an act of God's free grace wherein he pardons all our sins, and accepts us as righteous in his sight, only for the righteousness of Christ imputed to us, and received by faith alone' (Q. 33). In verse the same truth has been well stated in these words:

> The best obedience of my hands
> Dare not appear before Thy throne
> But faith can answer law's demands
> By pleading what my Lord has done.

IMPUTATION – THE OLD TESTAMENT GOSPEL

I move on now to refer to one common way in which this gospel is subverted today. It is by the claim that there is more than one 'gospel' in the New Testament. Salvation by imputed righteousness may be one of them but it is only Paul's doctrine. It is said that the whole idea of a legal change of status by imputation may be in his epistles, but it is not found elsewhere and is not the simple gospel of Christ. What those who speak in this way fail to take into account is that Paul has already met a very similar objection to his teaching on justification. Modern authors are not the first to accuse the apostle of teaching a novelty and of being out of harmony with the rest of Scripture. That charge was first made by the Jews themselves and in answering it Paul shows that what is alleged to be unique to him is the plain teaching of the Old Testament.

The unbelieving Jews saw only the righteousness of God as revealed in law; they missed another witness in their own Scriptures. Paul himself had once missed it but no longer. He writes: 'By the deeds of the law no flesh will be justified in his sight, for by the law is the knowledge of sin. But now the righteousness of God apart from the law is revealed, *being witnessed by the law and the prophets*, even the righteousness of God which is through faith in Jesus Christ to all and on all who believe' (*Rom.* 3:20–22, my italics). Not content to leave this simply as an assertion, Paul goes on in Romans chapter 4 to show that Old Testament believers were *never* accepted by God in terms of law-righteousness. 'For what does the Scripture say?' he asks, and answers with a quotation from Genesis 15:6, 'Abraham believed God, and it was accounted to him for righteousness' (*Rom.* 4:3). Then, turning to David, he proves from the words of Psalm 32 that David knew 'the blessedness of the man to whom God imputes righteousness apart from works' (4:6). Indeed, the apostle shows that the very ordinance of circumcision, upon which the Jews so much relied, cannot be understood apart from imputed righteousness.

Paul returns to the same subject in Romans 10 when he says that the unbelieving Jews were 'ignorant of God's righteousness.' The reference, as already said, is not to God's righteousness in the law, but to the righteousness which is his gift in Christ. The Jews should have known this, he argues, because God's justifying righteousness, as opposed to works-righteousness, is there in their own Scriptures: 'For Moses writes about the righteousness which is of the law,' and he goes on to quote Leviticus 18:5. But for the righteousness of the gospel Paul quotes Moses again, this time from Deuteronomy 30:11–14, 'Do not say in your heart, "Who will ascend into heaven" (that is, to bring Christ down from above), or, "Who will descend into the abyss" (that is, to bring Christ up from the dead). But what does it say? "The word is near you, even in your mouth and in your heart" (that is, the word of faith which we preach)' (*Rom.* 10:6–8).

The Jews missed justification in the Old Testament because they missed Christ there. From the very Fall of man the gospel was announced in terms of sacrifice, of substitution, of satisfaction for guilt by its transference, and of a transference which took place by imputation. In the truth of the altar, and the shed blood, the people were taught that God was willing to treat sinners as though they had done personally what Another was to do for them. With the eye of faith Old Testament worshippers were to look beyond the typical sacrifices to Christ himself. So we read, Abel offered a sacrifice 'by faith'; so Noah 'became heir of the righteousness which is by faith'; so Abraham, says Christ, 'rejoiced to see my day' (*Heb.* 11:4,7; *John* 8:56). 'The scripture, foreseeing that God would justify the nations by faith, preached the gospel to Abraham beforehand, saying, "In you all the nations shall be blessed"' (*Gal.* 3:8).

In the same way all the prophets taught that righteousness is to be received as a gift in the Messiah. In words prophetic of the gospel age, God says through the prophet Isaiah: 'Look to me, and be saved, all you ends of the earth'; and it was in the righteousness of a suffering Saviour that believers were taught that this salvation would be found. The church therefore is to say: 'Surely in the LORD I have righteousness and strength. To him men shall come' (*Isa.* 45:22,24). God's repeated promise is, 'In the LORD all the descendants of Israel shall be justified, and shall glory . . . I bring near my righteousness; it shall not be far off, and my salvation shall not tarry; and I will place salvation in Zion for Israel my glory' (*Isa.* 45:25; 46;13). The intention of the Messiah's sufferings was plainly revealed in the Old Testament: he shall 'justify many; for he shall bear their iniquities' (*Isa* .53:11). In the prophet Jeremiah (23:5–6) we read: 'Behold, the days are coming, says the LORD, that I will raise to David a Branch of righteousness; a King shall reign and prosper . . . In his days Judah will be saved, and Israel shall dwell safely; Now this is his name by which he will be called, THE LORD OUR RIGHTEOUSNESS' (*Jehovah Tsidkenu*). The last sentence provided the text for M'Cheyne's hymn on his conversion which I have quoted above.

Daniel 9: 24 speaks of the same subject: 'Seventy weeks are determined for your people and for your holy city, to finish

the transgression, and make an end of sins, to make reconciliation for iniquity, to bring in everlasting righteousness.'

We must conclude that those who say that Paul's gospel
was a novelty are in the same position as his Jewish oppo-
nents. Missing Christ, they cannot rightly interpret the Old
Testament. For as J. C. Ryle has said, 'If you lose sight of
justification by Christ, a large part of the Old Testament
Scripture will become an unmeaning tangled maze.'[7] The
Jews read the Scriptures with a veil over their eyes. In Paul's
words: 'Their minds were hardened. For until this day the
same veil remains unlifted in the reading of the Old Testament, because the veil is taken away in Christ. But even to
this day, when Moses is read, a veil lies on their heart. Nevertheless when one turns to the Lord, the veil is taken away'
(*2 Cor.* 3:14–16).

It is the Christian who understands the words of George
Smeaton when he writes: 'The Son of God made flesh, and
obedient in life and death, is our righteousness before God.
Scripture knows of only ONE righteousness uniting God and
men, and the world has never seen another.'[8]

CONCLUSIONS

1. *Because imputed righteousness is directly contrary to human
pride and self-sufficiency it has always been opposed by a world
hostile to Christ.* Sometimes the attack comes in the name
of morality. It is said that, if God should pronounce the
believing sinner to be righteous on account of another's
righteousness and not his own, then such a justification
would be artificial and unreal. The idea of imputation, say
these critics, is a fiction. To such an argument the church's
responsibility is to respond in the language of the New Testament. The gospel of Christ is not presented to men as an

---

[7] Ryle, *Old Paths* (1878; reprint, Edinburgh: Banner of Truth, 1999),
p. 222–3.

[8] *The Apostles' Doctrine of the Atonement* (1870; reprint, Edinburgh: Banner of Truth, 1991), p. 123.

opinion for discussion. It is a revelation of mercy from heaven which cannot be rejected without incurring the greatest guilt. To hold to works-righteousness is to make the death of Christ a worthless thing, for 'if righteousness comes through the law, then Christ is dead in vain' (*Gal.* 2:21). The language of morality is only a cover to excuse the rejection of Christ and his cross. To despise justification by Christ is to perish (*Acts* 13:38–41).[9]

The danger exists that in view of hostility to the truth, Christians may be tempted to modify the biblical teaching on justification and to speak of it only as forgiveness without any reference to imputation. In the face of that temptation, what needs to be remembered is that we cannot disbelieve that Christ's righteousness is imputed without logically giving up the truth that our sins were imputed to Christ. The imputation of sin to Christ and the imputation of righteousness to believers are laid down in Scripture as *parallel* truths: 'For he made him who knew no sin to be sin for us, that we might be made the righteousness of God in him' (*2 Cor.* 5:21). The words teach unmistakably that Christ was made sin, not in his subjective experience but in his representative office; although personally sinless, he was counted guilty. In precisely the same way, that is by imputation, is the atoning obedience – the righteousness – of Christ reckoned to believers. Where imputation is minimized the whole gospel will sooner or later be undermined.

2. *The allegation that salvation through imputed righteousness discounts the place of moral living is best answered by the transformed living of Christians.* The gospel, rightly believed, far from displacing the necessity of holiness establishes it. In the words of William Cowper:

[9] To those to whom these words were first spoken Paul gave the clearest instance of unbelief: 'For those who dwell in Jerusalem, and their rulers, because they did not know him, nor even the voices of the prophets which are read every Sabbath, have fulfilled them in condemning him' (*Acts* 13:27).

> To see the law by Christ fulfilled
> And hear his pardoning voice,
> Changes the slave into a child,
> And duty into choice.[10]

It is reconciliation through the atonement that provides both power and motive for obedience. There have been those who have held that God sees no sin in those who are justified and therefore holiness of life need be no concern for the Christian. Such teaching has ever been rejected by orthodox Christianity as a dangerous error. It is true, God sees no sin in believers as a Judge to condemn them, but he sees it as a Father who will act to correct them. A parallel error is the belief that because obedience to the law is 'ended' for Christians as a means of acceptance before God, it is also ended as a rule for his life. But the law, ended for our justification, is far from ended in sanctification. It is the character of God, as revealed in the law, that is now written in the heart of a believer, so that he can say with Paul, 'I delight in the law of God after the inward man' (*Rom.* 7:22). It is by the gospel, the same apostle says, that 'we establish the law' (*Rom.* 3:31).

Wherever justification is preached such errors repeatedly arise. Richard Sibbes, in the seventeenth century, wrote on Hosea 14:4–5:

> We have an error crept in among some of the ignorant sort of people, who think that God sees no sin when he has once pardoned men in justification. . . . No; it is false, as appears in this place; for how can God heal that he sees not? He sees it not to be revenged on them for

[10] Where 'faith' is professed without a changed life, it is because there has been no regeneration. 'The faith whereby we are justified is such as is not found in any but those who are made partakers of the Holy Ghost, and by him united unto Christ; whose nature is renewed, and in whom there is a principle of all grace, and purpose of obedience.' Owen, *Works*, vol. 5, p. 104.

it; but he sees sin, to correct it and to heal it. He sees it not after a revengeful, wrathful justice, to cast us into hell and damn us for it; but he sees it after a sort, to make us smart and lament for it, and to have many times a bitter sense of his wrath and forsaking, as men undone without a new supply of comfort and peace from heaven. Let a man neglect sanctification, daily sorrow and confession of sin, and now and then even craving new pardon for sins past, casting all upon a fantastic conceit of faith in their justification: what follows but pride, hardness of heart, contempt of others, and neglect of better than themselves, and proneness out of God's judgment, to fall from ill to worse, from one error to another? In this case the heart is false and deceitful. For while it pretends a glorious faith to look back to Christ, to live by faith, and lay all on him by justification, it winds itself out of all tasks in religion, sets the heart at liberty, neglects sanctification and mortification, and beautifying the image of God in them.[11]

These words are a reminder that while justification is at the centre of the gospel, it is not the whole gospel. Only when it is preached to the exclusion of other biblical truths can it become the means of belittling personal holiness.

3. *Because the doctrine of justification by Christ's righteousness is so uncongenial to the natural man, whenever unbelief has prevailed in the professing church it has been lost and has had to be rediscovered afresh.* It was largely lost to the Old Testament church

---

[11] Sibbes, *Works*, vol. 2, pp. 316-7. In his address on 'The Holy Spirit in Connection with Our Ministry,' C. H. Spurgeon has solemn words on how God saw sin in Moses, 'a man favoured of God beyond all others'; and he counsels his students: 'When you are fullest of the fruits of the Spirit bow lowest before the throne and serve the Lord with fear. "The Lord our God is a jealous God." Remember that God has come unto us, not to exalt us, but to exalt himself.' *Lectures to My Students*, Second Series (London: Passmore and Alabaster: 1877), pp. 21–2.

when Christ came into the world. It was lost again before the Reformation of the sixteenth century. It was lost in England before the Evangelical Revival of the eighteenth century. How the truth dawned upon Wesley and Whitefield is well known, but it was the same truth which made other leaders of that period the men they were.

John Berridge, a fellow of Clare College, Cambridge, and vicar of Everton, has left on record what a discovery this truth was to him at the age of forty-two. For thirty years, he said, he had endeavoured to blend the law and the gospel and unite Christ's righteousness with his own. 'I preached up sanctification very earnestly for six years in a former parish,' he writes to a friend, 'and never brought one soul to Christ. I did the same at this parish for two years, without any success, but as soon as ever I preached Jesus Christ, and faith in his blood, then believers were added to the church continually.' Berridge burned all his former sermons and shed tears of joy over their destruction.[12] The discovery of Thomas Chalmers, when he was minister of Kilmany in Fife, was very similar.[13]

James Buchanan has commented well on how the natural man is ignorant of the gospel and how it must therefore come to every generation as something amazingly new:

> It was new to ourselves – surprising, startling, and affecting us strangely, as if it were almost too good to be true – when it first shone, like the beam of heaven's own light into our dark and troubled spirits, and shed abroad 'a peace which passes all understanding'. It will be equally new to our children, and our children's children,

[12] *Works of John Berridge* (London: Simpkin, 1838), pp. 10, 357.

[13] 'I am now most thoroughly of opinion', Chalmers wrote to his brother [14 Feb. 1820], '. . . that on the system of "Do this and live", no peace, and even no true and worthy obedience, can ever be attained. It is, "Believe on the Lord Jesus Christ, and thou shalt be saved." When this belief enters the heart, joy and confidence enter along with it.' W. Hanna, ed., *A Selection from the Correspondence of Thomas Chalmers*, Edinburgh, 1853.

when they come to know that they have sins to be forgiven, and souls to be saved; and to the last sinner who
is convinced and converted on the earth, it will still be
as 'good tidings from a far country' – as 'cold water to a
thirsty soul' . . . it comes into contact, in every succeed-
ing age, with new minds who are ignorant of it, but
need it . . . and when they receive it . . . they will learn
from their own experience that the old truth is still the
germ of 'a new creation' – the spring of a new life, a
new peace, a new hope, a new spiritual existence.[14]

4. *Because of abounding error and ignorance of Scripture there
is danger today of ministers becoming engulfed in all kinds of
controversies.* But here is a doctrine which goes to the root of
the greatest issue of all, namely, human pride and self-righteousness.[15] In bringing forward Christ's righteousness we
therefore proclaim truth which goes to the very heart of
things. Here is a dispute into which we ought to enter and
for which, as the Reformers, we ought to be prepared to die.
Speaking of the Reformers and justification by faith, it has
been rightly said: 'It was mainly to the influence of this one
truth, carried home to the conscience "in demonstration of
the Spirit and with power", that they ascribed their success,
under God, in sweeping away the whole host of scholastic
errors and superstitious practices by which, in the course of
many preceding centuries, men had corrupted the simpler
faith and worship of the primitive Church.'[16]

This is the great controversy from which the devil would
seek to drive us by engaging us in lesser issues.

[14] James Buchanan, *The Doctrine of Justification* (1867; reprint, London:
Banner of Truth, 1961), pp. 2–3.

[15] 'It was long ere Paul could renounce all the things that were gain to
him, and prize the righteousness of Christ only. It is not then a doctrine
pleasing to flesh and blood, but altogether contrary, for it driveth a man
to self-judging, a self-abhorrency, a self-renunciation, and makes Christ
to be all in all.' Anthony Burgess, *The True Doctrine of Justification* (London,
1654), p. 305.   [16] Buchanan, *Justification*, p. 9.

5. *In the light of the history of this doctrine there is good reason for us to ask whether the weakness of our evangelistic preaching is not related to our contemporary deficiency in its presentation.* It is true that the consequences of faithful preaching are with God and not with us, but are we sure that we are faithful in making salvation by Christ's righteousness as clear and prominent as it ought to be? Here is the only message truly relevant to the reality of the condition of fallen men and women. Every offer of hope to individuals which is based upon moral education, self-improvement, or religious devotion, is an empty hope. It needs divine power to change human nature and it is this teaching alone which is 'the power of God to salvation to everyone who believes' (*Rom.* 1:16).

To the most degraded, to those upon whom even an immoral society looks with shock, the gospel speaks not of the possibility of gradual improvement but of an immediate reconciliation for the very worst, through receiving the righteousness of Christ. The dynamic of evangelism lies with this truth. It was the preaching of Christ's righteousness which brought salvation into the moral cesspool of the first century and it has ever been the same. We have therefore good reason to ask whether the small results of preaching in the present day are not connected with our weak hold of this message.

Of one thing we can be sure: every new flood-tide of spiritual blessing has been brought in by the fervent proclamation of the righteousness which Christ has secured for believing sinners by his death. Today men and women live as they have always done in the fear of death, possessed with the suspicion that the deeds of this life may follow them and be found displeasing to God. They fear that there is more that they ought to have done or to have been. The thought which came to the dying king, Louis XIV of France, is by no means uncommon. Amidst shortening periods of consciousness he looked back on his pleasure-seeking life, and asked his priest, Père Tellier, to give him absolution for all his sins. 'Do you suffer much?' Tellier asked. 'No,' replied the king, 'that's what troubles me. I should like to suffer more for the expiation of my sins.' Such is the religion of the natural man, looking to himself to the last.

What a difference we see in the last hours of J. Gresham Machen who died of pneumonia in a North Dakota hospital on January 1, 1937. The previous night he had spoken to a friend of a vision he had enjoyed of being in heaven, 'Sam, it was glorious; it was glorious.' And on the very morning of his death he sent a telegram to another friend, John Murray, repeating the grounds of his assurance, 'I am so thankful for the active obedience of Christ. No hope without it.'[17] This is the way of salvation. It leaves every believer saying with Paul, 'God forbid that I should glory except in the cross of the Lord Jesus Christ'; 'Not having my own righteousness, which is from the law, but that which is through the faith of Christ, the righteousness which is from God by faith' (*Gal.* 6:14; *Phil.* 3:9).

---

[17] *Collected Writings of John Murray,* vol. 3, p. 64.

ADDITIONAL NOTES

GEORGE HERBERT, 1593–1633:
JUDGEMENT

Almightie Judge, how shall poore wretches brook
   Thy dreadfull look,
Able a heart of iron to appall,
   When Thou shalt call
For ev'ry man's peculiar book?

What others mean to do, I know not well;
   Yet I hear tell,
That some shall turn thee to some leaves therein
   So void of sinne,
That they in merit shall excell.

But I resolve, when thou shalt call for mine,
   That to decline,
And thrust a Testament into thy hand:
   Let that be scann'd.
There thou shalt find my faults are thine.[18]

JOHN BUNYAN, 1628–88:
MY RIGHTEOUSNESS IN HEAVEN

'One day, as I was passing in the field, and that too with some dashes on my conscience, fearing lest yet all was not right, suddenly this sentence fell upon my soul, Thy righteousness is in heaven; and methought withal, I saw, with the eyes of my soul, Jesus Christ at God's right hand; there, I say, as my righteousness; so that wherever I was, or whatever I was adoing, God could not

---

[18] From *The Temple,* 1633, in *Works of George Herbert,* ed. F. E. Hutchinson (Oxford: Clarendon Press, 1941), pp. 187–8.

say of me, He wants [lacks] my righteousness, for that was just before him. I also saw, moreover, that it was not my good frame of heart that made my righteousness better, not yet my bad frame that made my righteousness worse; for my righteousness was Jesus Christ himself, the same, yesterday, and to-day, and for ever.

'Now I could look from myself to him, and should reckon that all those graces of God that were now green in me, were yet like those cracked groats and fourpence-halfpennies that rich men carry in their purses, when their gold is in their trunks at home! Oh, I saw my gold was in my trunk! In Christ, my Lord and Saviour!'[19]

CHARLES SIMEON, 1759–1836:
CONVERSION TESTIMONY, 1779

'My distress of mind continued for about three months, and well might it have continued for years, since my sins were more in number than the hairs of my head, or than the sands upon the sea shore; but God in infinite condescension began at last to smile upon me . . . in Passion week, as I was reading Bishop Wilson on the Lord's Supper, I met with an expression to this effect: "That the Jews knew what they did when they transferred their sin to the head of their offering." The thought rushed into my mind, What! may I transfer all my guilt to another? Has God provided an offering for me, that I may lay my sins on his head? Then, God willing, I will not bear them on my own soul one moment longer. Accordingly I sought to lay my sins on the sacred head of Jesus; and on the Wednesday began to have a hope of mercy; on the Thursday that hope increased; on Friday and Saturday it became more strong; and on the Sunday morning (Easter-day, April 4) I awoke early with those words upon my heart

---

[19] From *Grace Abounding to the Chief of Sinners* (1666), in *Works of John Bunyan,* vol. 1 (Banner of Truth edition, 1991), pp. 35–6.

and lips, "Jesus Christ is risen to-day! Hallelujah! Hallelujah!" From that hour peace flowed in rich abundance into my soul.'[20]

MARTIN BOOS, 1762–1825:
WORDS HE NEVER FORGOT

'In 1788 or 1789 I visited a sick person, who was respected for her deep humility and exemplary piety. I said to her, "You will die very peacefully and happily." "Why so?" she asked. "Because you have led", I replied, "such a pious and holy life." The good woman smiled at my words and said, "If I leave the world relying on my own piety, I am sure I shall be lost. But relying on Jesus my Saviour, I can die in comfort! If I listened to you, what would become of me? How could I stand before the Divine tribunal, where every one must give an account even of her idle words? Which of our actions and virtues would not be found wanting if laid in the Divine balances? No; if Christ had not died for me, if he had not made satisfaction for me, I should have been lost for ever, notwithstanding all my good works and pious conduct. He is my hope, my salvation, and my eternal happiness." '[21]

FRANCES RIDLEY HAVERGAL, 1836–79:
PERSONAL TESTIMONY, 1864

'God seemed to help me wonderfully to read and say the right things; I felt that He did so. But while talking to her, the feeling grew stronger daily, that what was true of her was true of me also, especially when we thought over Romans 3:22. I do not think I ever before ventured to really believe

---

[20] William Carus, *Memoirs of the Life of the Rev. C. Simeon* (London: Hatchard, 1848), pp. 8–9.

[21] *The Life of Martin Boos, A Roman Catholic Clergyman in Germany* (London: Religious Tract Soc., n.d.), p. 19.

that Christ's righteousness was imputed even to me; but I knew, I was sure, that I believed in Jesus, and so there seemed no alternative but to accept the glorious belief that "the righteousness of God" being "upon all and unto all them that believe" was upon me too. It used to seem "too good to be true" for me; but how could I doubt God's word? Then a great tide of sorrow came over me for having ever been so disbelieving; it seemed so very wrong to have doubted, that it threw other phases of sinfulness into comparative shade. And so that 10th of July was one of the happiest days I ever had.'[22]

[22] *Letters of the Late Frances Ridley Havergal* (New York: Randolph, 1885), pp. 29–30.

4

THE CROSS – THE PULPIT
OF GOD'S LOVE

'The cross was a pulpit in which Christ
preached his love to the world.'
AUGUSTINE

'Let us remember that God's glory displays itself more illustriously in the Gospel than in the Law, – and that his invitation is now full of love, but that formerly there was nothing but the greatest terrors . . . The Gospel contains nothing but love, provided it be received by faith.'

JOHN CALVIN, *Commentaries on the Epistle of Paul to the Hebrews* (Edinburgh: Calvin Translation Society, 1853), pp. 331–2.

'I was standing on the 10th December, 1846, at the end of my father's house, and meditating on that precious word that has brought peace to countless weary ones: "God so loved the world, that he gave his only begotten Son, that whosoever believeth in him should not perish, but have eternal life" (*John* 3:16). I saw that God loved me, for I was one of the world. I saw the proof of his love in the giving of his Son Jesus. I saw that "whosoever" meant anybody and everybody, and therefore me, even me. I saw the result of believing – that I would not perish, but have everlasting life. I was enabled to take God at his word. I saw no one, but Jesus only, all in all in redemption. My burden fell from my back, and I was saved. Yes, saved!'

JOHN MACPHERSON, *Life and Labours of Duncan Matheson: The Scottish Evangelist* (Kilmarnock: Ritchie, n.d.), p. 26.

The faith and work of the gospel ministry centre on the atonement. The purpose of gospel preaching is to make known what God has done in the cross of Jesus Christ. The evangel *is* 'the preaching of the cross' (*1 Cor.* 1:18). Paul states with an oath that his office as a preacher was for the setting forth of the vicarious sufferings of the Son of God, 'who gave himself a ransom for all, to be testified in due time. Whereunto I am ordained a preacher and an apostle' (*1 Tim.* 2:6–7). Accordingly, he writes to the Corinthians: 'I determined not to know anything among you, save Jesus Christ and him crucified' (*1 Cor.* 2:2); 'I delivered unto you first of all that which also I received, how that Christ died for our sins' (*1 Cor.* 15:3). Paul's hearers in Galatia could be described as people 'before whose eyes Jesus Christ has been evidently set forth, crucified' (*Gal.* 3:1). Such is the supremacy of this message that the apostle invokes the curse of God upon any teaching which would add anything to the completeness of what Christ did when he 'gave himself for our sins'(*Gal.* 1:4, 8–9). As George Smeaton has commented on that curse:

> Were the atonement not the principal matter of the gospel, and the highest exhibition of the united wisdom, love and faithfulness of God, – in a word, the greatest act of God in the universe, – that terrible anathema on its subverters would seem to us something inexplicable, if not intolerable.[1]

Smeaton goes on to characterize the ministry of all the apostles in these words:

[1] *The Apostles' Doctrine of the Atonement* (1870; reprint, Edinburgh: Banner of Truth, 1991), p. 19.

Their symbol was the cross; their boast was the cross: they could not live without it; they could not die without it . . . In preaching such a doctrine they exposed themselves to the loss of reputation, to hardships and peril, to persecution and death. But they held on their way, undeterred and undaunted.[2]

If this was apostolic Christianity then we are bound to examine ourselves as to whether our emphasis corresponds with it. The question is all-important because, if God gives this pre-eminence to the cross, it must follow that where there is hesitancy or uncertainty in preaching the death of Christ, there is bound to be a serious weakening, if not a nullifying, of the chief purpose of the gospel ministry. There is much discussion today about how evangelism may be advanced, but in the midst of all the discussion one finds too little consideration of the question whether the cross constantly holds the same position in our message as it very evidently did in that of the apostles.

There is an additional reason why a re-examination of our priorities is needed. Across the English-speaking world there has been a considerable recovery of the doctrinal beliefs which were prominent in the Puritans and the older evangelicalism. In that school of belief there was no doubt concerning the place given to the death of Christ. 'The cross, I see, is that chiefly which moves the sinner,' said John MacDonald, 'the Apostle of the North'.[3] More fully, Thomas Chalmers wrote:

The doctrine of the atonement, urged affectionately on the acceptance of the people, and held forth as the great stepping stone, by which one and all are welcome to enter into reconciliation and a *new life* (for a fully declared gospel is the very reverse of Antinomianism)

[2] Ibid., pp. 16, 20.
[3] John Kennedy, *'The Apostle of the North': The Life and Labours of Dr MacDonald* (London: Nelson, 1866), p. 122.

I hold to form the main staple of all good and efficient pulpit work.[4]

The men who spoke in this way were commonly men whose preaching was marked by evangelistic passion and the anticipation of success. In contrast, while we are thankful for the doctrinal recovery which has been taking place, it has to be questioned whether we have seen a parallel recovery in gospel preaching. If we prize the beliefs of a former age why should it be that we fall so far short of that earlier generation in the winning of souls? When due acknowledgement is made of divine sovereignty and of the hardness of our times, it may be a dangerous assumption to suppose that our weakness as evangelists has no connection with anything doctrinal. Our understanding of the cross is an area where we hope – over against a shallow evangelism – that we are at our strongest, but that very assumption may add to our danger. And where that danger lies was pointed out by Professor John Murray when he wrote not long before his death:

> The passion for missions is quenched when we lose sight of the grandeur of the evangel. . . . It is a fact that many, persuaded as they rightly are of the particularism of the plan of salvation and of its various corollaries, have found it difficult to proclaim the full, free, and unrestricted overture of gospel grace. They have laboured under inhibitions arising from fear that in doing so they would impinge upon the sovereignty of God in his saving purposes and operations. The result is that, though formally assenting to the free offer, they lack freedom in the presentation of its appeal and demand.[5]

This is tantamount to saying that while 'many' hold to the same confession of faith as the men I have quoted, they do

[4] W. Hanna, ed., *A Selection from the Correspondence of Thomas Chalmers*, Edinburgh, 1853, p. 329.

[5] John Murray, 'The Atonement and the Free Offer of the Gospel,' *Collected Writings*, vol. 1, pp. 59, 81.

not resemble them in the freeness with which they preach the cross. Jonathan Edwards believed it is 'past all contradiction' that Christ 'died to give all an opportunity to be saved',[6] and he urged his hearers, 'Accept of the offered love of him who is the only-begotten Son of God.'[7] Yet it is at this very point that there is now uncertainty in some Reformed circles.

Two Truths

Uncertainty in preaching Christ and the cross arises, as John Murray pointed out, from the difficulty of relating the Scriptures that speak both in particular and in universal terms. Both are to be found in Scripture, as many passages show:

Scripture teaches a definite atonement: that is to say, Christ died with the purpose of saving those whom the Father had given him — a number not vague or indefinite but sure and certain. Thus he says, 'I lay down my life for the sheep' (*John* 10:15); and Paul directs the elders at Ephesus 'to feed the church of God, which he has purchased with his own blood' (*Acts* 20:28). The effect of the death of Christ is definite, there is a 'purchased' people; his sufferings secured reconciliation and freedom from condemnation for all those whose sins he bore, the same number for whom he was 'made sin' are 'made the righteousness of God in him' (*2 Cor.* 5:21). So those whose place he took become the inheritors of all that he accomplished for them: 'By one offering he hath perfected for ever them that are sanctified' (*Heb.* 10:14; see also *Rom.* 8:32). In the words of the Westminster Confession (8:viii): 'To all those for whom Christ hath purchased redemption, he

---

[6] Jonathan Edwards, *Works*, vol. 13, *The 'Miscellanies,'* ed. Thomas A. Schafer (New Haven: Yale University Press, 1994), p. 174. This truth, he adds, 'Calvinists themselves never denied.' A. A. Hodge asserts it in his *Evangelical Theology* (1890; reprint, Edinburgh: Banner of Truth, 1976), p. 219.

[7] *Works of Jonathan Edwards*, vol. 2 (1834; reprint, Edinburgh: Banner of Truth, 1974), p. 933.

doth certainly and effectually apply the same.' William Cowper has stated the same truth memorably in his hymn, 'There is a fountain filled with blood':

> Dear dying Lamb, Thy precious blood
> Shall never lose its power,
> Till all the ransomed Church of God
> Be saved, to sin no more.

But if gospel texts speak of the death of Christ in terms of the particular, there are others which direct us to the universal: the message of the cross is to be presented to all in order that they may believe and be reconciled to God. The same God who 'now commands all men everywhere to repent' (*Acts* 17:30), assures every hearer of his willingness to pardon all who trust in Jesus. His direction to preachers is not that they command repentance in all, but confine the invitation to faith and forgiveness to a few. Rather *both* are to be presented together, 'repentance unto remission of sins should be preached in his name among all nations' (*Luke* 24:47).[8] In other words, the good news of a provided forgiveness is to be as universally proclaimed as is the command to repent:

'Come unto me all you that labour and are heavy laden, and I will give you rest'(*Matt.* 11:28).
'Preach the gospel to every creature' (*Mark* 16:15).
'This is his commandment that we believe on the name of his Son Jesus Christ' (*1 John* 3:23).
'Whosoever will, let him take the water of life freely' (*Rev.* 22:17).

---

[8] 'Those who deny the free overture of grace must rob the demand for repentance of its gospel implications. Denial dismembers Jesus' word, "repentance unto remission of sins" and it contradicts the plain import of Paul's "all everywhere".' John Murray, *Collected Writings*, vol. 1, p. 60. In translating 'unto remission', Murray is following a commonly recognized variant reading but his point holds good irrespective of whether it is 'and' or 'unto'.

Here then are two strands of truth: a redemption that is definite and yet good news and invitations that are to be addressed to all. So the question is, how do these two things, one particular and the other universal, stand related to each other? Can both be true? To that question we will return later, but more fundamental issues need to come first.

At Calvary We Learn of Forgiveness Consistent with Holiness and Justice

The entrance of sin into the human race created a problem with respect to the character of God in his dealings with men. Yet it is a problem about which we have no interest or comprehension until we come to be convicted that our sin deserves God's wrath and displeasure. Only when we are brought to see something of the enormity of sin do we discover why God's view of it is so different from our own. God loves righteousness with all the intensity of his being. And to love righteousness is necessarily to hate what is its opposite – in this his character is a pattern for us, 'Ye that love the Lord, hate evil' (*Psa.* 97:10). It is God's love of holiness which makes his judgment upon sin certain (*Psa.* 11: 6–7). He 'will by no means clear the guilty' (*Exod.* 34:7). He 'will render to every man according to his works' (*Rom.* 2:6). Because he is holy and just he will never fail to act against the moral evil that is an affront to all that he is.[9]

Such is the problem created by sin. If God were to pardon sin without upholding his righteousness he would cease to be God; merely to waive the penalty that sin deserves would be to deny his perfection. How then can he be true to himself, how can he vindicate his holiness, how can he remain God, *and* at the same time forgive sin? How can he be righteous

---

[9] 'When God "swears in his wrath", that is, swears by that essential attribute of His nature which leads Him to hate and punish sin, no doubt can be entertained that this is a quality or property of God (*Psa.* 95:11). It is a perfection having its root in the moral excellence of God.' Smeaton, *Apostles' Doctrine of the Atonement,* p. 312.

and not judge sin in righteousness? To put the same problem in another way, what can undo our past sin and remove its demerit in the sight of God? The whole world has no answer. It is a problem that no created intelligence can solve. An awakened conscience tells a man that even the omnipotence of God cannot undo the guilt of sin.

Only revelation can supply the answer and that answer can be stated in a single word: substitution – an exchange of places, a transference of responsibility – this is the good news to be proclaimed. The One has taken the place of the many, the sinless for the guilty: 'The LORD hath laid on him the iniquity of us all' (*Isa.* 53:6); 'The Lamb of God which takes away the sin of the world' (*John* 1:29); the Saviour who came 'not to be ministered unto but to minister and to give his life a ransom for many'(*Matt.* 20:28). God set forth Christ Jesus 'to be a propitiation' – a securing of divine favour – 'through faith in his blood' (*Rom* 3:25). 'Through this man is preached unto you the forgiveness of sins, and by him all that believe are justified from all things from which ye could not be justified by the law of Moses' (*Acts* 13:38–39).

Here is a foremost truth disclosed at Calvary: God has upheld and vindicated his holiness! In the sufferings of Christ the divine justice which obstructed blessing coming to those who deserve judgment has been satisfied. There is now favour and reconciliation for the very worst who has 'received the atonement' (*Rom.* 5:11). The pledge of God to pardon all who believe is bound up with the glory of his Son. In the cross God is both 'just and the justifier of him which believeth in Jesus' (*Rom.* 3:26), and there is no higher way for a sinner to glorify God than by trusting in Christ. In the words of John Owen, 'He was lifted up between heaven and earth, that all creatures might see that God had set him forth to be a propitiation.'[10] Accordingly the work of gospel preaching is to implore men on Christ's behalf to 'be reconciled to God' (*2 Cor.* 5:20). As Charles Hodge says, this

[10] *Works of John Owen*, vol. 9, p. 594.

does not mean, 'Reconcile yourselves to God', for the word is in the passive:

> 'Be reconciled,' that is, embrace the offer of reconciliation. The reconciliation is effected by the death of Christ. God is now propitious. He can be just and yet justify the ungodly. All we have to do is not to refuse the offered love of God.[11]

The last sentence brings us to another foremost truth.

BY CHRIST CRUCIFIED THE LOVE OF GOD AND HIS WILLINGNESS TO SAVE IS TO BE MADE KNOWN TO ALL PEOPLE

To assert that the message of the cross is *wholly* one of divine love (as some have done) is to destroy its meaning. For it is only in the recognition of the holiness of God that the sufferings of Christ, which brought forth the cry, 'My God, My God, why have you forsaken me,' can be truly understood. Apart from divine justice that cry is inexplicable. In the words of Thomas Robinson, 'Sin is nowhere seen so terrible, nor the law so inflexible, as in the cross of Christ.'[12]

Yet if we ask why God was moved to exercise his holiness and justice in such a manner, at such a cost, in the sacrifice of his own beloved Son for our sins, the answer is 'God so loved the world'. And it was love that led Jesus first to undertake his sufferings, and then to invite all men to enter into the love which his death proclaims. It is the Puritan Thomas Watson who quotes the words of Augustine, 'The cross was a pulpit in which Christ preached his love to the world.'[13] On the same subject John Owen writes: 'There is no property of

---

[11] Charles Hodge, *Second Epistle to the Corinthians* (1859; reprint, London: Banner of Truth, 1963), p. 147.

[12] *Suggestive Commentary on Romans,* vol. 1 (London: Dickinson, 1878), p. 239.

[13] Thomas Watson, *A Body of Divinity* (1692; reprint, London, Banner of Truth, 1958), p. 175.

the nature of God which he doth so eminently design to glorify in the death of Christ as his love.'[14]

This brings us inevitably to John 3:16, 'God so loved the world . . .' On this text Smeaton says: 'These words of Christ plainly show that the biblical doctrine on this point is not duly exhibited unless love receives a special prominence . . . If even justice were made paramount, the balance of truth would be destroyed.'[15]

But what is the love of God to which John 3:16 gives this prominence? Does it have reference to the elect only or to all men? Some have answered that its immediate purpose has to do with neither; because, they say, 'the world' here does not have numerical so much as ethical significance: it stands for 'the evil, the darkness, the sinner'.[16] God so loved those who are utterly contrary to himself that he gave his Son to die for them! As B. B. Warfield has written on the love of God in this text:

> It is not that it is so great that it is able to extend over the whole of a big world: it is so great that it is able to pre-vail over the Holy God's hatred and abhorrence of sin. For herein is love, that *God* could love the *world* – the world that lies in the evil one: that God who is all-holy and just and good, could so love this world that He gave His only begotten Son for it, – that He might not judge it, but that it might be saved.[17]

The same writer concludes: 'The whole debate as to whether the love here celebrated distributes itself to each and every man that enters into the composition of the world, or terminates on the elect alone chosen out of the world, lies

[14] *Works*, vol. 9, p. 604.

[15] Smeaton, *The Doctrine of the Atonement as Taught by Christ Himself* (1870; reprint, Edinburgh: Banner of Truth, 1991), pp. 45–6.

[16] See the usage of the word in John 7:7;14:17,22,27,30;15:18–19;16:8,20,33;17:14.

[17] 'God's Immeasurable Love' in B. B. Warfield, *The Saviour of the World* (1916; reprint, Edinburgh: Banner of Truth, 1991), p. 120.

thus outside the immediate scope of the passage.' But granting that the message of the cross is one of love to those who
by nature are the enemies of God, we are still faced with the
fact that the text provides no justification for limiting this
love to elect sinners. For if the elect are the 'world' that God
loves, why is it that only some out of that world ('whosoever
believes in him') come to salvation? There is surely a distinction in the text between the larger number who are the
objects of love and the smaller number who believe. It would
be a strange reading of John 3:16 to make those who believe
correspond exclusively with 'the world' that God loves. Such
a divine as John Calvin had no hesitation therefore in saying
on John 3:16:

> Although there is nothing in the world deserving of
> God's favour, he nevertheless shows he is favourable to
> the whole lost world when he calls all without excep-
> tion to faith in Christ, which is indeed an entry into
> life.[18]

If this is so, it is proof enough that there is a general proclamation of the love of God which comes to men in the
preaching of the cross. Individuals everywhere may be directed, as Nicodemus was directed, to God's love for the
unworthy. We are by no means dependent on John 3:16 alone
for this understanding. Surely the same truth shines throughout our Lord's ministry. He, 'the Friend of sinners', did not
limit love to the disciples, nor yet to those whom he knew
would become disciples. We read, 'When he saw the multitudes, he was moved with compassion for them'(*Matt.* 9:36).
Moreover we find this tender compassion individualized: of
the rich young ruler, who turned away from Christ in unbelief, we are explicitly told, 'Jesus, looking at him, loved him'
(*Mark* 10:21). What but that same love can explain such
words as, 'You will not come unto me that you might have

---

[18] Calvin, *The Gospel According to John, 1-10*, trans., T. H. L. Parker
(Grand Rapids: Eerdmans, 1979), p. 74.

life'(*John* 5:40)? Or the tears that accompanied, 'O Jerusalem, Jerusalem, thou that killest the prophets, and stonest them which are sent unto thee, how often would I have gathered thy children together, even as a hen gathereth her chickens under her wings, and ye would not!'(*Luke* 13:34; *Matt* 23:37)? 'Love towards *all mankind in general,*' John Owen wrote, is enforced upon us by the example of Christ's 'own love and goodness, which are extended unto all'.[19] And Owen encouraged his hearers to dwell on the 'love of Christ, in his invitations of sinners to come unto him that they may be saved'.[20]

Elsewhere the same writer says: 'There is nothing that at the last day will tend more immediately to the advancement of the glory of God, in the inexcusableness of them who obey not the gospel, than this, that terms of peace, in the blessed way of forgiveness, were freely tendered unto them.'[21]

Some have sought to escape from the force of Christ's example by referring it to his human nature and not to his divine. But as R. L. Dabney comments: 'It would impress the common Christian mind with a most painful feeling to be thus seemingly taught that holy humanity is more generous and tender than God.'[22]

Christ's example, that reveals the very character of God, remains the permanent standard for the church. The same love

---

[19] Owen, *Works*, vol. 15, p. 70. The italics are in Owen.

[20] *Works*, vol. 1, p. 422.   [21] *Works*, vol. 6, p. 530.

[22] R. L. Dabney, *Discussions: Evangelical and Theological,* vol. 1 (1891; reprint, London: Banner of Truth, 1967), p. 308. 'It is our happiness to believe that when we see Jesus weeping over lost Jerusalem, we have "seen the Father", we have received an insight into the divine benevolence and pity.' An evidence of this can be seen in the pleading of God with sinners in the Old Testament, e.g., 'For thus saith the Lord GOD, the Holy One of Israel; In returning and rest shall ye be saved; in quietness and confidence shall be your strength: and ye would not' (*Isa.* 30:15). 'Our utmost that we can, by zeal for his glory or compassion unto your souls,' writes Owen on proclaiming the invitations of the gospel, 'comes infinitely short of his own pressing earnestness herein.' *Works*, vol. 6, p. 517.

of which he spoke to Nicodemus, and which he showed to the multitude, lies in his command that 'repentance unto remission of sins should be preached in his name among all nations, beginning at Jerusalem' (*Luke* 24:47). And the apostles understood it when they preached indiscriminately to the Jerusalem sinners, who had rejected the Son of God, the astonishing news that God has sent Jesus 'to bless you, in turning away every one of you from his iniquities' (*Acts* 3:26).[23]

Universal gospel preaching is proof of the reality of universal divine love. It is the same love of which we read in Ezekiel 33:11:'As I live, saith the Lord GOD, I have no pleasure in the death of the wicked; but that the wicked turn from his way and live: turn ye from your evil ways; for why will ye die?' When the Pharisees complained of Christ, 'This man receives sinners, and eats with them,' Jesus responded by speaking of the character of God: he is like the father of the prodigal son who 'saw him and had compassion, and ran and fell on his neck and kissed him' (*Luke* 15:20).[24] Christ's unwillingness that men should be lost is the same as the Father's. He desires that all men everywhere should turn and live. As John Murray has written:

> There is a love of God which goes forth to lost men and is manifested in the manifold blessings which all men without distinction enjoy, a love in which non-elect persons are embraced, and a love which comes to its highest expression in the entreaties, overtures and demands of gospel proclamation.[25]

[23] For the way in which the gospel message is individualized in apostolic testimony see also *Acts* 2:38; 3:19; *Col.*1: 28; *1 Tim.* 2:4; *2 Pet.* 3:9.

[24] ' It would hardly be in accord with our Lord's intention to press the point that the prodigal was destined to come to repentance, and that, therefore, the father's attitude towards him portrays the attitude of God toward the elect only, and not toward every sinner as such.' Geerhardus Vos, 'The Scriptural Doctrine of the Love of God,' in *Redemptive History and Biblical Interpretation,* ed. R. B. Gaffin (Phillipsburg, NJ: Presbyterian and Reformed, 1980), p. 443.   [25] *Collected Writings,* vol. 1, p. 68.

We conclude that the death of Christ is to be preached to all, and preached in the conviction that there is love for all. 'In the gospel,' said an eminent preacher of the Scottish Highlands, 'the provision of God's love for the salvation of sinners is revealed and offered . . . Faith is a believing God as speaking to me – a receiving of what is said as true, because it is the testimony of God, and receiving it as true in its bearing on my own case as a sinner because it is addressed by God to me.'[26] Another Scots Calvinistic leader put it still more strongly in the words: 'Men evangelized cannot go to hell but over the bowels of God's great mercies. They must wade to it through the blood of Christ.'[27]

PARTICULAR AND GENERAL LOVE

'Particular' and 'general' are not words that have explicit biblical warrant. The love of God is not presented to us in Scripture in categories at once distinguishable from each other. As Donald Carson writes:

> We must not view these ways of talking about the love of God as independent, compartmentalized, *loves* of God . . . as if each were hermetically sealed off from the other . . . If you absolutize any one of these ways in which the Bible speaks of the love of God, you will generate a false system that squeezes out other important things the Bible says, thus finally distorting your vision of God.[28]

This admission is important. Language cannot reach the immensity of the reality; and yet the terms general and particular, or common and special, represent a distinction that can be justified, as it has in fact been by many teachers of the church. John Calvin preached it. He does not hesitate to speak of 'the

[26] MS sermon of Dr John Kennedy of Dingwall on Mark 16:16, preached on 10 January 1864.

[27] John Duncan, quoted in *'Just a Talker': The Sayings of Dr John Duncan,* p. 221.

[28] D. A. Carson, *The Difficult Doctrine of the Love of God* (Wheaton: Crossway, 2000), pp. 23, 75.

first degree of love' in redemption, and this, he says, 'extends to all men, inasmuch as Christ Jesus reaches out his arms to call and allure all men both great and small, and to win them to him.' This love he goes on to distinguish from 'special love'.[29] 'As he regards men with paternal love, so also he would have them to be saved.'[30] Puritans had no problem in speaking of 'God's unspeakable love to mankind', or in asserting that 'God hath a general love to all the creatures'.[31] Other Calvinistic preachers down to C. H. Spurgeon all made a similar distinction.[32] More recently Geerhardus Vos wrote:

> We certainly have a right to say that the love which God originally bears toward man as created in His image survives in the form of compassion under the reign of sin. This being so, when the sinner comes in contact with the gospel of grace, it is natural for God to desire that he should accept its offer and be saved.[33]

If a distinction between general and special love is correct,

[29] John Calvin, *Sermons on Deuteronomy* (1583; reprint, Edinburgh: Banner of Truth, 1987), p. 167. 'The second degree of love' is 'a special love unto those to whom the gospel is preached . . . the third love that God shows us: which is, that he not only causes the gospel to be preached unto us, but also makes us to feel the power thereof, so we know him to be our father and saviour.'

[30] Calvin, *Commentaries on Jeremiah*, vol. 5 (1855; reprint, Edinburgh: Banner of Truth, 1989), p. 423 (on *Lam.* 3:33).

[31] See, for instance, Thomas Manton on John 3:16 in *Works*, vol. 2 (1871; reprint, Edinburgh, Banner of Truth, 1993), p. 340; Hugh Binning, *Christian Love* (Edinburgh: Banner of Truth, 2004), p. 6.

[32] Further on Spurgeon and this whole issue, see my *Spurgeon v. Hyper-Calvinism* (Edinburgh: Banner of Truth, 1995).

[33] Vos, *Redemptive History*, p. 443–4. Vos adds: 'But this universal love should be always so conceived as to leave room for the fact that God, for sovereign reasons, has not chosen to bestow upon its objects that higher love which not merely desires, but purposes and works out the salvation of some.' This truth gives rise to the objection, How can God be said to desire what he does not effectively will to be accomplished? The only answer is that he does so desire, and that in the sovereignty of his grace, he

does it provide a solution to the problem of how the sufferings of Christ can be said to be both particular and universal? No, this is not a solution, for it provides no answer to the question as to how Christ can be sincerely offered to those whom he did not represent in his sufferings.

To provide an answer to that question some have argued that, if the invitations of the gospel are universal, then the atonement itself must also be universal. Propitiation must have been made for the sins of all men. Others have taken the opposite course. Believing that the atonement is definite and particular they proceed to deny any universal offer of salvation. They say Christ only meant the gospel invitation to be universal in order that by its proclamation the elect among all men may be gathered in. There is, according to this belief, no message of love for all.[34]

---

has not chosen to will the salvation of all men in the same manner. As John Howe says on Christ's tears over Jerusalem: 'It is unavoidably imposed upon us to believe that God is truly unwilling for some things, which he doth not think fit to interpose his omnipotency to hinder; and is truly willing of some things which he doth not put forth his omnipotency to effect.' 'The Redeemer's Tears Wept over Lost Souls', *Works of John Howe,* vol. 2 (London: Tegg, 1848), p. 359. A helpful exegetical study by John Piper, 'Are There Two Wills in God? Divine Election and God's Desire for All to Be Saved,' will be found in T. R. Schreiner and B. A. Ware, eds., *The Grace of God and the Bondage of the Will,* vol. 1 (Grand Rapids: Baker, 1995), pp. 107–131.

[34] This kind of objection has long been heard. Thomas Chalmers regretted the teaching of 'those Particular Redemptionists who explain away the universality of the gospel, by telling us that it only bears on some men in all nations.' *Sabbath Scripture Readings,* vol. 1 (Edinburgh: Sutherland and Knox, 1848), p. 173. For a powerful sermon by the same author on 'The Universality of the Gospel Offer,' see *Works of Thomas Chalmers,* vol. 10 (Glasgow: Collins, n.d.[1835?]). Chalmers was at the centre of the evangelical revival in Scotland in the early nineteenth century, yet he also believed in particular redemption and insisted against Thomas Erskine, 'All men are not pardoned – but all men have the pardon laid down for their acceptance.' See *Correspondence of Thomas Chalmers,* ed. W. Hanna, pp. 348–9.

These alternatives have their attraction in rendering consistent what we do not otherwise understand, but with the evidence of Scripture before us they cannot be right. The reality is that we are faced with truths that far outreach our understanding. Making that point on this subject, Calvin wrote on the words of Ezekiel 18:23: 'It is not surprising that our eyes should be blinded by intense light, so that we cannot certainly judge how God wishes all to be saved, and yet has devoted all the reprobate to eternal destruction.'[35] And on how God can be said to love in different ways Calvin says:

> True it is, that to speak properly, God has no divers affections: we must not imagine so: but I handle these matters according to our capacity, and we must consider of God's love according to our slenderness, because we cannot attain to his high majesty as is said afore, and therefore even he himself also uttereth himself to us according to our ability.[36]

Similarly, Thomas Crawford has said that the subject, 'far exceeds the power and compass of our faculties . . . it may be that the missing link that is needful, may be hidden from our view in that profound abyss of God's everlasting counsels which we cannot fathom.'[37]

Rowland Hill, the English evangelist at the end of the eighteenth century, was once present at 'a diet of catechizing' in Scotland. After he had also put some questions which were correctly answered, a grey-haired man asked if he might put a question to Mr Hill: 'Sir,' he said, 'can you reconcile the

---

[35] *Commentaries on Ezekiel*, vol. 2 (Edinburgh: Calvin Translation Soc., 1850), p. 247.

[36] Calvin, *Deuteronomy*, p. 167.

[37] Thomas J. Crawford, *The Doctrine of Holy Scripture Respecting the Atonement* (Edinburgh: Blackwood, 1888), p. 510. Smeaton speaks similarly: ' A special atonement and invitations sincerely made on the ground of it to mankind indefinitely are quite compatible. They will be found to meet at some point though their junction be beyond our present line of vision.' *Atonement Taught by Christ*, p. 380.

universal call o' the gospel wi' the doctrine o' a particler eleck?' Hill was right to reply promptly that he could not.

While the distinction between the general and the special or particular love of God does not, therefore, give us all the light we might ask for, it is nonetheless of much importance. It is necessary for believers to understand the special nature of God's love to them. 'The Son of God loved me and gave himself for me' (*Gal.* 2:20), is not a statement that gives security to all. To deny the special love of God, and to believe that Christ loves all men equally, is to suppose that Christ has done no more for those the Father has given to him than for mankind at large. But if Christians are no more loved than those who will finally be lost, the decisive factor in salvation becomes, not God's grace and love, but something in them, and their perseverance becomes dependent upon them-selves.[38] To widen the atonement, and to speak of it only in terms of general love, is to take away its *saving* power. The believer in Christ needs to know that the love which em-braces him is eternal, almighty, and immutable. It does not hang upon his faith for it went before faith.

However, if one facet of truth is needed by the believer, another is important for the unconverted. If there is no love except special love for the elect, then no one has any right to apprehend any love in God for them *before* they have evidence of their election, which is to say, before they are converted. And that would mean that preachers must not speak of the love of Christ indefinitely to all their un-converted hearers. Such an omission has to subvert gospel preaching. It would no longer be 'good news' for all – no longer an appeal 'not to refuse the offered love of God' – it would be a system closed to all except those who find some reason for faith other than the plain invitations of Christ.

The nature of conversion is an issue involved here. Are men brought into the kingdom of God by an action of God

---

[38] It was not an accident that Methodism departed from Protestant evangelicalism in rejecting the final perseverance of saints.

that by-passes the mind and will, or are those faculties involved in the great change? Does Christ draw men to himself irrespective of their thoughts and their consent? The scriptural answer has to be that conversion *includes* hearing and understanding; the Holy Spirit uses truth to convince of sin; that is the first work.

But conviction of sin is not enough to bring men to Christ. Conviction of sin only speaks of God's holiness, it tells the sinner nothing of God's willingness to pardon; it does nothing to remove the suspicion - common to fallen man – that God is against him and unconcerned for his happiness. For that further truth is needed. It is only the disclosure of love which can persuade the sinner of God's readiness and willingness to pardon, and thus the necessity that love be made known to all indefinitely in the free offer of the gospel. Love is the great attraction. Love stands foremost in the gospel appeal. 'It is not the over-heavy load of sin,' says John Bunyan, 'but the discovery of mercy . . . that makes a man come to Jesus Christ . . . Behold how the promises, invitations, calls, and encouragements, like lilies, lie round about thee! Take heed that thou dost not tread them under foot, sinner. With promises, did I say? Yea, he hath mixed all those with his own name, his Son's name; also, with the names of mercy, goodness, compassion, love, pity, grace, forgiveness, pardon, and what not, that he might encourage the coming sinner.' [39]

On the same point, John Owen wrote:

Christ draws none to himself whether they will or no; but he casts on their minds, hearts, and wills the cords of his grace and love, working in them powerfully,

---

[39] Bunyan, *Works*, vol. 1 (Edinburgh: Banner of Truth, 1991), pp. 286, 298. 'Men must see something in Jesus Christ, else they will not come to him.' (p. 295). A fine example of preaching that pleads with men can be seen in the closing pages of Bunyan's *Come and Welcome to Jesus Christ* (1681; reprint, Edinburgh: Banner of Truth, 2004), from which these quotes are taken.

working on them kindly, to cause them to choose him
. . . Drawing grace is manifested in, and drawing love
proceeds from, the sufferings of Christ on the cross.[40]

This love is to be proclaimed as 'good news' not to men as
elect but to men as sinners.[41] That is why any message that
would not include love to individuals until there is evidence
of their election turns the gospel upside down. It withholds
the very truth most conducive to bringing souls to rest in
Christ. Without question, history teaches us that the evangelists most used of God have all been men for whom love has
been the main theme.[42] Our sin must be discovered, says
Richard Sibbes, 'to drive us out of ourselves,' but then, 'there
must be a great deal of persuasion to still the accusing conscience of a sinner, to set it down, make it quiet, and
persuade it of God's love'.[43]

Persuading men of God's love is the great calling of the
Christian ministry. It is part of preaching 'to root out all the
secret reserves of unbelief concerning God's unwillingness to
give mercy, grace and pardon to sinners'.[44] It cannot be done
without conviction in the preacher that this love is a wonderful reality, and that it is to be pressed on all his hearers.

Yet, it may be asked, if this love is not necessarily saving,
should the distinction between 'general' and 'special' not be

---

[40] *Works*, vol. 9, p. 592,

[41] Ibid., vol. 6, p. 523. Owen is including both the universal and the
particular when he says that the freeness of God's mercy does not
interfere with the efficacy. 'Though he [God] proclaim pardon in the
blood of Christ indefinitely, according to the fullness and excellency of it,
yet he giveth out his quickening grace to enable men to receive it as he
pleaseth; for he hath mercy on whom he will have mercy. But this lies in
the thing itself; the way is opened and prepared, and it is not because men
cannot enter, but because they will not, that they do not enter.' p. 529.

[42] Evidence for this statement is vast; I give some of it in my book,
Pentecost – Today? (Edinburgh: Banner of Truth, 1998), p. 90–9.

[43] Sibbes, *Works,* vol. 2, p. 186.

[44] Owen, *Works*, vol. 6, p. 504.

made clear to people when the gospel is being presented? The answer has to be no, for Scripture itself makes no such distinction in the presentation of the gospel to the lost. And the reason why it does not do so is plain: it is not a doctrine either of special love or of general love that is to be offered to sinners; it is rather *Christ himself.* More than that, it is not ultimately preachers who offer Christ to others; but Christ – divine love incarnate – who speaks in the gospel and offers himself fully and freely to the most undeserving, if they will but receive him. 'Christ offers himself in mercy to the worst soul,'[45] even, as Whitefield used to say, to 'the devil's cast-aways'.

The relation of the preacher's role to Christ's is well stated by Robert Candlish:

> I go to the crowd of criminals, shut up in prison, under sentence of death; and my message is, not that in consequence of Christ's death I have now to offer them all liberty to go out free; – but that Christ himself is there, even at the door; in whom, if they apply to him, they will find One who can meet every accusation against them, and enrich them with every blessing. I refer them and point them to himself – to himself alone . . . I do not speak to them of a certain amount of atoning virtue purchased by the obedience and death of Christ, as if it were a store laid up for general use, from which they may take what they need. I speak to them of Christ as being himself the atonement, and summon them to a personal dealing with him accordingly . . . a present Saviour now, as well as then, having in his hand a special pardon and special grace for every one who will resort to him – and nothing for any who will not.[46]

---

[45] Sibbes, op. cit., p. 187. 'It is our office, thus to lay open and offer the riches of Christ.'

[46] Robert S. Candlish, *The Atonement:Its Reality, Completeness, and Extent* (Edinburgh: Nelson, 1861), pp. 232–3.

Candlish's point is of vital importance. Not only does evangelism not depend on the existence of a universal atonement, any making of saving faith to rest on a statement that 'Christ has died for you' is dangerously wrong. As Spurgeon, one of the foremost evangelists in English church history, said:

> You may believe that Jesus Christ died for you, and may believe what is not true; you may believe that which will bring you no sort of good whatever. That is not saving faith. The man that has saving faith afterwards attains to the conviction that Christ died for him, but it is not of the essence of saving faith. Do not get that into your head, or it will ruin you. Do not say, 'I believe that Jesus Christ died for me,' and because of that feel that you are saved. I pray you to remember that the genuine faith that saves has for its main element – trust – absolute rest of the whole soul – on the Lord Jesus Christ to save me, whether he died in particular or in special to save me or not, and relying, as I am, wholly and alone on him, I am saved. Afterwards I come to perceive that I have a special interest in the Saviour's blood.[47]

CONCLUSIONS

1. *This whole discussion shows how truth needs to be taught in its biblical proportions, and with consideration of the condition and circumstances of the hearers.* Not all truths are equally important for all and on all occasions. The so-called Five Points of Calvinism are important to distinguish certain truths from opposing tenets, but they are not all equally important for the presentation of the gospel to the lost. Whitefield was right to admire the words of John Bradford, 'Let a man go to the school of faith and repentance, before he goes to the university of election and predestination.'[48] The preaching of

[47] *Metropolitan Tabernacle Pulpit,* vol. 58, pp. 583–4.
[48] *George Whitefield's Journals* (1756; London: Banner of Truth, 1960), p. 491.

Christ crucified to the unconverted requires the presentation of his Person, the cost of his substitution for sinners, and the immensity of the divine love for sinners; it does not require explanations of the extent of the atonement. To quote Candlish again: 'It is irrelevant here to raise any question as to the extent, or even as to the sufficiency of the atonement. It is enough that it is sufficient for all who will avail themselves of it.'[49]

In this connection it is noteworthy that in the preaching of one of the most effective Calvinistic evangelists of the twentieth century, D. Martyn Lloyd-Jones, it was generally impossible to tell from his gospel preaching that he held to a particular and definite atonement.

2. *It is not the preacher's business to explain the unexplainable.* Where the Scripture sees no contradictions in its statements it is not our responsibility to answer objections that may be raised. For instance, 'How is it consistent with the unity of God's nature to speak of his possessing both general and particular love? How can the truth of his anger towards the wicked be compatible with the existence of any common love? Can compassion and wrath coexist in God's attitude towards sinners?'

Much error has come about through attempts to offer explanations of such questions. It ought to be enough, as I have said, to stand by what Scripture asserts. We are to be humble before the conviction that God's thoughts are far above our own. Truths that look contradictory to us are not so in the light of heaven. We are told, for instance, that God's wrath is revealed against the same men who are *also* the object of goodness and longsuffering that would lead them to repentance (*Rom*.1:18; 2:4). For Israel's rejection of the Saviour 'the wrath [was] come upon them to the uttermost'; yet God's compassionate entreaties towards them continued:

[49] Candlish, *The Atonement,* p. 202.

'To Israel he says, All day long I have stretched forth my hands unto a disobedient and gainsaying people' (*1 Thess.* 2:16; *Rom.* 10:21). It is of men under God's wrath that Scripture says he is 'not willing that any should perish, but that all should come to repentance' (*2 Pet.* 3:9).

These are truths to be preached without hesitation and without distracting needy souls with questions of controversy.

3. *Discussion of the doctrines of grace becomes dangerous when interest in them is more theoretical than practical.* Truth is given to men in order to their salvation (*2 Tim.* 3:15). If the presentation of the gospel ceases to be the first concern we have already gone wrong. To possess a knowledge of profound truths without *seeing* them at work in the salvation of sinners is not what Scripture commends. All knowledge that does not lead to practical love is to be pitied.

In this connection, words once spoken by William Roberts in a gathering of Calvinistic Methodist preachers in Wales, are worthy of repetition. Aspects of Calvinistic truth were under discussion, and the meeting was proceeding in such a way that Roberts believed their unity was being needlessly threatened. After a younger man had referred to the difficulty he found in preaching on election, Roberts rose to speak. He said he was glad to see that the young man evidently believed that 'there is a greater purpose to preaching than mere talking', and questioned whether they would ever be 'sufficient preachers' to preach election. 'I do not know who of us – if any – is such.' Then he went on:

> But should you ever attempt it, strive to view it yourself, and to so present it to your listeners, in the relationships in which you find it in God's Book. Particularly, do not keep it afar off in eternity; it will do no good to anyone there. Bring it down to the chapel, down to the midst of the people. There it will save. It is in its operation that we will understand election, if we will ever understand it.

Consider a large, complex machine, with its various wheels, pipes, hooks and chains, all interweaving and interlocking with one another. It is the engineer who understands its design and can explain it, in and of itself, its various parts, and the relationships of each part with the others so as to make one engine. But I can see it in operation. And an ordinary, illiterate man, knowing nothing of the laws of Mechanics and ignorant of the names which the engineer has for the various parts of the machine, he can make use of it and work with it, to achieve the end that was in view when it was designed and built. And it would be ludicrous to see those ignorant workers proceeding to argue amongst themselves as to the composition of the machine, rather than using it to purpose.

When you preach election, preach of it at work. Beware of speculating boldly and investigating in detail into the workings of the internal parts of the machine, and avoid bringing your listeners into the same temptation. Show the worth and glory of the machine by demonstrating it at work. Show the worth of the election of grace by depicting it as saving those who cannot save themselves. That is the view of it given in the Bible, and that, as far as I know, is the only worth it holds for the sinner. If this were not so I do not think the Gospel would acknowledge any relationship to it. But, on the contrary, upon understanding election properly, we find that it not only belongs to the Gospel but that it is one of the sweetest parts of it . . . it is life itself for such a dull, helpless, stubborn creature as myself that God has a provision, in his infinite grace, that meets my condition, and that he will never see in me anything that could turn out a disappointment to him, for he knew my whole history long before I knew anything of it myself.[50]

[50] *The Atonement Controversy in Welsh Theological Literature and Debate, 1707–1841,* Owen Thomas, translated by John Aaron (1874; first English

Calvinistic belief surely loses its attractiveness when the wisdom of this illustration is forgotten.

4. *If controversy among Christians on the atonement is sometimes unavoidable, let it be conducted in the most guarded language.* It is to be deeply regretted that this subject has too often led to God-dishonouring debate among Christians. Much time has been lost in argument and in the promotion of different views. But concern for purity in the faith can never justify believers in making the cross a subject of strife among themselves. We are shocked when we read that at Calvary there were soldiers gambling – 'casting lots' – over who should possess the Saviour's clothing. But our conduct is not so very different if we fall to wrangling about our crucified Saviour. In his day, when there were such disputes over the doctrine of the atonement, John Elias found it necessary to say:

> The conversation of many respecting the death of Christ is often very unbecoming. It is that of persons that have no corresponding feeling, no brokenness of heart and humility. They converse about it in a dry, carnal, and presumptuous manner. They never talk about it as the only way a person ever saw to save his life, when pursued by the holy law, and condemned by the justice of God.[51]

5. *No subject places higher demands upon the gospel preacher than this one.* If the cross is the pulpit from which the love of God is to be made known, why is it not more widely heard among us? Has our emphasis moved from the apostolic centre? Sometimes a lack of concentration on the love of

---

translation, Edinburgh: Banner of Truth, 2002), pp. 343–4. This book gives a sad demonstration of how unprofitable controversy may be.

[51] *John Elias, Life, Letters and Essays*, p. 362. The volume mentioned above, *The Atonement Controversy*, is replete with evidence that his words were not unnecessary.

God is justified by the argument that love is too prominent in the false religion of our times. It is true that all speaking of 'the love of God' apart from Christ is a false gospel, but the prevalence of the false ought to make us the more ready to preach the true. The confidence which non-Christians sometimes say they have in divine love is not in the love of God at all.

The source of our weakness as evangelists is that we are not living close enough to the fountainhead of love. Faithfulness and conscientiousness may be enough to enable us to say something on the law and judgments of God, but we cannot speak well of the love of God to sinners unless we are personally familiar with it and persuaded of it. What is at the forefront of our experience is going to be at the forefront of our preaching. It is 'divine love', writes Edwards, by which 'a minister of the gospel is a *burning light* . . . with ardent love to the souls of men, and desires for their salvation'.[52] 'Let him speak of love,' says Bunyan, 'that is *taken* with love, that is *captivated* with love, that is *carried away* with love . . . These are the men that *sweeten* churches and bring glory to God.'[53]

Of all the graces needed to make Christ known the greatest is love. The preachers who have had much of this grace, even though sometimes deficient in other respects, have been those owned of God to a remarkable degree. This is the reason why the Wesleyan Methodists were once so greatly used to deprive Satan of many of his subjects. They were right to sing:

> The arms of love that compass me
> Would all mankind embrace.

Love explains why men have been able to live with a passion for the conversion of others. 'He loved the world that hated him,' wrote Cowper of Whitefield, 'the tear that fell upon his Bible was sincere.' 'I could bear to be torn in pieces,'

[52] Jonathan Edwards, *Works*, vol. 2, p. 957.
[53] *Works*, vol. 2, pp. 39, 35.

said Henry Martyn, 'if I could but see eyes of faith directed to the Redeemer.'

Where is this love to be found but in the Saviour himself? Our prayer must be to be 'delivered from all coldness to Christ's death and passion,' and God answers that prayer by giving us a new, felt, understanding of texts we may long have known. The Scriptures can be illuminated afresh to us as they were once to an Australian Methodist, William Reeves. Before going to his trade as usual on the morning of August 16, 1846, the following occurred as he read John 3 in family worship:

> When I came to the exceeding precious lines, the 16th and 17th verses, the Lord in a most extraordinary manner broke in on my soul by the light of his Holy Spirit. He filled my whole soul with pure light, with fullness of joy, and holy love: all language fails to express what I felt. I saw and felt as I never saw before, that the Almighty did not love me in word only, but in deed and truth, in bestowing that unspeakable gift of his well-beloved Son: and I saw so clearly the precious love of his dear Son so sweetly blending with the Father's, that they became together one mighty ocean of unfathomable love.[54]

The cross remains the pulpit of God's love!

---

[54] Quoted in Robert Steel, *Doing Good: The Christian in Walks of Usefulness* (Edinburgh: Nelson, 1871), p. 80.

ADDITIONAL NOTES

JOHN CALVIN, 1509–64: GOSPEL PREACHING

'Isaiah had preached on the death and resurrection of our Lord Jesus Christ: as if he had displayed the banner to declare that everyone should come to be reconciled to God, and that poor sinners should be received to mercy, that their satisfaction and righteousness is altogether ready, and that God desireth nothing but to be merciful to those who seek him.'[55]

THOMAS CHALMERS, 1780–1847: GOD IS LOVE

'There is a moral, a depth and intensity of meaning, a richness of sentiment that the Bible calls unsearchable, in the cross of Christ. It tells a sinful world that God is righteousness; and it as clearly and emphatically tells us that God is love.

'But for the purpose of making this doctrine available to ourselves personally, we must view the love of God, not as a vague and inapplicable generality, but as specially directed, nay actually proffered, and that pointedly and individually to each of us. It is not sufficiently adverted to by inquirers, nor sufficiently urged by ministers, that the constitution of the gospel warrants this appropriation of its blessings by each man for himself . . . It is a message of good news to all people . . . The blessings of the gospel are as accessible to all who will, as are the water or the air or any of the cheap and common bounties of nature. The element of Heaven's love is in as universal diffusion among the dwelling-places of men, as is the atmosphere they breathe in. It solicits admittance at every door; and the ignorance or unbelief of man are the only obstacles which it has to struggle with. It is commensurate with the species; and may be tendered, urgently and honestly tendered, to each individual of the human family.'[56]

[55] Calvin, *Thirteen Sermons*, p. 61.
[56] *Works of Thomas Chalmers*, vol. 10, pp. 188–91.

THE OLD EVANGELICALISM

WILLIAM NEVINS, 1797–1835: THE EXTENT OF THE ATONEMENT

'In regard to the extent of the atonement, I would just say that it is so extensive that none will ever be lost by reason of any deficiency in it. It is extensive as it need be; so extensive, that on the ground of it, salvation is sincerely and freely offered to all; so extensive, that if all should accept the offer, all would be saved. Is not this extensive enough? It is limited only in this sense, that it was made with a special reference to those who will ultimately be saved by it. The foundation is broad enough to receive every soul – all the souls of all men. And all the sins of all these souls, though they be very many and very great, Christ's blood has still efficacy to cleanse away. Therefore, let each one come to Christ, and secure himself an interest in the atonement. Let this be the first anxiety – the first work. Does anything equal it in point of importance?'[57]

JOHN BONAR, 1799–1863: THE UNIVERSAL OFFER AND THE COMPASSION OF GOD

'Two things are evidently required, in order that these calls may be warrantably addressed to all, and all may have full warrant to comply with them. 1st, That there should be a Saviour provided – and 2nd, That that Saviour being provided, his salvation should be freely offered to us. Christ is an all-sufficient Saviour – having all that sinners need. Christ as thus all-sufficient is freely offered to all, – and this offer is conveyed to us, upon the testimony of God, and comes to each as "the word of salvation" sent to himself.

'The call to come is thus itself the assurance of welcome. As it would be presumption to come without an invitation, so it is presumption to hesitate when that invitation is sent . . . Yes, Christ is God's gift to mankind sinners. The cross is God's ordinance for the salvation of men, and Christ is dead for you to come to – for you to live by. God calleth you by ten thousand expostulations and

---

[57] *Select Remains of the Rev. William Nevins* (New York: Taylor, 1836), p. 139.

entreaties which he sends in his Word. Christ calleth you by his sufferings – by his death – by his tears of compassion – and by his entreaties of grace. The Holy Spirit calleth you by every one of those words of mercy and of warning, and by every conviction and impression which they awaken in the heart. Thy God hath found thee out, not with words of condemnation, but with words of mercy. His words are all as fresh and full of love as if first now, and first by you, they have been heard in human language. With these words of gracious compassion doth he once more overtake you – beseeching you to turn and live - assuring you that in no wise you shall be cast out. O sons of men, his words mean all that they say, and infinitely more than human words can say; they are drops of the compassion of God . . . God directly, personally, and earnestly beseeches us to be reconciled to him - eternal life in offer, Christ in offer, everlasting blessedness in offer, and every one either receiving or rejecting these offers. Rest not until the voice of Christ to the sons of men be answered by you in the first breathings of the Spirit of adoption, "I will arise and go to my Father." '[58]

[58] 'The Universal Calls and Invitations of the Gospel Consistent with the Total Depravity of Man, and Particular Redemption,' sermon on Proverbs 8:4,6, in *The Free Church Pulpit* (Perth: Dewar, 1844).

5

WHAT CAN WE LEARN FROM JOHN WESLEY?

'The Methodist movement deserves to be studied, not only as one of the great events of the past century, but because its history may suggest hints as to the best method of dealing with some of those problems which are now forcing themselves upon the attention of the church. Within the most part of Christendom "there remaineth yet much land to be possessed"; There are huge masses of heathenism to be reclaimed. How are they to be reached?'

British and Foreign Evangelical Review,
(ed. George Smeaton), vol. 11 (1862), p. 303.

'I have been reading, recently, Southey's *Life of John Wesley* and have been greatly impressed with it. I see more clearly than ever that every true spiritual revival is not the result of man's witness, but is determined by God.'

D. M. Lloyd-Jones: The First Forty Years, 1899–1939,
Iain H. Murray (Edinburgh: Banner of Truth, 1982),
p. 157.

Whether we are young Christians or older ones, we are all prone to fall into mistakes, but there are some mistakes into which young Christians are more particularly liable to fall. One of my mistakes at that age often recurs to me: when in my twenties, and in all the enthusiasm of discovering the writings of the Reformers and Puritans, I decided to carry out a purge of my infant library. The books that went were not by liberals but included such items as a set of Edward Irving's *Works*, the *Commentary on the New Testament* by Adam Clarke, and some of the books of G. Campbell Morgan. Somehow the sermons of John Wesley survived the purge. I think this omission was due to sentiment rather than principle, for Wesley's sermons were one of the first serious Christian books I ever possessed. But even Wesley did not wholly escape the sifting. I regret to say I exchanged a fine china figure of him for a second-hand set of Daniel Neal's *History of the Puritans*.

As we get older we slowly recognize the origin of such youthful excess. It lies in the confidence born of immaturity that we can draw a definite line between the profitable and the unprofitable, that we can put all the worthy and all the unworthy in their respective theological pigeon holes. But we have to learn that authors do not fall into such neat arrangements; many straddle across our would-be divide. One such 'straddler' was Richard Baxter who left us these wise comments in his later years:

> I now see more good and more evil in all men than heretofore I did. I see good men are not as I once thought they were, but have more imperfections. And the nearer approach and fuller trial doth make the best

appear more weak and faulty than their admirers at a distance think.[1]

It is a grand pernicious error to think that the same man's judgments must be followed in every case. And it is of grand importance to know how to value our guides, as the cases vary.[2]

The last quotation from Baxter is particularly relevant to the subject before us. When I previously wrote on Wesley[3] I overlooked the testimony of what was one of the most decidedly Calvinistic journals in the world, the *British and Foreign Evangelical Review* during the editorship of William Cunningham and George Smeaton. It contained a number of appreciations of Wesleyan Methodists, one of which I have quoted above. But there was also this caution:

When God wants men for a special exigency or a particular field, he brings them forward amply qualified for the work committed to their charge. These men, as we have said, were not fitted either by nature or culture, or experience, for doctrinal reformers. And hence, we believe, that Methodism was never commissioned for this specific work . . . it travelled out of its legitimate sphere when it undertook the work of reforming the creed of Christendom . . . its heavenly mission, though by no means less important, was not distinctly doctrinal.[4]

I have begun with personal testimony, and the way I want to approach our subject is to repeat some lessons that I believe I have been learning or relearning from Wesley and the Methodists in more recent years.

---

[1] *Reliquiae Baxterianae*, Part 1 (London, 1696), p. 130.

[2] *The Cure of Church-divisions* (London, 1670), p. 216.

[3] Iain H. Murray, *Wesley and Men Who Followed* (Edinburgh: Banner of Truth, 2003).

[4] *British and Foreign Evangelical Review*, vol. 11, p. 30.

What Can We Learn from John Wesley?

WESLEY IS A NECESSARY REMINDER OF HOW UPBRINGING
AND EDUCATION PREJUDICE OUR MINDS.

As is common knowledge, Wesley was born in the Church of
England rectory at Epworth, Lincolnshire, in 1703. Both his
parents, Samuel and Susanna Wesley, were ardent supporters
of the Established Church and their principles were strongly
impressed on their ten children. So Wesley could affirm, 'I am
an High Churchman, the son of an High Churchman.'[5] Even
after his conversion to evangelical belief, he wrote in his
Journal for March 31, 1739: 'I could scarce reconcile myself at
first to this strange way of preaching in the fields . . .
having been all my life (till very lately) so tenacious of every
point relating to decency and order, that I should have
thought the saving our souls almost a sin if it had not been
done in a church.' It was the same background that, years
later, led Charles Wesley to insist that he must be buried in
'consecrated ground'.

What is not so well known is that Wesley's grandfathers had
been Puritan preachers and both had become Dissenters on
the passing of the Act of Uniformity in 1662. That date drew
the line that has continued ever since between the Established
Church and Nonconformity. Wesley's paternal grandfather,
the first John Wesley, was a faithful pastor in Dorset, a friend
of Joseph Alleine; and, like Alleine, he suffered imprisonment
for the truth. His maternal grandfather was the eminent Dr
Samuel Annesley, one of the leading London Puritans,
ejected from St Giles, Cripplegate, in 1662, and later pastor
of a Dissenting congregation until his death in 1695. So both
Wesley's parents, born in the 1660s, grew up in a Dissenting
environment. Yet by the time they married in 1688 they had
both rejected the position of their parents and become devo-
tees of the national Church.

[5] *Letters of John Wesley*, ed. John Telford, vol. 6 (London: Epworth,
1931), p. 156. The context of the quotation has to do with 'notions of
passive resistance and non-resistance' in which, he says, he 'was bred up'
from childhood.

Not enough information has survived to explain how Samuel and Susanna Wesley, from two such families, could embrace principles so different from those of their parents. But one thing probably contributed to their change of mind. By the last quarter of the seventeenth century in England the Puritan tradition was less attractive than it had been in earlier years. Puritan witness had been overtaken by internal controversies over doctrine, by an over-scrupulous regard for points of church government, by fragmentation into parties, and by too much engagement in politics.

Speaking of 'miscarriages' among Puritan congregations, John Owen wrote in 1668:

> Some have been ready to condemn all that go not along with them in every principle, yea, opinion or practice. And every day slight occasions and provocations are made the ground and reason for severe censures; but nothing is more contrary to the meek and holy spirit of Christ.[6]

John Wesley's mother, Susanna, was to record this memory of the Dissenters she knew in her youth:

> I have been well acquainted with many predestinarians and have observed two sorts of people amongst them. The one were serious and, I believe, sincerely desirous of salvation, and striving to enter by the strait gate into the kingdom of heaven. These were generally much dejected and (excepting a few) always seeking after marks of grace, being doubtful of their own election often upon the point of despair, being ignorant of that true gospel liberty which is attainable in this life and which many, who hold universal redemption do actually enjoy.
>
> Others, and they the far greater number, were very confident of their own election, thought it a great sin to make any doubt of it, and could not patiently hear it questioned. These were commonly sunk in carnal secu-

[6] *Works*, vol. 6, p. 591.

rity and without scruple gave in to all manner of self-indulgence, fancying that what would be sin in a reprobate would be none in them.[7]

No doubt there is an element of prejudice in these words (which were written in support of her son against Whitefield's Calvinism), but the fact is that Susanna Wesley's words coincide with the perception of the Puritans that was common in the eighteenth century. And this image and caricature was strengthened by the state of numbers of the Dissenting churches. It was not among the Dissenting churches that the Evangelical Revival began. For the most part there was little zeal for evangelism shown among them. As Henry Rack has written, Dissent 'became a static, ingrown, hereditary (though also declining) creed'; for Wesley it seemed to be 'a hole-in-the-corner, static, localized form of religion'.[8]

So Wesley grew up in a home, a university, and a country, which identified the weakness of Dissent with the Calvinism of the Puritans. To us that may seem a classic case of confusion of identity, yet we have to remember that the Calvinism, of which the Dissenting chapels of the eighteenth century were the supposed representatives, was too often of a non-evangelistic kind. It was not difficult for observers to look at existing conditions in many Dissenting 'meeting houses' and conclude they were the consequence of predestinarian beliefs. Indeed it was from some of these chapels that the idea was promoted that the gospel should not be stated in terms of a 'free offer' to all men, that God has no love for the non-elect, and that Christ was not weeping over men's rejection of salvation when he said, 'O Jerusalem,

---

[7] *Some Remarks on a Letter from the Reverend Mr Whitefield to the Reverend Mr Wesley, In a Letter from a Gentlewoman to her Friend* (London, 1741), quoted in *Susanna Wesley, The Complete Writings*, ed. Charles Wallace, Jr (New York: OUP, 1997), p. 470. Frank Baker has proved that Mrs Wesley was the author of this originally anonymous piece.

[8] Henry D. Rack, *Reasonable Enthusiast: John Wesley and the Rise of Methodism* (London: Epworth, 1989), pp. 35, 38.

Jerusalem . . . how often would I have gathered thy children together, even as a hen gathereth her chickens under her wings, and ye would not!' (*Matt.* 23:37).[9]

Reading Wesley we may ask, How could a Christian be so prejudiced against Calvinism as he was? Part of the answer has to be that he did not understand the term as Whitefield, or you and I, understand it. But I believe it is profitable to remember that prejudice and distorted vision is common to us all as fallen men. It can exist in the best and most sincere of Christian men. This does not excuse Wesley's prejudice. It was a serious fault. As J. C. Ryle wrote,

> That Wesley would have done better if he could have thrown off his Arminianism, I have not the least doubt; but that he preached the gospel, honoured Christ, and did extensive good, I no more doubt than I doubt my own existence.[10]

It seems to me there is a lesson here that we can learn from Wesley. Prejudiced he certainly was, but his failure in this regard should lead us to think how far we may be guilty of the same fault. Thomas Scott, who was as sound an evangelical as one is likely to find, wrote in 1795:

> I believe there are many things unscriptural among us all; that is either defective, redundant, or erroneous: but human nature is very fallible; ten thousand circumstances produce prejudices, which warp the judgment; and the Lord seems to illuminate his people but in part.[11]

---

[9] A leader in promoting this teaching was Joseph Hussey, of whose writings John Newton said, 'I frequently found more bones than meat, and seasoned with much of an angry and self-important spirit.' See my *Spurgeon v. Hyper-Calvinism*, p. 118.

[10] J. C. Ryle, *Christian Leaders of the Eighteenth Century* (1885; reprint, Edinburgh: Banner of Truth, 1978), p. 86.

[11] *Letters and Papers of the Rev. Thomas Scott*, ed. John Scott (London: Seeley, 1824), p.176. Many eminent failures in this regard exist in church

I am sorry I did not understand this in younger years. Spurgeon built a library on better principles than mine. Listen to his wisdom and humour in his *Commenting and Commentaries:*

> I have placed next to Gill in my library Adam Clarke, but as I have no desire to have my rest broken by wars among the authors, I have placed Doddridge between them. If the spirits of these two worthies could descend to the earth in the same mood in which they departed, no one house would be able to hold them. Adam Clarke is the great annotator of our Wesleyan friends; and they have no reason to be ashamed of him, for he takes rank among the chief of expositors . . . like Gill, he is one-sided, only in the opposite direction to our friend the Baptist. The use of the two authors may help to preserve the balance of your judgments.[12]

WESLEY HAS SOMETHING TO TEACH US ON THE RELATION-SHIP BETWEEN ZEAL FOR THE GOSPEL AND CHURCH GOVERNMENT, PROCEDURES, AND PRACTICES.

Let me begin by reminding you of the kind of government that slowly became the church structure of Wesleyan Methodism. The seventeenth century had seen proposals for various types of church government but here was something quite different. It followed the pattern of neither the Church of England nor the Dissenters. It began with Whitefield and Wesley itinerating around the country, a practice Wesley was to continue for fifty years. He went, not where he was invited to go, but wherever he believed providence led him.

---

history: Augustine's sacramentalism; Luther's insistence on consubstantiation; Calvin's encouragement of the civil powers to punish error; Baxter's confusion on justification.

[12] C. H. Spurgeon, *Commenting and Commentaries: Two lectures, a catalogue of Bible commentaries and expositions* (1876; reprint, London: Banner of Truth, 1969), pp. 9–10.

For acting in this way both men were accused of arrogating to themselves the apostolic office. Who ever heard of preachers itinerating in this manner in a country where there were already hundreds of churches? What Church of England bishop spoke, as Wesley did, of looking 'upon all the world as my parish'?[13]

But this itinerating had other consequences. Many were affected by the preaching and as they often had no one else to care for their spiritual lives they looked to Whitefield and Wesley. Whitefield declined to set up any new structure, in part because that was not his gift, but Wesley began to organize a network of societies. To belong to them you did not have to be of any particular denomination but you had to be a person 'fleeing from the wrath to come', and conscientious about living a strict Christian life.

These societies were soon far too many to be nurtured by one man and so Wesley needed many men whom he called 'Assistants'. In fact, they were all preachers, irregular ones indeed for no one had ordained them – neither bishops, presbyteries, nor local churches. In addition, these Assistant preachers, instead of having the care of one society, were required to be itinerants like Wesley himself. The country was divided up into circuits and in a yearly conference the Assistants were appointed to an area, perhaps a few hundred miles square. Usually there were two itinerant preachers to a circuit and they worked there for one, two or at the most three years. The senior of the preachers in each circuit was the Superintendent. While these Assistants were the regular ministers of the word, who gave all their time to the work, the societies also had help from men known as 'local preachers' who earned their living by other employment.

So it was that a pyramid structure came into existence with Wesley and the annual Conference at its head. He arranged

---

[13] The phrase, he explained to his brother Charles, meant, 'that in whatever part of it I am, I judge it meet, right, and my bounden duty, to declare unto all that are willing to hear the glad tidings of salvation'.

that on his death the authority he had exercised should be transferred into the hands of one hundred of his Assistants and so the same pattern continued, the Conference placing the itinerant preachers in the circuits year by year. In due course the societies thus united formally became the Methodist Church.

Now to these Methodist views on the ordering of the life of the churches there are two main objections that can be made. The first is the one that was raised repeatedly in the eighteenth century, and the second is the one we are more likely to raise today. Let us take the common eighteenth-century objection first. It was the charge that the Methodist procedures disrupted the authority of the Church and promoted disorder.

Wesley's answer was that commitment to the gospel takes a higher priority than the upholding of church order. It was enough for him that the arrangements he encouraged proved effective in the salvation of sinners. He saw an itinerant ministry as essential because in large areas of England the majority of the people heard no saving gospel. The Methodist rule, said Wesley, was to evangelize, 'wherever they had a prospect of saving souls from death'. Thus when an Anglican clergyman accused him of ignoring good church order, he replied that the work of saving souls was a higher priority, and he asked his critic:

> What is the end of all *ecclesiastical order*? Is it not to bring souls from the power of Satan to God? And to build them up in his fear and love? *Order*, then, is so far valuable as it answers these ends; and if it answers them not it is worth nothing. Now I would fain know, Where has *order* answered these ends? Not in any place where I have been: not among the tinners in Cornwall, the keelmen at Newcastle, the colliers in Kingswood or Staffordshire; not among the drunkards, swearers, sabbath-breakers of Moorfields, or the harlots of Drury Lane. They could not be built up in the fear and love of

God while they were open, bare-faced servants of the devil.[14]

To the criticism that he was guilty of condoning and encouraging non-ordained preachers he gave a similar reply: 'Soul-damning clergymen lay me under greater difficulties than soul-saving laymen.' 'Give me one hundred preachers who fear nothing but sin and desire nothing but God, and I care not a straw whether they be clergymen or laymen.'

But let us come, secondly, nearer home and consider our own objection to the Methodist pattern. I think it can be stated like this: Instead of beginning with a scriptural pattern for the order of the church, the Methodist structure was surely an evolution in response to circumstances; that is to say, its justification rested on expediency rather than on the text of Scripture. Does this not mean that it was a form of church government based upon pragmatism? In contrast with that approach, our sympathies are more with the thinking of the Puritans, and we look for scriptural authority before anything is sanctioned in the churches. Is it not the case that a policy of expedience has contributed largely to the weakness of modern evangelicalism on the subject of the church? Should we not rather insist on acting on biblical principles, doing what is right regardless of consequences, even though, in Spurgeon's phrase 'the heavens should fall'.

Wesley's reply to us would be to say that he was not by-passing Scripture, on the contrary he was putting first what Scripture puts first, that is, the success of the gospel, according to Paul's rule: 'I am made all things to all men, that I might by all means save some. And this I do for the gospel's sake' (*1 Cor.* 9:22–23). Or take the words of Paul in 1 Timothy 1:5, where he is talking about the charge or command laid upon Timothy for the right administration of God's work, and he says of the great object in view, 'the end – the goal – of the commandment is love.' As Patrick Fairbairn

---

[14] *Works of John Wesley,* vol. 26 (Oxford: Clarendon Press, 1982) p. 206.

paraphrases the words, we are 'put in trust with the scheme of God for the well being of men, and so having love for its grand aim – love in the fullest sense – love to God, and love to mankind as the objects whose present and eternal good it contemplates'.[15] Wesley would argue that what they did fulfilled that injunction.

We may meet this argument by saying that love and church order are not to be put over against each other, rather we must follow Scripture on both. But to be fair to Wesley we need to ask, is the revelation in Scripture equally clear and emphatic with regard to both? Is there a pattern of church government so definite, complete and inflexible that no variations are to be permitted out of love to souls? Is it possible that the pattern best for one age or place is not necessarily the best in its entirety for another? The fact that the Puritans could not agree among themselves on *one* pattern has to raise doubt whether Scripture is as informative as they wanted to believe. The truth is there were simple questions to which these good men gave different answers. For instance, Was the church in Jerusalem in apostolic times made up of several congregations or was it only one? Or again, Was the 'presbytery' that appointed Timothy to office a group of presbyters belonging to one congregation, or was it representative of several congregations in a wider geographical area? Such questions remained unsettled in the century that preceded Wesley for the good reason, I think, that the New Testament does not give us information decisive enough to settle them. After the insoluble debates of the seventeenth century it has to be a brave man that insists that the Bible gives us more than some general principles for the ordering of the churches.

---

[15] Patrick Fairbairn, *Commentary on the Pastoral Epistles* (1874; reprint, Edinburgh: Banner of Truth, 2002, as *1 & 2 Timothy and Titus*), p. 79. Reproving the zeal of some who wanted to enforce uniformity in matters of church government, Owen observed: 'I know the end of all Christ's institutions is to increase love.' *Works*, vol. 9, p. 269.

The system Wesley inaugurated, instead of reviving debates on whether churches should be Episcopal, Independent, Presbyterian or whatever, aimed first at spreading the gospel by every available means. And the Methodist structure was flexible enough to operate effectively across the world – whether in England, or among the black slaves of the American South, or in Fiji, Tonga and other islands of the Pacific. What is beyond dispute is that in gospel effectiveness Wesleyan Methodism often outstripped other bodies; it reached slaves, soldiers, convicts and cannibals; it gave birth to vibrant churches which multiplied themselves as missionary agencies. This should at least make us cautious about dismissing the structure in terms of mere expediency. Testimonies to the usefulness of the Methodist system, and its itinerant preachers, come from many quarters. Speaking of the evangelistic outreach that marked Methodism, a writer in the *British and Foreign Evangelical Review*, at the time when it was edited by William Cunningham, wrote this high tribute:

> In perhaps no denomination of Christians is this doctrine better understood, and more consistently carried out, than among the Wesleyan Methodists; and with all their errors of opinion, and all their faults of administration, they have, in consequence, done more for the propagation of the gospel at home and abroad, in England, in America, and among the heathen, than any other sect at present existing.[16]

I am not about to suggest that we should all exchange our church structures for the one-time Methodist pattern. But I think Wesley prompts us to re-examine the relationship between zeal for the salvation of souls and church practices and procedures. We are prone to think that variations and changes in church order means laxity, but could it be that we need to re-examine what is most suited for the advance of the gospel in our generation? Is it not possible we could be

---

[16] *British and Foreign Evangelical Review,* vol. 7, p. 940.

in danger of allowing theory to prevent the introduction of changes that could be of blessing to people who are presently lost and far from God?

Lest anyone should suppose that Wesleyan church practice was simply the result of theological laxity let me remind you that in some features the practice had a parallel in what John Knox himself advocated in Reformation Scotland. Knox had 'Readers' and 'Exhorters' besides ordained ministers; he advocated weekly congregational meetings that were more akin to Methodist class meetings than to later Presbyterianism; and he had 'Superintendents' who had the care of a circuit of congregations.[17]

At some points it also needs to be said that the Methodist system was more scriptural than ours. They would, for example, have been shocked at the way we so nearly restrict our gospel preaching to church buildings. Open-air preaching may not always today have the same usefulness that it had in the eighteenth century, but ways have to be found to reach the masses who will never enter our buildings.

Further, the Methodists were closer to the New Testament than we often are in their view of the gospel minister. Wesley's critics cried that the office had to be upheld. He did not disagree but insisted that the authenticity of a man's ministry does not depend in the first place upon office. Churches or Colleges cannot make gospel ministers. There must be a divine calling that has to be seen in the presence of unction, commitment to Scripture and the evident usefulness in the salvation of souls. Wesley believed the Puritan saying, 'They are the best ministers that carry people unto heaven.'

Wesley was accused of lowering the position of the minister. It is true that men were sometimes admitted as Assistants and itinerants who were unworthy, but taking the early Methodist history as a whole, failures were not the norm.

---

[17] See *The First Book of Discipline,* David Calderwood, *History of the Church of Scotland,* vol. 2 (Edinburgh: Wodrow Soc., 1843); *The Liturgy of John Knox* (Glasgow: University Press, 1886).

The men who constituted the norm were often men of a standard which puts us to shame. The life of an itinerant preacher was a far harder one than the life of a man settled quietly to minister just to the needs of a local congregation. The itinerant had to find a pulpit wherever he could, whatever the weather, whatever the hostility. He was far more on horseback than ever he was at a fireside. Self-denial and sacrifice were a regular part of his existence, and, being married, he could not continue unless he had a wife of equal spiritual determination. We might think that they sometimes carried self-discipline too far, but there is no denying that they came closer than most to Paul's description of the gospel ministry in 2 Corinthians 6:4–9: 'In all things approving ourselves as the ministers of God, in much patience, in afflictions, in necessities, in distresses, in stripes, in imprisonments, in tumults, in labours, in watchings, in distresses . . . By honour and dishonour, by evil report and good report; as deceivers yet true; as unknown, and yet well known; as dying and behold we live.'[18]

Whatever we think of Methodism as a denominational structure we need to remember the regret expressed by John Brown of Haddington over denominational controversies among the Presbyterians of Scotland:

Alas! that we did not *chiefly* strive to pray better, preach better, and live better, than our neighbours.[19]

[18] In another respect Wesley gave higher importance to the gospel minister (by whatever name he is called) than we sometimes see today. He did not hold the idea that the Scriptures speak of presbyters who are not preachers, who only rule and yet have the same office. That was the reason why, before his death, he did not put a plan in place which would have allowed the societies to appoint their own ministers. Had that been done, it would have meant, he believed, giving laymen a role of leadership, calling and dismissing ministers as they pleased.

[19] *Memoir and Select Remains of the Rev. John Brown*, ed. William Brown (1856; reprint, Edinburgh: Banner of Truth, 2004, as *The Life of John Brown, with select writings*), p. 71n.

Is not this the same as saying that zeal for the gospel did not always come first?

In Wesley and Methodism We Are Taught That the Persuasion of the Love of God for Men Makes Churches Truly Evangelistic

George Smith, one of the best Methodist historians of the nineteenth century, asked the question whether it was the Methodist form of church organisation that was the key to their effectiveness. And his answer was a definite No![20] Rather, he said, the key was to be found in the level of piety that was pervasive in Methodism in its best days, and if the characteristic of that piety had to be reduced to one word, the word would have to be love, love to God and men. The constant prayer of the Methodists was

> Kindle a flame of sacred love
> On the mean altar of my heart.

In this their leader was their example. With justice it is said, 'Men could not hear Wesley preach, and yet doubt whether God loved them and desired their salvation.'[21] This was the belief that held priority in Wesley's life. When a critic condemned him for not recognizing that there were churches enough and ministers enough to reclaim all sinners in the land, Wesley replied:

One plain reason why, notwithstanding all these churches, they are no nearer being reclaimed is this —

[20] Smith asserts that 'the spiritual power of Methodism, the grand secret of its continued existence and success,' was 'the experience of personal godliness.' 'The Methodists', he says again, 'are not schooled in controversy; but in the art of teaching sinners the way to flee from sin and to find salvation in Christ, they are the best instructed people in the world.' *History of Wesleyan Methodism*, vol. 3, fourth ed. (London: Longmans, 1866), pp. 497–8.

[21] Richard Green, *John Wesley, Evangelist* (London: Religious Tract Society, 1905), p. 259.

they never come into a church, perhaps not once in a twelvemonth, perhaps not for many years together. Will you say (as I have known some tender-hearted Christians), 'Then it is their own fault'; and so it was my fault and yours when we went astray and were like sheep that were lost. Yet the Shepherd of souls sought after us, and went after us into the wilderness. And 'oughtest not thou to have compassion on thy fellow servants, as he had pity on thee?' Ought not we also 'to seek,' as far as in us lies, 'and to save that which is lost'? Behold the amazing love of God to the outcasts of men! His tender condescension to their folly![22]

And Wesley died as he had sought to live. It is sometimes said that his last action at the age of eighty-seven, on the morning of Wednesday, March 2, 1791, was singing. But that is not quite true. His last action was to direct that copies of his sermon, 'The Love of God to Fallen Man', should be 'scattered abroad and given to everybody'.[23]

This same spirit marked his men. When Gideon Ouseley died the last text he quoted was, 'God is love', a testimony, said his biographer, 'that, in life and strength, he had made to resound in the ears of many a thousand'. The dying words of William Hamilton were these: 'If I could shout so that the world might hear, I would tell them of the goodness and love of God my Saviour.' William Bramwell, who was privileged to preach in powerful revivals in Yorkshire, advised colleagues:

[22] Ibid., p. 323 quoting from Wesley's *Appeals to Men of Reason and Religion*.
[23] Which sermon of Wesley's this was is not clear to me. It is interesting to note that in an issue of the *Arminian Magazine* (London: Paramore, 1785), Wesley printed an 'Extract from a Sermon on God is Love' by Jonathan Edwards, which he introduced with the words, 'The following is the most remarkable discourse I ever saw upon the subject; and gives a full answer to one of the capital objections frequently made against Christianity.'

Get all your nature moulded into love: lose self in God, and dwell there. In your preaching, discover by every word and look the strongest affection for the congregation, and let everything declare your earnest desire for their salvation . . . Preach in an encouraging way . . . Dwell much on the love of Jesus.

John Smith (1794–1831) of Cudworth, Yorkshire, is a typical example of this kind of preaching. James Dixon says of him:

To have listened to John Smith expatiating on sin, announcing its threatenings, piercing and transfixing the soul of the evil doer, bringing home with tremendous force his artillery upon all the defences of the unconverted, opening up the regions of lost spirits – listening to all this, it would at once be thought that the same mind could not equally excel on the opposite tack. But this was certainly the case. His proclamation of the love of God was never neutralized in its breadth and fullness by refinements, by limitations and definitions, by any kind of reservations, as if this grace and love did not belong to some, and ought to be cautiously fenced round against their approach. Nothing of this nature occurred. His whole soul seems to have been roused to the highest possible tension, when dwelling on this subject. His sentences were ingots, masses of concentrated thought. God! The very term indicates fullness – perfection – infinity. God exists in peerless majesty, in incomprehensible being, in unfathomable mystery. Love! The love of God! No human being can fathom this: even its developments, as in the gift of Christ, and the wonderful provisions of man's salvation, lie infinitely beyond the reach of the human mind. John Smith was right in not attempting to refine on a subject so great, and in limiting himself to the task of a simple but full and pathetic declaration of this love. This he did in words of fire. The readiness of the love of God to save; the freedom of his grace; His nearness, presence, and power; the illimitable and universal extent of the Divine compassion; the inference that none are too bad, too miserable, for God to reach, and that all, however guilty, might be saved by this love – were intelligible points. These were seized by our preacher. He handled them, as is well known, with wonderful effect.[24]

If it is doubted whether such extracts give a representative idea of Methodist ministry, then there are very many biographies where more confirmation can be found. George Smith, in 1863, wrote of the number of these biographical works as 'immense', and regarded them as 'the clearest, brightest, and best public proof of the continued existence of spiritual life among us'.[25] But the question is, what made them this type of men? In part, the answer is that they knew the love of God shed abroad in their hearts by the Holy Spirit. But there is another part to the answer that is more controversial and perhaps more challenging to us. Wesley and the men who followed him believed it was essential to their duty as gospel preachers to believe in the love of God for all men. This belief was the main reason for his opposition to what he understood as Calvinism. Wesley thought that Calvinism

[24] Introductory Essay to *Memoirs of the Life, Character, and Labours of the Rev. John Smith,* Richard Treffry, twelfth edition (London: Wesleyan Conference Centre, 1881), pp. xxx–i. A passing sentence from Smith's correspondence in 1826 gives an idea of the blessings which he saw: 'Although our increase of members has not been very great – two hundred – we have four hundred and forty seven on trial' (p. 136). Not unconnected with such experience are such words as these: 'My soul has fast hold on God. He is mine, and I am His. I have had, of late, some very gracious Divine communications. I am looking for brighter, more penetrating and soul-transforming manifestations of God. I want, "beholding as in a glass the glory of the Lord," to be "changed into the same image from glory to glory, even as by the Spirit of the Lord"' (p. 171).

[25] Smith, *History of Methodism*, vol. 2 (London: Longmans, 1863), pp. 667–8.

believed in a divine love exclusive to the elect and that God viewed all the rest of mankind only in wrath. If that was true, then the gospel was to be preached to all men, not because God has any love or desire for the salvation of all, but only as a witness that would add to their condemnation.

Too much Calvinism in the eighteenth century corresponded with that kind of thinking. In its anxiety for strict orthodoxy it was careful not to give unconverted sinners the idea that God loved them, that there was a Saviour provided for them, that God was not willing that they should perish. It is clear enough that Wesleyans had to contend with that type of thinking. John Nelson, one of Wesley's Assistants, for instance, reports this encounter with a Dissenting minister who held the view I have just stated. When this man had affirmed to Nelson that there was no love in God for mankind as such, Nelson replied:

> Tell me, Sir, did you ever feel the love of God in your own soul? If you did, I appeal to your conscience, whether at that time you did not find love to every soul of man. Now, this was not your nature, but the nature of God; and if one drop of the bucket could so swell your soul, what must that ocean be from which it came?[26]

The trouble with 'labels' is that they can mean different things to different people and be used in different senses. So it is with 'Arminianism' and the point is well made in the well-balanced theological journal, already quoted, when it was edited by the Free Church of Scotland theologian, George Smeaton. In an article reviewing the Wesleyans we read:

> They call themselves Arminians; but it is perfectly obvious that their theology differs widely from that of Limborch, and Whitby, and Warburton, and all the recognized Arminian divines of Holland and England.

---

[26] *Journal of Nelson,* pp. 182–3 (London: Mason, 1846).

THE OLD EVANGELICALISM

. . . They differ widely and radically in principles and in results; whereas when we hear the gospel preached by a Methodist, we feel that it is the very same to which we love to listen, and are accustomed to hear as Presbyterians. . . . Man's ruin by the fall, his native depravity and alienation from God, his absolute need of a Saviour, and utter inability to save himself, the necessity of regeneration by the Holy Spirit, justification, not by works, but by faith alone in the blood and righteousness of Jesus, the free offer of the gospel to every human being without money and without price, the necessity of holiness, not to merit heaven, but to become meet for it — these articles constituted the very burden of their preaching.[27]

The label of 'Calvinism' is equally open to more than one meaning. There is some excuse for Wesley being confused over what is the authentic thing, for true Calvinism is not the narrow thing to be found in parts of eighteenth-century Dissent. The latter was not Whitefield's Calvinism. 'God is loving to every man,' said Whitefield.[28] Calvin himself preached, 'Jesus Christ offers himself generally to all men without exception to be their redeemer.'[29]

Puritans could speak similarly.[30] Thomas Watson, after quoting the words of Augustine, 'The cross was a pulpit, in

[27] Review of *Annals of the American Pulpit (Methodist)*, in the *British and Foreign Evangelical Review,* vol. xi (London: Nisbet, 1862), pp. 301–2. For further discussion of the same point see 'Arminianisms' in *Collected Shorter Writings of J. I. Packer,* vol. 4 (Carlisle: Paternoster Press).

[28] Letter to Wesley of Dec. 24, 1740, in *George Whitefield's Journals* (London: Banner of Truth, 1960), p. 585. In the same letter Whitefield asks perceptively, 'Mr Wesley perhaps has been disputing with some warm narrow-spirited men that held election, and then infers, that their warmth and narrowness of spirit was owing to their principles?' (p. 577).

[29] See John Calvin, *Sermons on Deuteronomy*, p. 167; and his *Commentary* on John 3:16.

[30] See above, p. 110–11. The Westminster divines were agreed that 'the gospel, where it cometh, doth tender salvation by Christ to all,' and, in the words of Edmund Calamy, 'It is most certain that God is not the cause

which Christ preached his love to the world,' went on to say:
'That Christ should die, was more than if all the angels had
been turned to dust; and especially that Christ should die as
a malefactor, having the weight of all men's sins laid upon
him . . . Christ shed his blood to heal those that crucified
him.'[31]

These authors all believed in the sovereignty of grace; they
did not hold that God loves mankind with the identical love
with which he loves the church, but they knew that the
gospel which is to be addressed to every creature is a real
expression of divine love and compassion. John Owen could
call upon all his hearers to 'consider the infinite condescension and love of Christ, in his invitations and calls of you to
come unto him for life.'[32] Great is the mystery, but it is men
themselves who exclude themselves from the loving Saviour!
Wesley was surely right in believing that if there is no love of
God to be proclaimed to all men then there is no real gospel
for all men. John Knox once wrote:

> By what means Satan first drew mankind from the
> obedience of God, the Scripture doth witness: To wit,
> by pouring into their hearts that poison, that God did
> not love them.[33]

The business of gospel preaching surely involves addressing
this 'poison'. Preachers are not simply to present Christ in
terms of facts, merely as a witness, but men are to be pleaded
with, to be beseeched to be reconciled to God; and such

---

of any man's damnation. He found us in Adam, but made none sinners.'
Minutes of the Sessions of the Westminster Assembly of Divines, edited by A. F.
Mitchell and J. Struthers (Edinburgh: Blackwood, 1874), pp. lx–lxi.

[31] Thomas Watson, *Body of Divinity*, p. 175.

[32] *Works*, vol. 1, p. 422. 'He is as able to save us as he is ready and willing . . . The testimonies which he hath given us unto his goodness and
love are uncontrollable' (p. 424).

[33] *Works of John Knox*, ed. David Lang, vol. 5 (Edinburgh: James Thin,
1895), p. 24.

preaching is not possible unless *the preacher himself* is possessed with the conviction that there is a divine love abundantly willing to receive all those to whom he speaks. Too often the Calvinism of eighteenth-century Dissent was not an evangelistic force because it lacked this. It did not have the biblical or emotional capability to persuade men of Christ's willingness to embrace all. Certainly God's wrath upon sin must be preached, there was no deficiency among the Methodists on that score, but it is in the message of love, not wrath, that faith finds a resting place. In the words of the Scots Puritan, William Guthrie, 'A man is not to question the Lord's willingness to receive men. Unless a man knows so much he will not dare to adventure the whole weight of his salvation upon Christ Jesus.'[34] On the same point John Owen wrote:

> Though men profess that God is gracious, yet their aversation that they have unto him and communion with him doth abundantly manifest that they do not believe what they say and profess . . . Let us not entangle our own spirits by limiting his grace. . . . We are apt to think that we are very willing to have forgiveness, but that God is unwilling to bestow it . . . And to this end serves also the oath of God – namely, to root out all the secret reserves of unbelief concerning God's unwillingness to give mercy, grace, and pardon unto sinners.[35]

Wesleyan Methodism contained a number of errors and mistakes but there was something great in its message that the Spirit of God was pleased to own, first in England and then across the world, and in that it put its emphasis on the truth at the heart of the New Testament, that 'God is love'.

A PARALLEL WITNESS FROM SCOTLAND

There is strong confirmation of the truth of what I am saying from another part of the United Kingdom in the

---

[34] Guthrie, *The Christian's Great Interest*, quoted by Adam Philip, *The Devotional Literature of Scotland* (London: Clarke, n.d.), p. 44.

[35] *Works*, vol. 6, pp. 400, 502–4.

eighteenth century. What was the most effective evangelistic movement in Scotland in that century? The answer has to be the movement represented by Thomas Boston, the Erskines and the Secession Church. What was the difference between these men and the moribund Calvinism that existed in many parts of the national Church in Scotland? The answer is the place of the love of God in gospel preaching. These 'Marrow-men', as they were called, were Calvinists – they believed in the love of God to the elect, but they knew that if love is *only* for the elect then it cannot be a message for all men. Sinners would need to know they are believers (and therefore elect) before they believed in any love for them! This would leave no message of love to be preached to unbelievers as such. The Marrow-men relit an evangelistic fire in Scotland with the conviction that the ground of faith, set forth in the gospel, is not God's love to the elect, but his love extended to all men in the invitation; it is 'such a love as sinners, under the notion of sinners, may rely upon as exhibited in the gospel'. There is a 'call to every one to believe this love, and to take hold of this lover'.[36] 'God offers Christ cordially and affectionately in the gospel; his very heart goes out after sinners in the call and offer thereof.'[37]

> The general call and offer of the gospel reaches every individual person, and God speaks to every sinner as particularly as though he named him by his name and surname. Remission of sins is preached to *you*, we beseech *you* to be reconciled, the promise is unto *you*; and for my part I do not know what sort of gospel men make, who do not admit this.[38]

[36] John Brown, *Gospel Truth Accurately Stated and Illustrated* by James Hogg, Thomas Boston, Ebenezer Erskine, and Ralph Erskine and others (Glasgow: Blackie, 1831), p. 390. Dr John Macleod speaks of this book as a valuable compendium 'for anyone who wants to learn what the teaching of Boston and his fellows was which told so much upon the thinking of Evangelical Scotland'. *Scottish Theology* (Edinburgh: Banner of Truth, 1974), p. 160.

[37] Ibid., p. 365.   [38] Ibid., p. 355.

Boston and the Secession men opened a door for the people of Scotland that a narrow theology had almost shut. They held that, while the gospel is effectual for the elect, its revelation of Christ is for all: 'Mankind sinners indefinitely are the objects of the administration. The extent of it is not founded upon election, but on the sufficiency of Christ's obedience and death for the salvation of all.' Then, 'to confirm this truth, which is glad tidings for all sinners of Adam's race,' Boston goes straight to that wonderful evangelistic passage, John chapter 3. He says that, as God instituted an ordinance for Israel for their healing in the wilderness,

> without excepting any that needed healing . . . So all mankind being bitten by the old serpent the devil . . . God has appointed Jesus Christ the ordinance of heaven for their salvation, and has made a grant of him as such, to all of Adam's lost posterity who will make use of him for that purpose, by looking to him in the way of believing, without excepting in this grant, any, if they are but of the world of mankind, John 3:14, 15, 16.[39]

And it is love that so led God to act towards mankind.

> Where true love is, there is an aptness to communicate; the lover cannot see the beloved want what he has. God's love is giving love: 'He so loved the world, that he gave his only-begotten Son,' *John* 3:16. Christ's love is also such; he loves indeed . . . You are welcome to it. He has it not to keep up, but to give out, and to whom but to needy sinners.[40]

Or listen to these words from another evangelical leader in Scotland on the gospel offer:

> It confers on every sinner who hears the gospel, a *Divine* right to trust . . . This offer is such, as not only

---

[39] *The Whole Works of Thomas Boston*, ed. S. M'Millan , vol. 1 (Aberdeen: King, 1848), p. 352.

[40] Ibid., vol. 9, pp. 172–3.

warrants, but obliges, every hearer of the gospel, on pain of eternal punishment, to embrace it. . . . God, as the God of matchless and immense love, makes an absolutely free offer of Christ, and of himself in Him, to sinners of mankind indefinitely (*John* 3:16). As long as a sinner apprehends God to be his infinite, and implacable enemy, and to be designing his eternal destruction, his enmity to him will continue; and while his enmity to God remains in all its strength, it will be impossible for him to place the smallest confidence in him. But if the convinced, trembling sinner be once persuaded that God in Christ is a God of grace, mercy and love toward him, then he will be encouraged to trust in him . . . he will cheerfully entrust his salvation to him (*Psa.* 36:7).[41]

Here are Scots Calvinists agreeing with John Wesley on perhaps the most crucial verse in the New Testament for evangelism. What Wesley did not know was that John Calvin also agreed with him on John 3:16, as I have shown elsewhere in these pages.[42] But my point is to emphasize that the recovery of a gospel open to all had the same effect in Scotland as it did among the Wesleyans. In the words of James Walker: 'Boston and the Marrow-men, first of all among our divines, entered fully into the missionary spirit of the Bible; were able to see that Calvinistic doctrine was not inconsistent with world-conquering aspirations and efforts.'[43]

[41] John Colquhoun, *A View of Saving Faith* (Edinburgh: Thomsons, 1824), pp. 130, 148.

[42] See above, p. 112. Also on that verse: R. L. Dabney, 'God's Indiscriminate Proposals of Mercy,' in *Discussions*, vol. 1, pp. 312-3; and J. C. Ryle, *Expository Thoughts on John*, vol. 1 (1869; reprint, Edinburgh: Banner of Truth, 1987), pp. 158-9. Ryle quotes the words of Bishop Davenant: 'The general love of God toward mankind is so clearly testified in Holy Scripture, and so demonstrated by the manifold effects in God's goodness and mercy extended to every particular man in this world, that to doubt thereof were infidelity, and to deny it plain blasphemy.'

[43] James Walker, *The Theology and Theologians of Scotland* (Edinburgh: T. & T. Clark, 1872), p. 60.

In recent times it has been common for Calvinists to think they have nothing to learn from Wesley but this was not always the case. To think thus is not to know what Methodism was at its best. Better informed Calvinists never held that opinion, and have understood why it was used to reach multitudes of men and women with the gospel.

Wesley would tell us that the key was heartfelt persuasion of the love of God for men. Sometimes God takes unexpected teachers to remind us of great truths. The way in which the Spirit of God honoured the preaching of the early Methodists must make us check whether there is not a doctrinal reason for our deficiency as evangelists. The best accounts of Methodist preaching make humbling reading: they were men who lived very close to the love of Calvary; that same love entered into them deeply and we should not be ashamed to sit at their feet. Without their spirit we will be Calvinists without passion for the winning of souls.

WESLEY CHALLENGES US ON THE FOCUS OF OUR DOCTRINE OF SANCTIFICATION

I do not mean here to digress into an examination of Wesley's belief that Christian − *not* sinless − perfection can be sought and obtained by the Christian. In my judgment there was a considerable mistake in his thinking,[44] but before we set aside his standpoint we need to remember that in *pursuit* of that attainment Wesley was essentially biblical. The aim was right: 'You therefore must be perfect, as your heavenly Father is perfect' (*Matt.* 5:48, ESV).

Wesley was rightly afraid of a Christian profession that treated regeneration and justification as though they represented the final state of the Christian instead of the beginning. Warnings from authors of other periods show this was not a danger peculiar to the eighteenth century. Calvin taught that we are 'not to labour feebly or coldly in urging

[44] I have written on this in *Wesley and Men Who Followed*, p.232–46.

perfection.'[45] John Duncan, in the nineteenth century, was of the same mind; his biographer says: 'He did not care to speak strongly against the doctrine of Christian perfectibility in this world. "I have less quarrel," he said, "with a man holding the doctrine of perfection; but I would not like to see a man who thinks himself perfect." '[46]

Setting aside here, how and when 'perfection' is attained, and whether the translation 'completeness' is not in most instances a better rendering of the original Greek, I want to speak rather of its nature. What is the chief feature of the condition belonging to those of whom Paul speaks when he says 'as many as be perfect'(*Phil.* 3:15, AV; 'mature', ESV)? For Calvin it was maturity of faith; for Wesley it was love, 'the bond of perfectness' (*Col.* 3:14, AV); 'love, which binds everything together in perfect harmony' (ESV); 'love, which is the perfect bond of unity' (NASB). 'By perfection,' wrote Wesley, 'I mean perfect love, or the loving of God with all the heart,' or, more briefly elsewhere, 'a mature happy Christian'.

There is, of course, no antithesis between faith and love in sanctification. They ever belong together and grow together: 'the work of faith and the labour of love'; 'faith working through love'(*1 Thess.* 1:3; *Gal.* 5:6, etc). The Holy Spirit directs the believer's faith to Christ and to his love, and the stronger that faith, the stronger the love, for 'We love, because he first loved us' (*1 John* 4:19). Faith in the truth looks

---

[45] *Institutes*, 4:1:20. Quoted by R. S. Wallace, 'Progress towards Perfection,' in *Calvin's Doctrine of the Christian Life* (Grand Rapids: Eerdmans, 1959), p. 322.

[46] A. Moody Stuart, *Recollections of John Duncan* (Edinburgh: Edmonston and Douglas, 1872), p. 174. Duncan would have been pleased that Wesley did not profess to have obtained what he sought, nor did another Methodist that Duncan once met and whom he sought to deliver from Arminianism. The man, says Moody Stuart, was a sea captain and no match for the theologian, yet he ended the argument effectively with these words to Duncan, 'I have really enough to do, Sir, to fight with the world, the flesh, and the devil, and I shall not fight any longer with you'! p. 193.

without, love is the grace that works within for building up the body of Christ (*Eph.* 4:16).[47]

Wesley's writings are strong in their emphasis that 'the fruit of the Spirit is love'. The outworking is to be seen in the life of his Societies, in the hymns they loved, and in the sufferings and self-sacrifices they willingly accepted. By this teaching a generation of Christians was raised up for whom the practice and the enjoyment of Christian love was the first duty. While, at points, the formulation of their doctrine was skewed, many of these men and women proved the truth of the words of a later evangelist: 'The highest type of Christian is a loving and lovable one: such a one will exercise for good an influence that none other can ever possess.'[48]

The eighteenth century saw revival in the churches and at the heart of revival there is ever a recovery of love. Wesley was by no means alone in this priority. George Whitefield shone in love, as Wesley testified in preaching his funeral sermon. 'It is manifest', said Jonathan Edwards, 'that love is . . . the very essence of Christianity.'[49] In Wales, William Williams wrote, 'Love is the greatest thing in religion, and if that is forgotten nothing can take its place.'[50] And Thomas Charles, a successor to Williams, agreed: 'It is the leading passion of the soul. Like a general in an army, wherever it presses, all the rest will follow . . . In this respect the soul greatly resembles the Deity himself.'[51]

---

[47] See Owen's comment on this, *Works*, vol. 9, p. 268. 'A church full of love, is a church well built up.'

[48] *Richard Hobson of Liverpool: the Autobiography of a Faithful Pastor* (Edinburgh: Banner of Truth, 2003), pp. 246–7. Hobson also gives us these memorable words: 'I once said to an intelligent Christian Scotchman, "Tell me how you hard-headed Scotchmen could listen to Moody." His answer was, "Who can resist love".' (p. 191).

[49] Edwards, *Treatise on Grace* (Cambridge: James Clarke, 1971), p. 43.

[50] Quoted by D. M. Lloyd-Jones, *The Puritans: Their Origins and Successors* (Edinburgh: Banner of Truth, 1987), p. 187.

[51] *Thomas Charles' Spiritual Counsels* (Edinburgh: Banner of Truth, 1993), pp. 74, 77.

While, therefore, there is much that we can learn from Wesley, the truth is that all that was best in the Methodist leader was not unique to him. It will be found wherever there is true New Testament Christianity and true Christian experience. Archibald Alexander, shortly before his death, had good reason to write in a Preface to his last book:

> The author, in a long life, has found that real Christians agree much more perfectly in experimental religion, than they do in speculative points; and it is his belief, that a more intimate acquaintance among Christians of different denominations would have a happy tendency to unite them more closely in the bonds of brotherly love. May the time soon come when all the disciples of Christ shall form one great brotherhood under the name of Christians![52]

[52] A. Alexander, *Practical Sermons* (Philadelphia: Presbyterian Board of Publication, 1850), p. 6.

6

ASSURANCE OF
SALVATION

'Justification realised is the great vantage ground in striving after personal holiness; a happy consciousness of our acceptance in the Beloved is the great incentive to true obedience. Grasping pardon you grasp holiness. He who receives Jesus receives his Spirit. Love springs from faith; and he who realises most assuredly his standing in grace, walks most steadily in fellowship, works most cheerfully in obedience, and lives most freely in the liberties of holy joy.'

JOHN MACPHERSON,
Life and Labours of Duncan Matheson,
the Scottish Evangelist, p. 36.

'If you look to have such an evidence, light into, and absolute conviction of this matter, as shall admit of no doubts, fears, questionings, just occasions and causes of new trials, teachings and self-examinations, you will be greatly deceived. Regeneration induceth a new principle into the soul, but it doth not utterly expel the old; some would have security, not assurance . . . The constant conflicts we must have with sin will not suffer us to have always so clear an evidence of our condition as we would desire.'

JOHN OWEN, *Works,*
vol. 6, p. 593.

The Christian with assurance is a person who enjoys the persuasion of a saving relationship with God through Jesus Christ. The statement is simple yet the subject of assurance involves no small mystery and it has been a matter of repeated controversy.

Sometimes the controversy has centred on the dangers of assurance and whether it is even desirable for Christians to profess to have it. May such confidence not lead to moral carelessness or to a sense of superiority over others? And are there not also many warnings in Scripture of individuals deceiving themselves by what is no more than a self-induced assurance? (*Isa.* 50:11; *Matt.* 7:22; 13:20). Is doubt about oneself not perhaps more consistent with Christian humility?

More often controversy over assurance has concerned how it is to be obtained. The Church of Rome, while denying that any certainty over personal salvation is possible, has directed individuals to put their confidence in the sacraments of the Church. Many once-Protestant denominations have lapsed into making baptism the means by which assurance can be mass-produced. Others, believing in the need for conversion, have come close to identifying assurance with the words an evangelist may give to those who publicly 'decide for Christ'. Jesus said, 'the one who comes to me I will by no means cast out' (*John* 6:37), and so what more assurance does anyone need who responds to the public appeal? Is this not 'taking God at his word'?

The long existence of such controversy is proof enough of the importance of the subject. Next to the issue, how one becomes a Christian, there can be no question more significant than, how does one know one is a Christian. All who take seriously the warnings of Scripture that the devil 'is a liar and the father of it,' and that he is able to speak as though he were 'an angel of light,' will understand his special interest in confusing and deceiving souls over the true answer.

THE TRUTH AND USEFULNESS OF ASSURANCE

That the New Testament makes the possession of assurance the common privilege of Christians is scarcely open to discussion. Textual evidence exists in abundance. The 'Helper' was promised to believers that they may know they are in Christ and Christ in them (*John* 14:20). That promise was fulfilled: ' The Spirit himself bears witness with our spirit that we are the children of God'; 'We are always confident, knowing that while we are at home in the body we are absent from the Lord'; 'Believing, you rejoice with joy inexpressible and full of glory'; ' We know that we are of God' (*Rom.* 8:16; *2 Cor.* 5:6; *1 Pet.* 1:8; *1 John* 5:19). The only argument that has been used against these and parallel texts is that they speak of something peculiar to the apostolic age. So some English bishops argued against the leaders of the evangelical awakening of the eighteenth century. Were the argument true, it would nullify the relevance of much of the New Testament and undermine its abiding value. The truth was rather, as John Wesley wrote, 'This great evangelical truth has been recovered which has been for many long years well nigh lost and forgotten.'[1]

All history confirms that what was so prominent in the New Testament church has also been marked in all periods when Christianity has been most vital and effective in the world. The gospel penetrated the gloomy paganism of the early centuries because the joy of its adherents caused men to ask 'a reason for the hope' that was in them (*1 Pet.* 3:15). The boldness first witnessed in Jerusalem was repeated across the Roman Empire and the effect among many who saw it was the same: 'They realized that they had been with Jesus' (*Acts*

---

[1] 'The Witness of the Spirit,' Discourse, *Works of John Wesley* (London: Wesley-Methodist Book-Room, n.d.), vol. 5, p. 124.

4:13). Exactly the same phenomenon re-appeared in the Reformation of the sixteenth century. Once again there was a body of Christians who *knew* that they belonged to Christ and their words of certainty fell with power on a doubting world. 'When I live in a settled and steadfast assurance about the state of my soul,' said Bishop Hugh Latimer, 'then I am as bold as a lion.' John Bradford, another martyr could say, 'If Queen Mary gives me my life, I will thank her; if she burn me, I will thank her.'[2]

Nor is it only in days of persecution that Christians have been able to speak in this way. Many believers, when dying, have been as ready as Richard Baxter to affirm that they were 'almost well'. William White, a country pastor in Virginia, on hearing from his doctor that he had only a few days to live, could declare, 'That's the best news I have heard in twenty years.'[3] A bed-ridden Methodist woman in Cornwall, and eager for 'home', told her attentive daughter that she was too weak to take a drink. 'Do not say so,' the daughter urged, 'you will be down among us again yet.' To which the response was, 'You are always a-foreboding!'[4]

Such testimonies harmonize with what Scripture emphasizes on the usefulness of assurance in the life of the church. The joy of salvation and effective living are bound up together (*Psa.* 51:12–13). John Bunyan was right in *Pilgrim's Progress* when he represented Christian as sleeping when his roll [assurance] was lost. 'But,' he further wrote, 'who can tell how joyful this man was when he had gotten his roll again! For this roll was the assurance of his life and acceptance at the desired haven . . . oh, how nimbly now did he go up the rest

[2] These instances are given by J. C. Ryle in his masterly chapter on Assurance in his book, *Holiness* (1879; reprint, Moscow, Idaho: Nolan, 2001, pp. 119–60).

[3] H. M. White, ed., *William S. White* (Harrisonburg, Va.: Sprinkle, 1983), p. 234.

[4] Quoted in Samuel Coley, *Life of the Rev. Thomas Collins* (London: Hamilton, Adams, 1868), p. 308.

of the hill!'[5] Summarizing the difference which assurance makes for the Christian, Spurgeon wrote:

> It is one thing to *hope* that God is with us, and another thing to *know* that he is so. Faith saves us, but assurance satisfies us. We take God to be our God when we believe in him; but we get the joy of him when we know that he is ours, and that we are his.[6]

THE HOLY SPIRIT AND ASSURANCE

Scripture makes plain that true assurance is always the result of divine action in an individual: 'The Spirit *himself* bears witness.' 'It is the Spirit who bears witness, because the Spirit is truth' (*1 John* 5:6). To believe this ought to lead to the recognition that there is profound mystery involved in the subject. We do not know how the Spirit of God dwells in the believer, nor how his work is conjoined with the believer's work without in any way diminishing human responsibility (*Phil.* 2:12–13). In this realm we must stick to biblical certainties:

1. The Holy Spirit lives in every Christian (*Rom.* 8:9). It is his work that causes regeneration and brings faith into existence. It is his witness that makes the truth real in a manner entirely unknown to the non-Christian (*John* 14:22; *1 Cor.* 2:12–14;). 'He that believes in the Son of God has the witness in himself' (*1 John* 5:10). It is because his presence is abiding that the warning has force: 'Do you not know that your body is the temple of the Holy Spirit who is in you?' (*1 Cor.* 6:19).

2. The indwelling of the Spirit is not therefore the special privilege of some Christians, experienced because of certain conditions they have fulfilled. Rather this high status belongs to all those for whom Christ died. It is Christ's redemptive

---

[5] Bunyan, *Pilgrim's Progress* (1895 ed., reprint, Edinburgh: Banner of Truth, 1977), p. 44.

[6] C. H. Spurgeon, *Cheque Book of the Bank of Faith*, entry for November 9.

work that has made us 'sons,' and 'because you are sons, God has sent forth the Spirit of his Son into your hearts' (*Gal.* 4:6). The Holy Spirit is present in the church because of the atonement and glorification of the church's head.

3. Error arises when teaching on the Spirit and assurance does not take into account *all* his work in the individual. His first action on individuals is not to comfort or to make them happy but the reverse. He does not give assurance to those who never knew their need or their danger. The starting point is: 'When he has come he will convict the world of sin, and of righteousness, and of judgment' (*John* 16:8). It is the 'broken hearted,' the 'captives,' the 'blind', and the 'bruised' who are the subjects of his work. 'Assurance' preceded by no conviction of sin is a dangerous thing. Hence the words of Luther to Melanchthon on discriminating between true and false converts that we have already quoted.[7]

Further, as the Spirit's action in convincing of sin must be taken into account, so must his work in sanctification. His goal is to produce moral likeness to Christ in the sons of God and any severance of assurance from the moral and the ethical is a major departure from the New Testament.

4. Assurance, unlike justification, admits of degrees, and of loss as well as progress. It is not a once-for-all single experience. To ascertain this fact from Scripture is necessary if confusion is to be avoided over the question, Does every believer possess assurance or does it belong to some Christians only? The answer has to be that while assurance in its essence belongs to all believers, all may not be able to discern it,[8] and in its strength it is to be found only in some. The New Testament both gives warrant for assurance in every

---

[7] See above p. 24.

[8] 'A man may want assurance and have grace, but he cannot slight assurance and have grace. He that is without it may be one of God's children, but he that doth not look after it, and is satisfied without it, certainly is none of that number.' Thomas Manton, *Complete Works,* vol. 7 (London: Nisbet, 1872), p. 120.

Christian and also speaks of full assurance. Hence believers are urged to attain to a firmer assurance in such texts as 2 Peter 1:10 and 1 John 5:13. It is of this full assurance that the *Westminster Confession* is speaking when it asserts: 'This infallible assurance doth not so belong to the essence of faith, but that a true believer may wait long, and conflict with many difficulties, before he be partaker of it.'[9]

To say this is not to deny that the 'witness' or testimony of the Spirit, spoken of in Romans 8:16, belongs to all Christians but it is to say that it is not uniform in strength. Robert Haldane observes on that verse:

> This testimony, although it cannot be explained, is nevertheless felt by the believer: it is felt by him, too, in its variations, as sometimes stronger and more palpable, and at other times more feeble and less discernible.[10]

Assurance, then, is not to be understood as one special experience, although special experiences may well mark the Christian life.

5. As the Spirit's work in the believer remains incomplete in this life – we have only 'the first fruits of the Spirit' (*Rom.* 8:23) – so, although assurance can be certain, it is never perfect while sin and ignorance remain within us. It is therefore not true teaching that represents assurance as bringing all the realities of heaven permanently into present Christian experience. The truth is that 'groaning' for the future and the aspiration, 'that I may know him', remain characteristics even of those filled with the Spirit (*Rom.* 8:23; *Phil.*3:10). However great our blessings here, as John Bunyan says, 'The milk and honey lie beyond this wilderness.' Or, to quote another who knew much of full assurance, Samuel Rutherford wrote:

> My Lord now hath given me experience (howbeit weak and small) that our best fare here is hunger. We are but

[9] *Westminster Confession of Faith*, 18:iii.

[10] Robert Haldane, *Exposition of the Epistle to the Romans* p. 363. On the same point see Owen, *Works*, vol. 6, p. 551.

at God's by-board in this lower house; we have cause to long for supper time, and the high table, up in the high palace. Lord hasten the marriage-supper of the Lamb![11]

THE TWOFOLD BASIS OF TRUE ASSURANCE

Few would dispute the assertion of the *Westminster Confession* that assurance is 'founded upon the truth of the promises of salvation'. That is to say, we gain assurance not by looking at ourselves, or anything within ourselves, but by looking to Christ alone, and to Christ as he is revealed to us in the promises of Scripture. By this means an individual may have assurance instantly upon believing the gospel. The gospel is that Christ has gone to the death of the cross for the full and certain salvation of all who come to God by him; that pardon, righteousness, and eternal life are free gifts, to be received solely by faith by those who can do nothing to qualify themselves. 'He that believes in the Son has everlasting life' (*John* 3:36).

Such a message, rightly received, contains assurance. The promises which warrant our trust and acceptance are the same promises upon which assurance is founded. That was true for the dying thief (*Luke* 23:43) and is true for all. We shall never hear more comforting words than those of Jesus when he says: 'I am the bread of life. He who comes to me shall never hunger, and he who believes in me shall never thirst' (*John* 6:35). And of those of the apostle, 'Whoever

---

[11] *Letters of Samuel Rutherford*, ed. Andrew A. Bonar (1891; reprint, Edinburgh: Banner of Truth, 1984), p. 387. His allusion, of course, is to the hierarchical manner of sitting in the dining halls of castles. Elsewhere he writes on the same point: 'His kisses and His visits to His dearest ones are thin-sown. He could not let out His rivers of love upon His own, but these rivers would be in hazard of loosening a young plant at the root; and He knoweth this of you. Ye should, therefore, frist [postpone] Christ's kindness, as to its sensible and full manifestations, till ye and He be above sun and moon. That is the country where ye will be enlarged for that love which ye dow [can] not now contain.' Ibid., p. 367.

believes in him will receive remission of sins' (*Acts* 10:43). God's gift of his Son has nothing to do with what we are in ourselves: 'It is of faith that it might be according to grace, so that the promise might be sure to all the seed . . . Therefore, having been justified by faith, we have peace with God, through our Lord Jesus Christ' (*Rom.* 4:16; 5:1).

So assurance turns on *believing*. 'For we who have believed do enter into that rest' (*Heb.* 4:3). 'Though now you do not see him, yet believing, you rejoice' (*1 Pet.* 1:8). And the Christian will never get beyond the promises of Christ as the sure ground of peace. As Martyn Lloyd-Jones once wrote:

> It is grace at the beginning, grace at the end. So that when you and I come to lie upon our deathbeds, the one thing that should comfort and help and strengthen us there is the thing that helped us at the beginning. Not what we have been, not what we have done, but the grace of God in Jesus Christ our Lord. The Christian life starts with grace, it must continue with grace, it ends with grace.[12]

The Puritans have been accused of giving too little place to faith in the gospel as the ground of assurance. The charge has arisen in part because they did not believe that it was the *only* ground or basis of assurance. But they held that it was the *chief* ground and indeed the foundation of all else.[13] One of the best-known of Puritan writers on assurance, Thomas Brooks, speaks thus of faith:

> 'The God of hope', saith the apostle, 'shall fill you with all joy and peace in believing.' That is, whilst you are in the exercise and actings of faith, the God of hope shall

---

[12] D. M. Lloyd-Jones, *Spiritual Depression: Its Causes and Cure* (London: Pickering and Inglis, 1965), p. 132.

[13] See the 'Rule' Owen gives in vol. 6, pp. 564–6, 'Mix not foundation and building together.' The foundation is 'Christ alone, mere grace and pardon in him. Our building is in and by holiness and obedience, as the fruits of that faith by which we have received the atonement.'

fill you with that joy that is 'unspeakable and full of glory', and with the 'peace that passes understanding'.

Faith is the key that unlocks paradise, and lets in a flood of joy into the soul. Faith is an appropriating grace, it appropriates all to itself; it looks upon God, and says with the psalmist, 'This God is my God for ever and ever,' Psa .63:1, and 48:14. It looks upon Christ and says, 'My beloved is mine and his desires are towards me,' Cant. 8:10. It looks upon the precious promises and says, These 'precious promises' are mine, 2 Pet.1:4. It looks upon heaven and says, 'Henceforth is laid up for me a crown of righteousness,' 2 Tim.4:8; and this fills the soul with joy and peace . . . Faith sees in Christ a fullness of abundance and a fullness of redundancy; and this fills the heart with glorious joy.

Ah, Christians! believing, believing is the ready way, the safest way, the sweetest way, the shortest way, the only way to a well grounded assurance, and to that unspeakable joy and peace that flows from it.[14]

Puritan teaching on assurance did not, however, stop at that point. The sentence from the *Confession* we have already quoted continues by saying that assurance is also 'founded upon . . . the inward evidence of those graces unto which these promises are made'. Clearly this is something additional to what has already been stated. We have said that the simple promises of the gospel are the basis both for saving faith and for assurance; these promises are not 'inward evidence' but the written, objective words of Scripture. So the question arises: If we have these promises, and promises which speak to us of the fullness of Christ and the perfection of his work, why do we need anything more? Can there be any place for a *second* basis of assurance? The nature of salvation and the testimony of Scripture ought to confirm that there is.

---

[14] *Works of Thomas Brooks*, vol. 2 (1861–7 ed., reprint, Edinburgh: Banner of Truth, 1980), p. 359.

A true experience of salvation includes two things: a change of status in the sight of God – Christ *for* us; and a change of nature – Christ *in* us. One of these things without the other is no salvation according to Scripture, and so the second, a change of nature, is to be seen as *confirmation* of the reality of the first. A 'believer' without a Saviour who is transforming his life is no believer at all. Thus Paul can challenge the church at Corinth with the words: 'Examine yourselves whether you be in the faith. Prove your own selves. Do you not know yourselves, that Jesus Christ is in you – unless indeed you are disqualified [i.e., no Christians at all]' (*2 Cor.* 13:5).

Peter strikes the same note when he teaches that advancing to a fuller assurance is related to diligent action on the part of believers (*2 Pet.* 1:5–10). The fullest scriptural evidence on this point is to be found in the First Epistle of John. With regard to the words found in his Gospel, John says: 'These are written that you may believe that Jesus is the Christ, the Son of God, and that believing you may have life in his name' (*John* 20: 31). The Gospel record is to produce faith. But in his Epistle John is not so much dealing with the way of salvation as he is with the issue, how professing believers may know that their faith is real. The emphasis is different: 'These things I have written to you who believe in the name of the Son of God, that you may know that you have eternal life' (*1 John* 5:13).

To make this knowledge clear John has much to say on the inward evidence of grace in a believer: 'Now by this we know that we know him, if we keep his commandments. He who says, "I know him," and does not keep his commandments, is a liar, and the truth is not in him . . . We know that we have passed from death to life, because we love the brethren. He who does not love his brother abides in death . . . By this we know that we love the children of God, when we love God and keep his commandments. For this is the love of God that we keep his commandments' (*1 John* 2:3–4; 3:14; 5:2–3).

'LEGALISM'

It has been argued that to introduce subjective evidence of grace in the life as a basis of assurance leads straight to legalism, because it turns attention from Christ to self, from his work to our own. By way of answer it needs to be conceded that there is a type of assurance teaching that does lead to an unhealthy subjectivism and legalism. Legalism means obeying God's law in order to move him to love us and accept us. Such aberrant teaching leads to putting sanctification in the place of justification. But the obedience of which John speaks, and which confirms the reality of grace, is not of that type at all. It is obedience springing *from love*, 'We love him because he first loved us' (*1 John* 4:19, see *Psa.* 116:1–2). The love of God, rightly believed, leads to holiness and it does so in a way which is the very opposite of legalism.

The need for obedience, if there is to be assurance, is bound up with the necessity for the Christian to maintain a 'good conscience'. A conscience 'without offence' means a life bound to obedience (*Acts* 24:16). This obedience becomes a part of assurance, not because of our actions in themselves but rather because the Holy Spirit witnesses *by conscience* to the sincerity of the believer's desire to please God. 'Our glorying is this,' writes the apostle Paul, 'the testimony of our conscience that we conducted ourselves in the world in simplicity and godly sincerity, not with fleshly wisdom, but by the grace of God' (*2 Cor.* 1:12). And John says: 'Beloved, if our heart does not condemn us, we have confidence towards God' (*1 John* 3:21).

So Paul does not teach that 'faith' is all that need concern the Christian. If 'faith *and a good conscience*' are not kept together the end result will be 'shipwreck' (*1 Tim.* 1:19). The *Confession of Faith* of the Calvinistic Methodists of Wales introduces a helpful addition to the *Westminster Confession* at this point. In the course of a section 'Of Peace of Conscience,' it states: 'Though peace of conscience is not founded on the man's experience, the purity of his motives, or the strictness of his life, pure motives and a strict walk in the ways of God are very helpful to keep and enjoy peace of conscience.'[15]

Bunyan was not then turning Mr Honest into a legalist when he writes of him:

> Then Mr Honest called for his friends and said unto them, I die . . . Now the River at that time over-flow'd the banks in some places, but Mr Honest in his life-time had spoken to one Good-Conscience to meet him there, the which he also did, and lent him his hand, and so helped him over. The last words of Mr Honest were, *Grace Reigns:* So he left the World.[16]

The New Testament makes a clear connection between godliness and assurance. To professing believers Paul has no hesitation in saying, 'If you live according to the flesh you will die; but if by the Spirit you put to death the deeds of the body, you will live' (*Rom.* 8:13). Paul's own testimony on the necessity of the mortification of sin is so strong that its plain sense has been too often disputed. Literally, in 1 Corinthians 9:27, he writes: 'I give my body a black eye, and I make it a slave lest in any way, after having preached to others, I myself should be rejected.'[17] The words teach that not only assurance, but salvation itself, is inconsistent with a life-style of moral laxity. An assurance accompanied by careless living is counterfeit. It has been claimed that the word 'rejected' (*adokimos*), thus interpreted, would mean that Paul himself had no assurance. But they do not indicate that at all. They mean rather that diligence and obedience are necessary to the preservation of assurance, and that without this there can be no expectation of maintaining a peaceful conscience. 'It is

---

[15] *Confession of Faith of the Calvinistic Methodists, or the Presbyterians of Wales*, Section 32.

[16] *Pilgrim's Progress*, p. 375.

[17] The translation is that of R. C. H. Lenski, *1 and 2 Corinthians* (Minneapolis: Augsburg, 1961), p. 385.

only those who are conscious of this constant and deadly struggle with sin, to whom this assurance is given. It is the indolent and self-indulgent Christian who is always in doubt.'[18] The Puritans had no hesitation in teaching, 'A man may at the same time live the life of faith in the righteousness of Christ, yet walk with an holy fear and trembling, lest he be an hypocrite or castaway.'[19]

Those who conclude that because works and obedience have no place in the believer's justification, therefore they need have no place in assurance, are therefore in serious error. Christ teaches emphatically that the assuring work of the Spirit and the comfort of his presence is related to obedience: 'He who has my commandments and keeps them, it is he who loves me. And he who loves me will be loved by my Father, and I will love him and manifest myself to him' (*John* 14:21). J. C. Ryle is commenting on this same truth when he writes: 'I bless God that our salvation in no wise depends on our own works . . . But I never would have any believer forget that our SENSE of salvation depends much on the manner of our living. Inconsistency will dim our eyes and bring clouds between us and the sun.'[20]

A THIRD WAY TO ASSURANCE?

There have been Christian teachers of eminence who would remain very dissatisfied with all that has been said so far. They do not question that there is a form of assurance available to

[18] Charles Hodge, *Exposition of 1 Corinthians*, p. 169. Jonathan Edwards charges those who deny this teaching, and call it 'legalism', with being 'the most dangerous opposers of pure humble Christianity'. *Religious Affections* (1746; reprint, London: Banner of Truth, 1961), p. 245.

[19] Anthony Burgess, *Spiritual Refinings*, Part II (London, 1654), p. 173.

[20] *Holiness*, p. 145. On the same point Thomas Brooks writes: 'Though no man merits assurance by his obedience, yet God usually crowns obedience with assurance . . . Assurance is a choice part of a believer's happiness, and therefore God will never give it out of a way of holiness. "The Lord has set apart for himself the man that is godly," *Psa.* 4:3.' *Works*, vol. 2, p. 415.

Christians on the twofold basis already stated, but they hold that both of these are inferior to something better, namely, 'the witness of the Holy Spirit'. In the former cases, they say, a believer reaches assurance by a process of reason and logical deduction. He argues with himself: 'I read and believe the promises and I have assurance'; or, 'I examine myself and I find within evidence of the grace of God in my life'. But the highest form of assurance, they argue, is when the Spirit 'immediately and directly' speaks to the soul, convincing a believer with a flood of light and love of his inheritance in Christ, and this pre-eminently they call 'the witness' or 'testimony of the Spirit'.

Much has been written on this point and it is necessary to clarify where the issue lies. It is not whether special manifestations of the love of God to the soul are a reality and known among God's people. Records of such experiences are plentiful in the history of the church. Jonathan Edwards carefully details such an experience in the case of his wife, Sarah.[21] Biographies of martyrs and evangelists speak of the same thing. That is not the question. Nor is the question whether 'the testimony of the Spirit' is essential to assurance. The *Westminster Confession* agrees that it is. The difference lies in the issue whether that testimony is *distinct from* the twofold basis already stated or whether it is normally concurrent.

While there have been eminent teachers of the view that the witness of the Spirit is something distinct, and of pre-eminent importance, we believe there are three serious objections to this teaching:

1. The way this teaching is presented commonly includes the argument, as given above, that, by promises and seeing inward grace, the Christian can arrive at assurance for himself, whereas the 'witness of the Spirit', understood as something separate and wholly God-given, has to be a higher, more certain thing. Such a 'witness' is thus made the

---

[21] *Works* (Banner of Truth edition), vol. 1, pp. lxii–lxviii.

form of assurance to which every Christian should aspire.[22]
The former ways to assurance are said to be 'mediate' while
this is 'immediate'. But a contrast of this kind is unhelpful
and, we think, unbiblical. There can be no assurance of any
real kind without the Holy Spirit. At every stage of Christian experience his work is essential. We cannot command
faith. It is the Spirit who 'lights the lamps of promise' and
enables the believer to appropriate them. This is true for all
Christians and it is well illustrated in the struggle in which
John Bunyan slowly came to assurance. He had the promises
yet he could not 'suck comfort and peace' from them until he
had help from heaven, then 'methought that every word was
a mighty word unto me'. 'The Scriptures now also were
wonderful things unto me.'[23]

Similarly the believer cannot rightly see the grace of God
in his life, nor obtain assurance from it, unless the Spirit
testifies with that grace. Paul did not teach Christians to prize
'the testimony of our conscience', in 1 Corinthians 1:12,
because that testimony was something they could arrive at by
themselves. 'Although there are habits of grace always resident
in the hearts of saints,' says Brooks, they 'cannot act of themselves, there must be renewed strength imparted to set them
on work.' There must be 'the concurrent presence and assist-
ance of Christ.'[24] 'O Christians,' he says in other places, 'till

[22] There is an important distinction among teachers of this view which
I am not here considering. Antinomians have commonly despised any
assurance other than by immediate witness and rejected the need for any
personal obedience. Their language is, 'Having assurance by God's Spirit,
what needs evidence by inherent grace? This is to light a candle when the
sun shines.' Reformed teachers who have given prominence to the witness of the Spirit as a third way to assurance are not to be confused with
Antinomians.

[23] Bunyan, 'Grace Abounding', in *Works*, vol. 1, see pp. 32–8. 'A man
may read the promises over and over a thousand times, and yet never be
affected, delighted or taken with them, till the Spirit of the Lord set them
home upon his soul.' Brooks, *Works*, vol. 3, p. 477.

[24] Brooks, *Works*, vol. 5, p. 470.

the Spirit of the Lord shine upon your graces, you will still be in the dark.'[25] 'Without all controversy, it is as much the office of the Spirit that witnesses to a man his sanctification as it is to witness to him his justification, *1 Cor.* 2:12: *1 John* 4:13-14.'[26]

When a third and 'superior' way to assurance is taught, the inevitable tendency seems to be to lessen the importance of what is given most prominence in the New Testament. This was a major reason why Jonathan Edwards and David Brainerd were so strongly against those who insisted that assurance must be seen in terms of an 'immediate witness'.[27]

2. If there is a superior third way to assurance to be sought by all believers, then there must be scriptural teaching to direct us. But when the alleged textual evidence is brought forward it is unconvincing. It alleges, for instance, that 'the seal' or 'earnest of the Spirit' refers to such assurance as belongs only to some Christians; and the words of Ephesians 1:13 , 'Having believed, you were sealed with the Holy Spirit of promise', are quoted as evidence that there is a particular, post-conversion experience of the Spirit to be sought. That text, however, does not naturally support such an interpretation; the weight of biblical evidence points rather to 'the seal' the believer receives being the Holy Spirit *himself* who indwells every Christian (the original Greek requiring no time lapse between believing and sealing).[28]

The words of Romans 8:16, 'The Spirit himself bears witness with our spirit,' have similarly been used as a proof

---

[25] Ibid., vol. 3, p. 477.   [26] Ibid., p. 471.

[27] Edwards, *Works* (Banner of Truth ed., vol.2,) pp. 448–50. Edwards, *Religious Affections,* pp. 159–65. See also my *Jonathan Edwards: A New Biography* (Edinburgh: Banner of Truth, 1987), pp. 264–7, 489–90.

[28] On Ephesians 1:13, a number of Puritans took the view I am opposing, and its most eminent modern advocate was Martyn Lloyd-Jones. John Owen came to disagree with those who referred sealing to a post-conversion experience. For his thinking, see Sinclair B. Ferguson, *John Owen on the Christian Life* (Edinburgh: Banner of Truth, 1987),

text for a distinct and higher assurance, experienced only by some. But the context of the verse is plainly dealing with the Spirit's work in all Christians (*Rom.* 8:4–5; 9–14), and the Greek aorist tense for 'received' in verse 15 most naturally points to the once-for-all receiving of the Spirit at regeneration. So Romans 8:16 would introduce a major change of theme if the words 'bears witness' apply only to some Christians. Further, the text itself speaks not of a single experience but of something on-going; and not of 'immediate witness' but of a witness conjoined with the Christian's own consciousness.[29] The comment given above by Haldane on this witness 'as sometimes stronger and more palpable' appears to us the more satisfactory. To quote Thomas Charles, the Spirit 'bears a joint-witness or testimony, according to his own will, at the time and in the degree he pleases'.[30]

This is by no means to deny the reality of high spiritual experiences, such as those which Edwards records of his wife, it is only to say that the unusual is not to be made normative. The comment of William Guthrie is characteristic Puritan wisdom on this point. The Puritans knew the reality of special manifestations of the love of God. Thus, after speaking of assurance in the manner we have done above, Guthrie says:

There is a communication of the Spirit of God which is sometimes vouchsafed to some of his people which is

---

pp.121-4. I am not, of course, arguing here that the Christian's experience of the Holy Spirit is complete at conversion, only that the Scriptures teach no *one* additional experience. See my *Pentecost – Today? The Biblical Case for Understanding Revival* (Edinburgh: Banner of Truth, 1998), pp. 117–33.

[29] A claim that we can clearly distinguish between our own spirit and the Spirit of God was another reason why Edwards opposed the teaching.

[30] *Thomas Charles' Spiritual Counsels*, p. 469. He adds: 'It is a bad sign of a man's state, that he is continually looking for the witnessing of the Spirit, or for what he so calls, and yet is negligent and unwatchful as to his spirit and conduct . . . The confidence that we are children, – and the obedience of children, – and the nurture of children, *go together inseparably.*'

besides, if not beyond, that witnessing of a sonship spoken before. It is a glorious divine manifestation of God unto the soul, shedding abroad God's love in the heart; it is a thing better felt than spoken of.

But he then adds:

This is the thing which doth best deserve the title of *sensible presence*; and is not given unto all believers . . . This is so absolutely let out upon the Master's pleasure, and so transient or passing, or quickly gone when it is, that no man may bring his gracious estate into debate for want of it.[31]

In other words, assurance of this kind should not be held up as the scriptural norm, nor be regarded as *the* meaning of Romans 8:16.

John Owen similarly believed that the Spirit may witness 'in a way of sovereignty, when and to whom he pleaseth', but he lays down the principle: '*If you are doubtful concerning your state and condition, do not expect an extraordinary determination of it by an immediate testimony of the Spirit of God.*'[32]

The well-known Puritans generally seem to treat this subject in the same way. John Flavel writes of times when 'God comes nigh to men', seasons which are 'the golden spots of our lives'. 'These seasons, I confess, do but rarely occur to the best of Christians, nor continue long when they do: Alas! This wine is too strong for such weak bottles as we are.'[33] These extraordinary times he does not identify as *the* witness of the Spirit:

The Spirit, indeed, assures by witnessing to our adoption; and he witnesses two ways.

[31] William Guthrie, *The Christian's Great Interest*, pp. 108–9.
[32] *Works*, vol. 6, p. 594. This quotation comes from a volume published in 1668; for an earlier and different view on the Spirit's testimony, see his statement of 1657, *Works,* vol. 2, pp. 241–2.
[33] *Works of Flavel*, vol. 3, pp. 568–9.

(1) Objectively, i.e. by working those graces in our souls which are the conditions of the promise, and so the Spirit and his graces in us, are all one: the Spirit dwelling in us is a mark of our adoption. Now the Spirit cannot be discerned in his essence, but in his operations; and to discern these is to discern the Spirit; and how these can be discerned, without serious searching and diligent watching of the heart, I cannot imagine.

(2) The other way of the Spirit's witnessing is effectively, i.e., by irradiating the soul with a grace-discovering light, shining upon his own work . . . he first infuses the grace, and then opens the eye of the soul to see it.[34]

These quotations from Guthrie and Flavel point to another reason why Scripture does not present assurance as one special or extraordinary experience. It is, as they say, that the feelings accompanying such experiences, while wonderful to the believer at the time, do not last. John Wesley's well-known experience on 24 May 1738 is a case in point. He tells us that at Aldersgate Street in London, as someone was reading Luther's Preface to the *Epistle to the Romans:*

About quarter before nine, while he was describing the change which God works in the heart through faith in Christ, I felt my heart strangely warmed. I felt I did trust in Christ, Christ alone for salvation; and an assurance was given me that He had taken away *my* sins, even *mine*, and saved *me* from the law of sin and death.

[34] Ibid., p. 434. See also, vol. 3, pp. 57–9. It is a pity that the nineteenth-century edition of Flavel's *Works*, now reprinted, does not date his various books and so it is hard to check on any change or development in his thinking. Anthony Burgess treats the above subject at some length and writes: 'Some divines do not indeed deny the possibility of such an immediate testimony, but yet they conclude the ordinary and safe way, is to look for that testimony which is by the effects and fruits of God's Spirit.' *Spiritual Refining: or, A Treatise on Grace and Assurance* (London, 1652), p. 52.

Yet the following January the same man wrote: 'I am not a Christian now ... I *feel* this moment I do not love God; which therefore I *know* because I *feel* it ... Again, joy in the Holy Ghost I have not ... Though I have constantly used all the means of grace for twenty years, I am not a Christian.'[35]

What is still more strange is to find Wesley using the same language of non-assurance more than a quarter of a century later. To his brother he wrote in a despondent letter of 27 June 1766, 'I have no *direct* witness, I do not say that I am a child of God.'[36] It is hard to avoid the belief that Wesley's problem was connected with his *identifying* assurance too closely with a special work of the Spirit, and that his occasional despondency was due to what he failed to *feel*. 'There is no clear evidence that Wesley ever received the kind of "assurance" that he was looking for', writes one of his more recent biographers. 'The self-doubts and laments at the lack of experience of God and the assurance of salvation by the evidence of his feelings show him searching for such experiences and searching in vain.'[37]

[35] *Journal of John Wesley,* ed. Nehemiah Curnock, Standard Edition (London: Kelly), vol. 1, pp. 475–6; vol. 2, pp. 125–6. It is regrettable that, amid all the good that Wesley did, his teaching on the witness of the Spirit seems to have remained confused. See his *Letters,* vol. 4, p. 170, and *Letters of Henry Venn* (1835; reprint, Edinburgh: Banner of Truth, 1993), pp. 227, 474.

[36] *Letters of John Wesley,* ed. John Telford (London: Epworth, 1931), p. 16. Parts of the original letter were written in shorthand or in Greek.

[37] Rack, *Reasonable Enthusiast,* pp. 545, 549. By the 'direct witness' Wesley clearly meant *felt* assurance. See his words on John Matthews who 'had the witness in *my* sense for several months' (*Letters,* vol. 4, p. 280). What is missing in Wesley's teaching is Owen's direction, '*Learn to distinguish between faith and spiritual sense*' [i.e., feeling], *Works,* vol. 6, p. 561. This does not mean that the Puritans disregarded feeling, only that it should not be put in the wrong place. Robert Bolton wrote of 'many' of a true heart, 'who while they labour, and long with insatiable greediness (and I blame them not) for a sensible assurance, and feeling apprehension of God's favour; do too much neglect and disregard that comfort which

It would be quite wrong to interpret these quotations as showing a failure of personal religion on Wesley's part. He expresses normal Christian experience when he writes in another place: 'I see abundantly more than I feel. I want to feel more love and zeal for God.'[38] His failure lay in his formulation of the doctrine of assurance, a formulation that made a present and on-going assurance virtually impossible.

To a desponding Christian, who had regarded 'the direct witness' as supremely important, John Newton once gave the following counsel:

> What you complain of in yourself, comprises the best marks of grace I can offer. A sense of unworthiness and weakness, joined with a hope in the Saviour, constitutes the character of a Christian in this world. But you want the witness of the Spirit; what do you mean by this? Is it a whisper or a voice from heaven, to encourage you to believe that you may venture to hope that the promises of God are true, that He means what He says, and is able to make His word good? Your eyes are opened; you are weary of sin; you love the way of salvation yourself, and love to point it out to others; you are devoted to God, to his cause and people. It was not so with you once. Either you have somehow stolen these blessings, or you have received them from the Holy Spirit. While you are slow to believe what the Lord has promised, you are expecting and hankering after what he has not promised. What He has done for you amounts to the best witness of the Spirit ... Be as much humbled as you please, but do not expect to be an angel while you are in the body. Depend upon it, if you walk closely with God forty years, you will at the end of that time have a much lower opinion of yourself than you have now.[39]

---

their faith might afford them upon good grounds.' *Directions for a Comfortable Walking with God* (London, 1638), p. 321.

[38] *Letters*, vol. 7, p. 319. In the same letter he says, 'I go on in an even line, being very little raised at one time or depressed at another.'

[39] *Letters of John Newton*, pp. 388-9.

UNBALANCED TEACHING

I have argued that to make a third way of assurance *the way* is not in accord with biblical teaching. That Scripture calls believers to closer and higher communion with God is not in doubt, but that we are called to reach such a state by *one* experience (however it is described) is teaching which unbalances the New Testament. At the same time, it has also to be said that if either of the two bases of assurance is pressed to the exclusion of the other, then unbalance of another kind will also follow. If all that people hear is of the promises of Christ, and that the sole Christian duty is faith in the promises, there will sooner or later develop a superficial assurance amounting to 'easy believism'. Such a condition has come to prevail in churches at various times and the remedy has been to bring forward the challenge to self-examination and the necessity of inward grace. As already said, more than faith is required in true Christian living – self-denial, the mortification of sin, and 'giving all diligence' are also duties which bear a relation to assurance (*Rom.* 8:13; *2 Pet.* 1:5).

There have been times in church history when those who *professed* to believe, on hearing powerful teaching on the nature of Christian living, have been compelled to abandon their profession and to seek Christ in truth for the first time.

But danger also lies in giving too much attention to the second basis of assurance. The Puritan emphasis on the need for self-examination and diligence in order to assurance has at some periods been taught too exclusively and in such a manner that an unhealthy, subjective form of legalism begins to reign in the churches. Owen speaks strongly of how 'the peace of many' is disturbed because they mix 'their obedience, duties, mortification of sin, and the like' with the foundation of mere grace.[40] Under such teaching, personal holiness almost comes to be looked upon as the basis on which one is accepted of God and, not surprisingly, Christian joy disappears. An imbalance of this kind led many

[40] *Works*, vol. 6, p. 565.

Scottish churches into a spiritual bondage. A typical example of this is given in the *Life of Robert Haldane*. One of his contemporaries was a merchant in Edinburgh by the name of John Campbell who came to be much used of God. But before the period of his greater usefulness, Campbell was locked up in the kind of introspection I have described. We read:

> For many years he had known and believed the truth, but his views of Christ had been rather sought in the reflection of the inward work of the Holy Spirit in his heart than in the contemplation of the finished righteousness of Christ, and he had neither peace nor joy in believing. . . . At last, to use his own earnest words in a remarkable letter published by John Newton, 'The cloud which covered the mercy-seat fled away, Jesus appeared as he is! My eyes were not turned *inward,* but *outward,* The Gospel was the glass in which I beheld him. . . . I now stand upon a shore of comparative rest. Believing, I rejoice. When in search of comfort, I resort to the testimony of God; this is the field which contains the pearl of great price. Frames and feelings are, like other created comforts, passing away. What an unutterable source of consolation is it that the foundation of our faith and hope, is ever immutably the same! – the sacrifice of Jesus as acceptable and pleasing to the Father as ever it was! . . . Formerly the major part of my thoughts centred either upon the darkness I felt or the light I enjoyed. Now they are mainly directed to Jesus, what he hath done, suffered and promised.'[41]

---

[41] Alexander Haldane, *Lives of Robert and James Haldane*, pp.127–8. Duncan Matheson gives a similar testimony: 'I had begun in the Spirit, and wanted to be made perfect in the flesh. . . . My eyes were fixed within myself, and my comfort drawn from my frames. The Spirit's work in me was the ground of my peace, rather than the work of Christ in our room.' *Life and Labours of Matheson*, p. 35.

The whole situation brightened in Scotland when the priority of direct faith in Christ, made known in his free promises, was again restored to the first place. One of the men responsible for this change was John Colquhoun of Leith (1748–1827), who wrote in his fine *Treatise on Spiritual Comfort:*

> To trust simply in the Lord Jesus for salvation to himself, is the *principal* mean which the disconsolate Christian should employ for attaining spiritual comfort. Without this, no other means will be of the smallest avail. . . . If the disquieted Christian, then, would recover spiritual consolation, let him 'hold the *beginning* of his confidence, steadfast unto the end'. . . . Let him come frequently to Jesus, the Consolation of Israel, and come every time, as if it were the first time.[42]

More recently R. A. Finlayson, another Scot, wrote on the same point:

> No assurance that we may possess is to supersede or supplant a life of direct faith in the Son of God. The Christian can never afford to live either on his first committal to Christ, or on his present feelings, or on his obedience of life. He must be looking unceasingly by faith to the Son of God. Faith must maintain its living contact. It must never degenerate into a mere believing in believing, a believing in our salvation, a believing in prayer, or any other of the spurious objects of faith. Faith in faith is not the same as faith in the Lord Jesus Christ. When this happens the peace and joy that are the fruits of assurance may be lost: we are resting on a moribund experience of yesterday.[43]

---

[42] John Colquhoun, *Treatise on Spiritual Comfort* (Edinburgh: Ogle, 1814), p. 263.

[43] R. A. Finlayson, *Reformed Theological Writings* (Fearn, Ross-shire: Christian Focus, 1996), p. 114.

Where an imbalance on the subject of assurance exists, it is by no means easy to remedy, and much wisdom is needed lest teaching goes too far in another direction. Sometimes what needs to be recovered is the direction, 'For one look at self, take ten looks at Christ.' At other times, when orthodoxy has lost the power of godliness, and multitudes are mistaken in thinking they are looking to Christ, another note has to be pressed. Sometimes churches languish for lack of any insistence on the need for a *felt* faith in Christ; at other times a form of excitement can be so popular that the need is to assert 'religion should not be a *rapture*, but a *habit*'.[44]

Sometimes needless controversy has arisen between authors who have lived at different periods and have not appreciated the situation which called for a different emphasis in writers of another time and place. An example of this is the way in which Asahel Nettleton, in early nineteenth-century New England, depreciated the value of Walter Marshall's book, *The Gospel Mystery of Sanctification*, first published in 1692 and frequently reprinted.[45] Marshall, a later Puritan, who wrote in different circumstances from those of Nettleton, was strong on the place of faith in the Christian life. In the ministry of a number of the earlier Puritans there was a different stress that led to such books as Thomas Shepard's *Parable of the Ten Virgins*. What needs to be remembered is that such men as Shepard were often labouring in parishes where faith of a nominal kind was prevalent.[46]

[44] *Select Remains of the Rev. William Nevins*, p. 386.

[45] See Bennet Tyler and Andrew Bonar, *The Life and Labours of Asahel Nettleton* (Edinburgh: Banner of Truth, 1975), p. 99.

[46] Robert Bolton, for instance, writes in the Epistle Dedicatory to his book, *A Discovery about the State of True Happiness* (1625): 'I endeavour and desire to come nearer and closer to men's consciences; and to tell them, that out of a conceit of their moral honesty, and outward religiousness, they may persuade themselves that they are rich and increased in spiritual store, and have no need for the attainment of heaven; when in deed and truth, as concerning the power of saving grace and sincere exercise of religion, they are wretched, and miserable, and poor, and blind, and naked.'

The differences here were all of emphasis, not of truth versus error. The duties of putting all our trust in Christ and of personal godliness belong together. Faith and works are contraries in justification but not in the living of the Christian life. As John Wesley once wrote to a friend: 'All who expect to be sanctified at all expect to be sanctified by faith. But meantime they know that faith will not be given but to them that obey. Remotely, therefore, the blessing depends on our works, although immediately on simple faith.'[47] This statement is equally applicable to assurance.

CONCLUSIONS

1. *It is a dangerous thing to make assurance consist of high degrees of feeling,* or 'sense', to use an older term. These are too impermanent and changeable to be made the foundation for anything enduring. The foundation has to be the Word of God, and in the exercise of faith there is a confidence and peace that endures. In the words of Thomas Charles: 'It is a mistake very injurious to us to set our *feelings* of comfort, or of no comfort, as our ground and rule in our communion with God, instead of the *word* of truth.'[48] Elaborating the same point, John Newton gave this advice:

> When young Christians are greatly comforted with the Lord's love and presence, their doubts and fears are for a season at an end. But this is not assurance; so soon as the Lord hides His face, they are troubled and ready to question the very foundation of hope.
>
> Assurance grows by repeated conflict, by repeated experimental proof of the Lord's power and goodness to save; when we have been brought very low and helped;

[47] *Letters,* vol. 4, p. 71.

[48] *Spiritual Counsels,* p. 445. 'Weak Christians,' says Thomas Brooks, 'making sense, feeling, and reason, the judge of their estates, they wrong, and perplex, and vex their precious souls, and make their lives a very hell.' *Works,* vol. 3, p. 56. Whitefield, the last person to deprecate feeling, makes the same point in his sermon on 'Marks of a True Conversion.'

sorely wounded and healed; cast down and raised again; have given up all hope, and been suddenly snatched from danger and placed in safety; and when these things have been repeated to us and in us a thousand times over, we begin to learn to trust simply to the Word and power of God, beyond and against appearances; and this trust, when habitual and strong, bears the name of assurance; for even assurance has degrees.[49]

On the same point Duncan Matheson observed: 'Young converts live more by sense than faith, and they must be taught that Jesus Himself, and not the comforts he gives, is their life. The weaning time is a critical period; then it is a man's Christian character is stamped.'[50]

2. *In seeking to aid professing Christians to attain to a clearer assurance it is always essential to remember that a number who lack assurance do so because they are not yet Christians at all.* Archibald Alexander, long experienced in this field, wrote:

In dealing with professors troubled with doubts, we are too apt to proceed on the assumed principle, that notwithstanding their sad misgivings and fears, they are at bottom sincere Christians, and have the root of the matter in them; while in regard to many, this may be an entire mistake, and we are in danger of cherishing them in a fatal delusion . . . The true reason why many

---

[49] Newton, *Letters*, p. 373. See Edwards' description of the nature of Brainerd's assurance, *Works*, vol. 2, p. 449. On young Christians being 'greatly comforted', the words of Thomas Brooks are worthy of being remembered: 'A man may at his first conversion have such a clear glorious manifestation of God's love to him, and of his interest in God, and his right to glory, that he may not have the like in all his days after.' And as a footnote he adds, 'I have conversed with several precious souls that have found this true by experience, and upon this very ground have questioned all, and strongly doubted, whether that they have not taken Satan's delusions for divine manifestations.' *Works,* vol. 2, p. 349.

[50] Macpherson, *Life of Matheson*, pp. 28–9.

professors have no comfortable evidence of their religion
is because they have none. They have never experienced
the new birth; and being still dead in trespasses and sins,
it is no wonder that they cannot find in themselves what
does not exist. I abhor a censorious spirit, which, upon
slight grounds, judges this and that professor to be grace-
less; but all my experience and observation led me to
believe that, in our day as well as in former times, the
'foolish virgins' constitute a full moiety of the visible
church.[51]

It is therefore needful for pastors to deal with counterfeit
assurance. 'As counterfeit gems do so shine and sparkle like
real jewels,' writes Brooks, 'that a man if he be not very careful may be cheated; so counterfeit grace, counterfeit holiness,
do so shine and sparkle, they do so nearly resemble real holiness, that a man may be easily mistaken, if he do not make a
narrow search.'[52] At the same time it is needful to show that,
in its essence, the evidence that shows a real Christian is eminently simple, 'entire trust in Christ for justification, and a
sincere and universal love of holiness, with a dependence on
the Holy Spirit for its existence, continuance and increase.'[53]

3. *A low esteem for the Holy Spirit, and a failure to seek the fullness of the Spirit, is a most common cause for weak assurance.* Many
people, says Guthrie, 'have not honourable apprehensions and

[51] Alexander, *Thoughts on Religious Experience*, pp. 287–8. Alexander
speaks about the common lack of assurance among Christians of Calvinistic persuasion in his day and says: 'It was not, I believe, always so with
those who cordially received the doctrines of grace and rested their souls
upon them. To say nothing about the joyful confidence and assured hope
of the apostles and primitive Christians, the members of the first reformed
churches seem to have derived from the pure doctrines of the Bible a high
degree of peace and joy. The same was the fact among the pious Puritans
of Old and New England, and the Presbyterians of Scotland in the best
and purest days of the Scottish Church.' (p. 286).

[52] Brooks, *Works*, vol. 4, p. 99.

[53] Alexander, *Religious Experience*, p. 289.

thoughts of the Spirit of God', and, while complaining of their lack, 'are not at pains to seek the Spirit in his outgoings, and few do set themselves apart for such precious receptions.'[54] Assurance and prayerlessness cannot belong together. But it has to be remembered that the aid of the Holy Spirit in the granting of peace, comfort and assurance, is ever related to the service of Christ: they are not blessings merely for personal enjoyment. To look for assurance without active labour for Christ is futile. 'The soul of the sluggard desires, and has nothing; But the soul of the diligent shall be made fat' (*Prov.* 13:4).

At the same time, just as the service and duties to which Christians are called vary, so will their needs. And so, also, the grace by which these needs are met will vary according to the duties to be fulfilled. When the special need of the disciples was boldness, this is what they asked for, and it was given (*Acts* 4:29–31). At other times the special need may be for love or patience. While courage has often been given to martyrs in a marked degree, and their mouths have been filled with praise, eminent Christians have frequently died in quiet peace and with no transports of joy. Thus an unknown layman, 'Master Peacock', at his martyrdom in the reign of Mary Tudor, could profess that the joy he felt was incredible, while such leading Puritan preachers as Thomas Hooker and Jeremiah Burroughs 'went away without any *sense* of assurance, or discoveries of the smiles of God'.[55]

Brooks writes of how God gives his children 'a sweet assurance of his favour and love, when he intends to put them upon some high and hard, some difficult and dangerous service'. He continues:

Thus God dealt with Paul. He takes him up to heaven and sheds abroad his love into his heart, and tells him he is a chosen vessel; he appears to him in the way and fills

[54] Guthrie, *Christian's Great Interest,* p. 114.
[55] Brooks, *Works,* vol. 2. p. 343. Italics for 'sense' added: they did not lack assurance.

him with the Holy Ghost, that is, with the gifts, graces
and comforts of the Holy Ghost, and straightway he falls
to preaching of Christ, upon exalting of Christ, to the
amazing and astonishing of all that heard him. And as
he had more clear, full, and glorious manifestations of
God's love and favour than others, so he was more
frequent, more abundant, and more constant in the
work and service of Christ than others, *2 Cor.* 11:21–
33.[56]

It should also be said that just as a lack of esteem for the
Holy Spirit militates against assurance, so does all deprecia-
tion of the importance of the need for biblical teaching and
particularly of the doctrines of grace. It was no accident that
in the sixteenth century the experience of assurance revived
simultaneously with the recovery of the truths called Calvinistic. In Calvin's own words:

> We may rejoice in this, that God will have pity upon us
> until the end, and that he will keep us: and although he
> suffer us to stumble, yea so as we fall, we shall be recov-
> ered and upholden by his hand. And how is it that we
> can trust in this? Without election it is impossible: but
> when we know that the Father has committed us unto
> the keeping of his Son, we are certain that we shall be
> maintained by him unto the end.[57]

4. *Assurance is of great importance.* The usefulness of a Christian will most commonly be in proportion to its strength.
Yet it is not, after all, to be the first pursuit of the Christian.
It is not something to be attained in itself; rather it is a
consequence of something else, namely a life directed to
communion with God, looking to Christ and conformity to
his likeness. Brooks likens joy, peace, comfort and assurance
to 'the Christian's wages' and says that weak Christians are

[56] Brooks, *Works*, vol. 2, p. 350.
[57] Calvin, *Thirteen Sermons*, p. 67.

'more taken up about their wages than they are about their work', as 'children mind more play-days than they do school-days'. 'Their work is waiting upon God, believing in God, walking with God, acting for God . . . They are none of the best servants that mind their wages more than their work, nor they are none of the best Christians that mind their comforts more than their homage and duty they owe to God.'[58]

In his portrait of David Brainerd, Jonathan Edwards depicts the outworking of this teaching in the life of his friend:

> It is to be observed that his longings were not so much after joyful discoveries of God's love, and clear views of his title to future advancement and eternal honours in heaven; as after more of present holiness, greater spirituality, a heart more engaged for God, to love, and exalt, and depend upon him. His longings were to serve God better, to do more for his glory, and to do all that he did with more of a regard to Christ as his righteousness and strength.[59]

---

[58] Brooks, *Works*, vol. 3, pp. 59–60.
[59] Edwards' *Works* (Banner of Truth edition), vol. 2, p. 450.

7

CHRISTIAN UNITY AND
CHURCH UNITY

'Whatever blame may or may not rest upon men for the existence of the various evangelical denominations in Christendom, let not the superintending hand of God therein be lost sight of. In our readiness to criticize former leaders – which charity requires us to believe were at least equally devoted to the Lord and as anxious to conform to his Word as we are – we need to be much on our guard lest we be found quarrelling with Divine providence . . . We are either very ignorant of history or superficial readers thereof, if we fail to perceive the guiding hand of God and his "manifold wisdom" in the appointing and blessing of the leading evangelical denominations . . .

'We have lived long enough and travelled sufficiently, to discover that no one "church", company, or man, has all the truth, and as we grow older we have less patience with those who demand that others must adopt their interpretation of Scripture on all points. . . .

'On first entering the school of Christ most of us expected to find little difference between members of the same family, but more extensive acquaintance with them taught us better, for we found their minds varied as much as their countenances, their temperaments more than their local accents of speech and that amid general agreement there were wide divergences of opinions and sentiments in many things. While all God's people are taught of him, yet they know but "in part" and the "part" one knows may not be the part which another knows. All the saints are indwelt by the Holy Spirit, yet he does not operate uniformly in them nor bestow identical gifts (*1 Cor.* 12:8–11). Thus opportunity is afforded us to "forbear one another in love"(*Eph.* 4:2) and not make a man an offender for a word or despise those who differ from me. Growth in grace is evidenced by a spirit of clemency and toleration, granting to others the same right of private judgment and liberty as I claim for myself. The mature Christian, generally, will subscribe to that axiom, "In essentials unity, in non-essentials liberty, in all things charity."'

A. W. PINK, quoted in *The Life of A. W. Pink,* Iain H. Murray (Edinburgh: Banner of Truth, 2004), pp. 306–11.

I deally, and in the eternal perspective, Christian unity and Church unity are the same, but in the realities of our present situation it is important that we understand the need for a distinction between the two. Christian unity has to do with the truth that all believers are members of the body of Christ. Christ has made that union a reality; its existence does not depend upon location, nationality, denomination or anything else. It is unity *in* Christ; it is the oneness for which he prayed in John 17 and the petition *has been* heard. Believers *are* all one in Christ Jesus. From this truth a false deduction is sometimes drawn, namely, that because believers are already one it is inconsequential whether or not they choose to belong to a particular congregation. The opposite conclusion is the one that should be drawn. For the New Testament shows that union with Christ comes to practical expression in the visible unity of believers in churches. Loyalty to Christ also entails commitment to a people, and it is in each local church that the unity of the body of Christ is normally to be seen.

Today, however, the term 'Church unity' does not commonly refer to the life of local churches. It more usually refers to unity *between* churches, and *between* denominations, and that is the sense in which I am using the term in what follows. 'Church unity,' so understood, is often referred to as though it were the same as Christian unity. I want to argue that the two things are not the same, and that confusion arises when they are treated as though they were.

There is much in the present situation that makes the subject an important one, and there is evidence enough that the devil knows the importance of frustrating unity among Christians.

DENOMINATIONS AND UNITY

When 'Church unity' is talked about, it commonly has reference *in the first instance* to matters of organization and corporate government: the unity envisaged is of an umbrella structure of one kind or another for the purpose of maintaining 'oneness'. The vision of the ecumenical movement was for such a unity, and this was regarded as being the same as the 'Christian unity' for which Jesus prayed. But the New Testament says nothing of the need for churches to be under a universal government in order to the preservation of a universal unity.[1] This last statement is not intended to be an argument that independency is *the* form of church government; the point I am making has been equally recognized by Presbyterian authors. It was A. A. Hodge who asserted, 'Christ never did make organization needful in the sense that our being Presbyterians is an essential of the Church.'[2] Or again, B. B. Warfield, in 'True Church Unity: What It Is', writes as follows of the unity of the churches of the first century:

> This unity was not organic, in the special sense of the word which would imply that it is founded on the inclusion of the whole Church under one universal government. The absence of such an organization is obvious on the face of the New Testament record, nor do its pages contain any clear promise or prominent provision for it for the future.[3]

[1] On the contrary, there may be warnings against any such thing. James B. Ramsey, writing of prophecy, said: 'Above all, any unity of visible organization, under one common head, is an impossibility; and the mere attempt to make this the test of the true church of God has been the source of untold disasters to the cause of truth and human happiness.' *Revelation: An Exposition of the First Eleven Chapters* (1873; reprint, Edinburgh: Banner of Truth, 1977), p. 446.

[2] A. A. Hodge, *Evangelical Theology*, p. 177.

[3] B. B. Warfield, *Selected Shorter Writings* ed. J. E. Meeter (Nutley, NJ:

Different opinions and different convictions exist among Christians on *how* the oneness of Christians everywhere should be manifested. There have been honoured names in the past that have thought there ought to be some visible oneness in government. But can it be possible that a matter, on which Scripture says so very little, is to be regarded as *essential* to Christian unity? The endless debates of past centuries in the quest of a common government, far from being productive of unity, have only illustrated how loyalty to Christ and Scripture may co-exist alongside conflicting convictions on matters concerning the external ordering of churches.

The denomination that has gone by the name of the Christian Brethren has argued that Christian unity and Church unity would be *one* if only there were no denominations at all and, accordingly, they set themselves to implement that noble vision. One reason it failed was that it did not do justice to an important fact: Christians today are *not* agreed over what constitutes 'the whole counsel of God'; there are scriptural issues which we do not all understand in the same way, and some of these issues are important enough to imply that if unity means putting together pastors and teachers who hold contradictory views then it would soon be no unity at all. This is the fact which has often given rise to denominations. Without wishing to 'unchurch' others,

---

Presbyterian and Reformed, 1970), vol. 1, pp. 299–307. See also R. L. Dabney, 'What is Christian Union?' *Discussions: Evangelical and Theological,* vol. 2 (1891; reprint, London: Banner of Truth, 1967), pp. 430–46; D. B. Knox, 'The Church and the Denominations,' in *Sent by Jesus* (Edinburgh: Banner of Truth, 1992), pp. 55–65. Free Church of Scotland leader, Donald Maclean, speaking of the revival of orthodoxy for which he looked in the last century, wrote: 'This revival may not necessarily result in denominational disintegration, but it will issue in interdenominational unity in the faith, which is the only unity the New Testament teaches Christians to aspire to.' *Aspects of Scottish Church History* (Edinburgh: T. & T. Clark, 1927), p. 175.

congregations that have shared a like understanding of the New Testament have believed that the Faith is best advanced by a common association, and such associations sooner or later become denominations, irrespective of what title they may choose.

Of course, not all denominations have come into existence in that way. Political reasons entered into the existence of the *national* Churches in England and Scotland, and one justification for these Churches was that they were necessary for 'the unity of the Church'. We think that claim cannot be defended by New Testament usage of the word 'church'. There the term has only two possible meanings: the church local or the church universal. When it is local churches that are referred to, the word is plural, ' the seven churches of Asia', 'the churches of Galatia, Macedonia', etc. The only justification for the singular, as in Acts 9:31 (where the most commonly accepted reading is 'the church throughout all Judea'), is that *all* believers are understood to be included. But where a denomination does not include *all* the believers of an area then it cannot qualify for the title 'church' in the New Testament sense of the word, whether it be national or any other association of churches. Denominations, as such, are not scriptural institutions; at best they are only approximations to the apostolic era and their justification ought to be that they stand for important biblical truths which could not be as effectively maintained by congregations lacking any connection.[4] It is a pragmatic argument arising from

[4] 'Denominations are called "churches," and this nomenclature misleads many . . . The denomination is an organizational structure to facilitate the fellowship of the church with Christians in other churches. To call a denomination a church is strictly inaccurate, and in furtherance of clarity of thought ought to be dropped, and the word "denomination" always substituted.' 'The Church, the Churches and the Denominations of the Churches,' in D. Broughton Knox: *Selected Works, vol.2, Church and Ministry,* ed. K. Birkett (Kingsford, NSW: Matthias Media., 2003), p. 96. To say this is not, of course, to say that denominational distinctives are insignificant.

conscientiously held convictions and from the recognition of the liberty of other Christians to think differently. Any idea that 'my denomination' exists because it is *the* Church, *the* representative of the true unity, and therefore the one that all other Christians ought to join, is utterly sectarian and destructive of Christian unity. As Spurgeon once said:

> Above all, we must not aim at unity by setting ourselves up as the Church, and styling all others 'sectaries'. This is to cement our walls with dynamite, and lay the foundations of peace upon barrels of gunpowder.[5]

WHEN CHURCH AND DENOMINATION ARE CONFUSED

It may seem trivial and quibbling to question whether the name 'Church' rightly belongs to any denominational grouping of churches. I agree it may not always matter, but the danger is that its use as part of a denominational title can unconsciously encourage an attitude that *equates* the denomination with the New Testament church. When this happens arguments can easily come to be used that allow no such distinction. For instance, when those who stay in denominations where the testimony is seriously mixed have been asked how they can justify remaining, they have been known to reply, 'Where in the New Testament does it say anything

[5] *Sword and the Trowel*, 1886, p. 518. Elsewhere he says: 'People try to get a visible form of that one Church: but I believe that is utterly impossible. The Church of Rome claims to be that one Church and we know what sort of a church that is . . . all schemes for comprehending all the saints of God in one visible Church must fail.' *MTP*, vol. 48, p. 340. This was the common opinion of English Nonconformists. Dinsdale T. Young wrote: 'All who love the Divine Lord and Saviour are truly one, and this is vastly more important than any mechanical unity . . . Denominationalism did not come about by chance, nor was it by any lapse from Christ that it eventuated. We must beware of confusing uniformity with Christian union. Fervent love is quite consistent with denominational distinctiveness.' *Stars of Retrospect* (London: Hodder and Stoughton, 1920), pp. 237–8.

about believers leaving *the church*?' The opinion may even be added that leaving the denomination is akin to schism. A recent article by Dr Packer,[6] in which he speaks of leaving the Church of England as 'lapsing into sectarianism', seems to be a slip that unhappily looks like such thinking.

But arguments from those on the 'separatist' side of the debate can proceed on a similar basis, viz., 'The Scriptures command that Christians withdraw themselves "from every brother that walks disorderly" (*2 Thess.* 3:6), therefore believers are being disobedient who remain in denominations where errorists are tolerated and even honoured.' The next step in this argument can be that we ought to have no fellowship or co-operation with those who are disobeying the biblical command by staying in 'mixed denominations'.

The case, however, does not appear quite so straightforward when a denomination ceases to be treated as the same as church. Certainly, withdrawal from a local congregation, where the disorderly and the false teacher have power, is a biblical duty, but the duty of withdrawal from a denomination is not *necessarily* equally clear. Regard for gospel opportunity, concern for numbers of Christians still within a denomination, and hope for the reversal of a situation, can be conscientiously held. Thus there have repeatedly been cases in church history where faithful men have done their utmost not to condone wrong and error, and have withdrawn from fellowship with unbelievers, yet they have remained in denominations where little or no discipline existed outside their own congregations. Such was the case with Wesley and Whitefield, and with Church of Scotland ministers who lived under the reign of Moderatism in the eighteenth century. They believed that *more good* was to be done for the gospel by their remaining than by their removal. We may disagree with their thinking (and no case can be made for Christians listening to, or supporting, unfaithful teachers), but, before we dismiss them for acting from 'expediency' rather than

[6] J. I. Packer, 'From 1966 to 2002?' in *Evangelicals Now,* March 2004.

Scripture, let us remember that the principles governing the existence of denominations are not so clear that all Christians should have had no difficulty in recognizing them. The mistake of the Scots Seceders of the 1730s, and their subsequent rejection of Whitefield, his 'corrupt Church [the Church of England]', and the Cambuslang revival, should be warning enough on this point.

The Church of Scotland in the eighteenth century was certainly a denomination in which the truth was seriously compromised and faithful men disagreed on how that situation was to be addressed. We read of how Dr John Erskine, one of the leaders of the evangelical party in the Church of Scotland at that time, acted within that denomination. Required by the Edinburgh Presbytery to preside at a service where a new minister was being settled by the patron, and not by the congregation, he protested in the following manner. On arriving at the church, after a walk of more than eight miles from Edinburgh, he was invited by the patron to take some refreshment before the service. This he declined to do. Once the proceedings were over, the invitation was renewed and with more insistence. We are told that

> his calm yet firm and solemn answer, was to this effect: 'I feel obliged by your politeness, my lord, but "if thou wilt give me half thine house, I will not go in with thee, neither will I eat bread nor drink water in this place, for so was it charged me by the word of the LORD" (*1 Kings* 13:7–9).' And the good doctor walked his way back to Edinburgh without a rest, or even a halt.

We may think John Erskine should have gone further with his protest but the fact is, to use M'Cheyne's words, 'Christ owned his work and shall we the sinful fellow-servants disown him?' Would we have refused fellowship with John Erskine if we had lived at that day? Doctrinal indifferentism is a great and dangerous evil but it is surely a mistake to treat evangelicals who remain in the mixed denominations as necessarily condoning it. John Newton, in discussing the

Seceders with a Scottish correspondent, once remarked: 'I believe all denominations, as such, abound with bigotry in favour of their own side, and that the ministers and private Christians in each, are more or less freed from it, in proportion as they are favoured with more of the unction of the Holy Spirit, and as they have more opportunities of observing his work carried on among other parties.'[7]

THE UNITY THAT COMES FIRST

To return then to the distinction between Church unity and Christian unity. The two are not the same. Church unity, in the sense of the bringing together of groups or denominations, may be desirable in some circumstances. But the 'bringing together' has primarily to do with questions of ministry, mutual eligibility, confessional standards, agreement over government and such like. Christian unity is a bigger thing: it overrides denominations; its existence is proved by 'a common faith and love' rather than by 'external conformity'.[8] Denominations are for time, Christian unity is for eternity. We *may* consider the advancement of Church unity a duty, and in one form or another we should all seek to promote it, but we *must* treat the upholding of Christian unity as our duty. The obligation is beautifully stated in Chapter 26 of the *Westminster Confession of Faith* which begins:

> All saints that are united to Jesus Christ their head by his Spirit, and by faith, have fellowship with him in his

---

[7] William Barless, *Sermons on Practical Subjects, with the Correspondence between the Author and the Rev. John Newton* (New York: Eastbourne, 1881), p. 559. It is said that when John Erskine once queried Newton on how he could remain in the Church of England, the latter replied that he could not understand Erskine's association with the leading Edinburgh Moderate, William Robertson (their respective congregations met in separate parts of the same building). M'Cheyne speaks of faithful servants who have 'inconsistencies of mind which we cannot account for' and 'prejudices of sect and education'.

[8] Dabney, *Discussions*, vol. 2, p. 434. See also Owen, *Works*, vol. 4, p. 147.

graces, sufferings, death, resurrection and glory. And being united to one another in love, they have communion in each other's gifts and graces; and are obliged to the performance of such duties, public and private, as do conduce to their mutual good.

From those words follows the catholic attitude so well stated by Robert M'Cheyne in his pages on 'Communion with Brethren of Other Denominations'.[9] His argument remains highly relevant, not least in Scotland where Christian unity has too often been subsumed under 'Church unity', as though the latter must always have the priority. And because Church unity has largely to do with ministers, differences between ministers come to *govern* the relationships of all Christians, so that I no longer have obligations of love and fellowship towards those who are not in my connection. Fidelity to Christ thus comes to be identified too exclusively with denominational loyalty, as happened with the Scots Seceders. I have already said that what makes denominations distinctive *may* be important, indeed *ought* to be important if a separate denomination is justified. I am advancing no case for a unity based on the lowest common denominator – but *what makes us distinctively Christian* has to be more important than any denominational distinctives. Dr John Duncan, no latitudinarian, wrote those fine words: 'I am first a Christian, next a Catholic, then a Calvinist, fourth a Paedobaptist and fifth a Presbyterian. I cannot reverse this order.'

The problem with the elevation of denominations (and even with independent churches) is that too commonly the order of biblical priorities comes to be reversed, so that I am *first* a Calvinist, or *first* a Presbyterian, an Anglican or a Baptist, and when this happens it is the wider Christian unity which suffers and Christ himself is dishonoured.[10] It used to

---

[9] *Robert Murray M'Cheyne: Memoir and Remains,* pp. 605–12.

[10] This point is relevant to the co-operation of Christians in agencies which are not under the authority of a church or denomination. Some have regarded all such 'non-church' agencies as illegitimate, as though

be said by some that classic Presbyterian Church order was the way to a wider unity. The multiplicity of Presbyterian denominations today – 750, it is said, in Korea alone – hardly confirms such an opinion. In the nineteenth century, James Hamilton, Presbyterian minister and friend of M'Cheyne, wrote a tract on Christian union that deplored what he saw in his own circles and beyond. It included this illustration:

> The more carnal a Christian is, the more sectarian he will be; and the more spiritual he is, the more loving and forbearing and self-renouncing are you sure to find him. And it is with Christian communities as with individual Christians. When the tide is out, you may have noticed, as you rambled among the rocks, little pools with little fishes in them. To the shrimp in such a pool his foot-depth of salt water is all the ocean for the time being. He has no dealings with his neighbour shrimp in the adjacent pool, though it may be only a few inches of sand that divide them. . . . When the tide is out – when religion is low – the faithful are to be found insulated, here a few and there a few, in the little pools of water that stud the beach, having no dealings with their neighbours of the adjoining pools, calling them Samaritans, and fancying that their own little communion includes all that are precious in God's sight. They forget for a time that there is a vast and expansive ocean.[11]

It is a spiritual change, not an ending of all denominations that is necessary to meet this failure which affects us all. Denominational distinctives, as such, need not prevent

---

there should be no work in mission, literature, etc. by Christians simply as Christians. The fact is that such agencies have been, and continue to be, much used of God.

[11] William Arnot, *Life of James Hamilton* (London: Nisbet, 1870), pp. 246–7.

Christian unity. Sometimes it is necessary and more biblical for denominations to stay apart.[12] Whitefield's societies and the Wesleyan Methodist societies of the eighteenth century, for example, could not effectively work together although they sought to respect one another. The doctrinal difference between them was too great and they were better acting separately. But Christian unity (as exemplified by the friendship of Whitefield and Wesley) transcended that difference. Such catholicity glorifies our common Saviour and is preparatory to that perfect oneness in love that is the final destiny of the church. Then the longing expressed by Archibald Alexander earlier in these pages will be fulfilled![13]

The words of A. A. Hodge are a good conclusion:

All claims that our Church is the one Church and only Church, are of the essence of schism; all pride and bigotry are of the essence of schism; all want of universal love, all jealousy, and all attempts to take advantage of others in controversy or in Church extension, are of the essence of schism. . . . It is not by the uniting of types, but by the unity of the Spirit; it is not by working from without, but from within outward; by taking on more of Christ, more of the Spirit, that we will realize more and more the unity of the Church in our own happy experience.[14]

[12] 'The only practicable scheme of church association is that which unites in one denomination those who are honestly agreed, while it leaves to all others who differ from them the same liberty of association and testimony. Does a certain separation of the parts of the visible church catholic result? I answer, it is the least of the possible evils.' Dabney, *Discussions*, vol. 2, p. 440. W. G. T. Shedd advances the same argument in a chapter, 'Denominational Unity Undesirable', *Orthodoxy and Heterodoxy* (New York: Scribner's, 1893).

[13] See above, p. 165.

[14] *Evangelical Theology,* pp. 182–3.

ADDITIONAL NOTE

JOHN OWEN OF THRUSSINGTON: UNIFORMITY AND UNITY

'Uniformity without religion, that is, without real vital religion, is worthless. Combined with true religion it is very valuable. But the *chief* uniformity that is wanted, is that of mind, heart, and spirit, as to things essential to salvation. We too often begin at the wrong end, labouring for uniformity in external matters, when we ought first to seek uniformity in principles, in essential doctrines and in spiritual experience. To amalgamate discordant elements is a vain attempt. They may be put in juxta-position, but they cannot mix. The church are the faithful, true Christians, and none but such can unite well together.'[15]

WILLIAM GIBSON: UNITY AND THE HOLY SPIRIT

'We learn from such a work of grace as that which has taken place in Ulster, *the true theory and solution of the problem of Christian unity*. Is it not to the Church an instructive, and to the world a convincing sight, which is exhibited at such a time of spiritual renovation? How often do we hear on platforms of "sinking of minor differences" and the like; and yet how rarely do we practise it, or make it manifest that we are one with all who hold by the Living Head, in faith, and hope and charity! But let a baptism of the Holy Ghost be given, and what before was a pleasing theory, beautiful to contemplate, impossible to realise, becomes without an effort an actual reality. Separations that threatened to last for ever yield to His glad advent.'[16]

[15] John Owen, *Memoir of Daniel Rowlands* (London: Routledge, 1848), p. 238.

[16] William Gibson, *The Year of Grace: A History of the Ulster Revival of 1859* (Edinburgh: Elliot, 1860), p. 379.

INDEX

Titles published by the Banner of Truth Trust are marked ★

Ability and responsibility, 22–23n, 46, 62
★*Advice for Seekers* (Spurgeon), 51n, 55n
★*Alarm to the Unconverted* (Alleine), 24n, 48n
Alexander, Archibald, 22n, 26, 30n, 165, 195–6, 213
  Life (J. W. Alexander), 30n
  Practical Sermons, 165n
  ★*Thoughts on Religious Experience*, 22n, 196n
Alexander, J. W., 30n
Alleine, Joseph, 23–4, 139
  ★*Alarm to the Unconverted*, 24n, 48n
  ★*Sure Guide to Heaven*, 24n
Antinomians, 183n
Apostle of the North, The (Kennedy), 104n
★*Apostles' Doctrine of the Atonement* (Smeaton), 89n, 103n, 108n
Appeals to Men of Reason and Religion (Wesley), 152n
Application of Redemption, The (Hooker), 28n
Arminian Magazine, 152n
Arminianism, varieties of, 155–6
Arnot, William, 212
  Life of James Hamilton, 212n

Annesley, Samuel, 139
Aspects of Scottish Church History, (Maclean), 205n
Assurance of salvation, 167–99
  the Holy Spirit and, 172–5
  sealing with the Spirit, 184–5
  twofold basis of, 175–81
  witness of the Spirit, the, 181–9
Atonement, Doctrine of Scripture respecting (Crawford), 118n
Atonement, The (Candlish), 122–4n
★*Atonement Controversy in Welsh Theological Literature and Debate,* (Thomas), 126–7n
Augustine, 101, 110, 156
Awakening, preaching and, 1–37

Baker, Frank, 141n
Barless, W., 210n
  Sermons on Practical Subjects, 210n
Basket of Fragments (M‘Cheyne), 21n
Baxter, Richard, 20, 137–8, 171
  Cure of Church Divisions, 138n
  Reliquiae Baxterianae, 138n
Berridge, John, 93
  Works, 93n
★*Biblical Doctrines* (Warfield), 44n, 62n

Binning, Hugh, 116n
  *Christian Love, 116n
Blair, Samuel, 3–4
Blair, William, 5n
*Body of Divinity (Watson), 110n,
  157n
Bolton, Robert, 24–5, 188–9n
  Directions for a Comfortable
    Walking with God, 188–9n
  Right Comforting of Afflicted
    Consciences, 25n
  State of True Happiness, 193n
Bonar, Andrew, 28
  *Life and Labours of Nettleton,
    193n
  *Letters of Rutherford, 175n
  *Memoir and Remains of
    M'Cheyne, 72
Bonar, Horatius, 80n
  God's Way of Peace, 80n
Bonar, John, 132–3
  Free Church Pulpit, 133n
Boos, Martin, 99
  Life, 99n
Booth, William, xi
Boston, Thomas, 159–60
  Whole Works, 160n
Bradford, John, 123, 171
Brainerd, David, 30–1, 184, 195n,
  199
Bramwell, William, 152
Brethren movement, 205n
British and Foreign Evangelical
  Review, 136, 138, 148, 156n
Brooks, Thomas, 176–7, 183–4,
  195n, 196–9
  *Works, 176n, 181n, 183–4n,
    194–9n
Brown, John (Haddington), 150n
  *Memoir and Select Remains,
    150n
Brown, John (Wamphray), 33–5
  Mirror for Saint and Sinner, 35n
Brown, John (Whitburn), 159n
  Gospel Truth Accurately Stated,
    159n
Buchanan, James, 93
  *Doctrine of Justification, 94n
Bunyan, John, 7n, 22, 31n, 97–8,
  120, 128, 171, 174, 180, 183
  *Pilgrim's Progress, 172n, 180
  *Works, 7n, 31n, 98n, 120n,
    128n, 183n
Bunyan Characters (Whyte), 36n
Burgess, Anthony, 2
  Spiritual Refinings, 2, 181n, 187n
  True Doctrine of Justification, 94n
Burroughs, Jeremiah, 197

Calamy, Edmund, 156–7n
Calderwood, David 149n
Calvin, John, 32, 102, 115–6, 118,
  131, 156, 161, 198
  *Commentaries on Jeremiah, 116n
  Commentaries on Ezekiel, 118n
  Commentary on John 1–10, 112n,
    156n
  Commentaries on Hebrews, 102
  Institutes, 163n
  *Sermons on Deuteronomy, 116n
    118n, 156n
  Thirteen Sermons on Election and
    Reprobation, 32n, 131n, 198n
Calvin's Doctrine of the Christian
  Life (Wallace), 163n
Calvinistic Methodism, 125–6
Cambuslang revival, 209
Campbell, John, 191
Candlish, Robert, 122–3
  The Atonement, 122n, 124n

Index

Carson, D. A., 115
  Difficult Doctrine of the Love of God, The, 115n
Carus, William, 99n
Chalmers, Thomas, 93, 103–4, 117n, 131
  Correspondence, 93n, 105n, 117n
  Sabbath Scripture Readings, 117n
  Works, 117n, 131n
Charles, Thomas, 164, 185, 194
  Spiritual Counsels, 164n, 185n, 194n
Charnock, Stephen, 44n, 74n
  Works, 44n, 45n, 74n
Cheque Book of the Bank of Faith (Spurgeon), 65–6n, 172n
Christian Brethren, 205n
Christian in Complete Armour, The, (Gurnall), 30n
Christian Leaders of the Eighteenth Century (Ryle), 142n
Christian Love (Binning), 116n
Christian's Great Interest (Guthrie), 158n, 186n, 197n
Christ's Doctrine of the Atonement (Smeaton), 111n, 118n
Clarke, Adam, 137, 143
Coley, Samuel, 171n
  Life of Thomas Collins, 171n
Collected Writings (Murray), 23n, 61n
Collins, Thomas, 171n
Colquhoun, John, 161, 192–3
  A View of Saving Faith, 161n
  Treatise on Spiritual Comfort, 192n
Commenting and Commentaries (Spurgeon), 143n
Confession of Faith (Calvinistic Methodist), 179–80

Conscience, preaching and, 6–15, 36–7
Conversion:
  nature of, 41–70, 72, 80–2, 119–23
  preaching for, 60–8
Corinthians, 1 and 2 (Hodge), 110n, 181n
Corinthians, 1 and 2 (Lenski), 180n
Counted Righteous in Christ (Piper), 83n
Cowper, William, 90, 107, 128
Crawford, Thomas J., 118
  Doctrine of Holy Scripture respecting the Atonement, 118n
Cross, the, displays the love of God, 101–133
Cunningham, William, 138
Cure of Church Divisions (Baxter), 138n

Dabney, Robert L., 6, 113
  Discussions: Evangelical and Theological, 113n, 161n, 205n, 210n, 213n
d'Aubigné, J. H. Merle, 80
Davenant, Bishop, 161n
Denominations and unity, 204–13
Deuteronomy, Sermons on (Calvin), 116n, 118n, 156n
Difficult Doctrine of the Love of God, (Carson), 115n
Directions for a Comfortable Walking with God (Bolton), 188–9n
Discussions: Evangelical and Theological (Dabney), 113n, 161n, 205n, 210n, 213n
Doctrine of Repentance (Watson), 20n
Dogmatic Theology (Shedd), 19n, 22n, 43n

Doing Good: The Christian in Walks of Usefulness (Steel), 129n

Duncan, John, 6, 11–12n, 17–18, 30n, 58, 115, 163, 211
  'Just a Talker', 18n, 58n, 115n
  Life (Moody Stuart), 6n
  Pulpit and Communion Table, 30n
  Recollections (Moody Stuart) 163n
  Rich Gleanings after the Vintage, 11–12n, 18n

Easy-believism, 190
Edwards, Jonathan, 4, 12–13, 106, 128, 152n, 182, 184, 185, 199
  Narrative of Surprising Conversions, 4
  Religious Affections, 181n, 184n
  Treatise on Grace, 164n
  Works, 4, 12–13, 31n, 106n, 128n, 182n, 184n, 195n, 199n
  Edwards: A New Biography (Murray), 184n
Election and Reprobation, Thirteen Sermons on (Calvin), 32n, 131n, 198n
Elias, John, 81–2, 127
  Life, Letters and Essays, 81, 127n
Epworth, Lincs., 139
Erskine, Ebenezer, 159
Erskine, Dr John, 209, 210n
Erskine, Ralph, 159
Evangelicals Now, 208n
Evangelical Theology (Hodge), 106n, 204n, 213n
Evangelism
  and awakening, 1–37
  and the love of God, 101–33, 151–62
  Spurgeon's example, 37–67

Ezekiel, Commentaries (Calvin), 118n
Fairbairn, Patrick, 146, 147n
  Pastoral Epistles, 147n
Fear of God, the, 3–6, 31, 66
Ferguson, Sinclair B., 184n
  John Owen on the Christian Life, 184–5n
Finlayson, R. A., 192
  Reformed Theological Writings, 192n
Firmin, Giles, 20
  The Real Christian, 20n
First Book of Discipline, 149n
Flavel, John, 7n, 186–7
  Works, 7n, 44n, 84n, 186–7n
Forgotten Spurgeon (Murray), 45n

Gill, John, 143
Gibson, William, 215
  The Year of Grace, 215n
Gifts of the Spirit (Vaughan), 52n, 57n, 60n
Gillies, John, 4n
  Historical Collections, 4n
God's Way of Peace (Bonar), 80n
Goodwin, Thomas, 29
  Works, 43n
Gospel Mystery of Sanctification (Marshall), 193n
Gospel Truth Accurately Stated (Brown), 159n
Grace of God and Bondage of the Will (Schreiner), 117n
Great Awakening, the, 3–4
Green, Richard, 151n
  John Wesley, Evangelist, 151n
Guide to Christ (Stoddard), 20n, 28n
Gurnall, William, 30

*Christian in Complete Armour,
    The*, 30n
Guthrie, William, 158, 185–6, 196–7
    Christian's Great Interest, 158n,
        186n, 197n
Guyse, John, 4

Haldane, Robert, 80, 174, 185
    *Lives of Robert and James
        Haldane* (A. Haldane), 80n,
        191n
    Romans, 84–5n, 174n
Hamilton, James, 212
    Life, 212n
Hamilton, William, 152
Havergal, Frances R., 99–100
    Letters, 100n
Heaven Opened (Winslow), 2
Hebrews, Commentaries (Calvin),
    102
Heppe, Heinrich, 43n
    Reformed Dogmatics, 43n
Herbert, George, 97
    Works, 97n
Hill, Rowland, 118–9
Historical Collections (Gillies), 4n
Hobson, Richard, 164n
    Autobiography, 164n
Hodge, A. A., 106n, 204, 213
    Evangelical Theology, 106n, 204n,
        213n
Hodge, Charles, 43n
    Romans, 84n
    1 Corinthians, 181n
    2 Corinthians, 110n
    Systematic Theology, 43n
Hogg, James, 159
Holiness (Ryle), 171n, 181n
Hooker, Thomas, 22, 28, 197
    Application of Redemption, 28n

Howe, John, 117n
    Works, 117n
Hunt, Bruce, 5n
Hussey, Joseph, 141n

Imputed righteousness, see
    Justification
Innes, A. Taylor, 6n
    John Knox, 6n
Institutes (Calvin), 163n
Irving, Edward, 137

Jeremiah, Commentaries (Calvin),
    116n
John 1–10, Commentary (Calvin),
    112n, 156n
John, Expository Thoughts (Ryle)
    161n
Johnson, T. C., 17n
'Just a Talker' (Duncan), 18n, 58n,
    115n
Justification, 71–100
Justification, Doctrine of (Buchanan),
    94n
Justification, True Doctrine of
    (Burgess), 94n

Kennedy, John, 115n
    The Apostle of the North, 104n
Knox, D. Broughton, 205n, 206n
    Selected Works, 206n
    Sent by Jesus, 205n
Knox, John, 6, 149, 157
    Works, 157n
Korea, 4–5, 212

Latimer, Hugh, 171
Law, preaching and, 8–16, 23–37,
    47–54, 64, 69
Lectures to My Students (Spurgeon),
    30n, 63n, 92n

Legalism, 179–81, 190–4

Lenski, R. C. H., 180n

  1 and 2 Corinthians, 180n

Liturgy of John Knox, 149n

Lloyd-Jones, D. Martyn, 9, 27–8,
  37, 64n, 69, 124, 136, 176,
  184n

  First Forty Years, The (Murray),
  136

  *Puritans: Their Origins and
  Successors*, 164n

  Preaching and Preachers, 64n

  Romans, Exposition, 9n, 37n,
  82–3n

  *Sermon on the Mount, Studies
  in*, 27n, 69n

  *Spiritual Depression: Its Causes
  and Cure*, 176n

Louis XIV, 95–6

Love of God, 30, 65, 101–33,
  151–62

Luther, Martin, 24n, 187

M'Cheyne, R. M., 21, 209, 210n,
  211–2

  Basket of Fragments, A, 21n

  Memoir and Remains (Bonar),
  72, 211n

MacDonald, John, 104

  Life (Kennedy) 104n

Machen, J. Gresham, 96

Maclean, Donald, 205n

  Aspects of Scottish Church History,
  205n

Macleod, John, 159n

Macpherson, John, 102n, 168,
  195n

Malan, Caesar, 22

  Life, Labours and Writings of,
  22n

Manton, Thomas, 116n

  Works, 116n, 173n

'Marrow men', 159–61

Marshall, Walter, 193

  Gospel Mystery of Sanctification,
  193n

Martyn, Henry, 129

Masters, Peter, 44, 61n

Mather, Increase, 20n

Matheson, Duncan, 102, 168, 195

  Life and Labours (Macpherson)
  102, 168, 191n, 195n

Matthews, John, 188n

Melanchthon, Philip, 24

Memoir and Remains of M'Cheyne
  (Bonar), 72, 211n

Methodism (Wesleyan), 27, 119n,
  128–9, 138–58, 162–5, 213

Metropolitan Tabernacle Pulpit, see
  Spurgeon, C. H.

Mirror for Saint and Sinner (Brown)
  35n

Moderatism, 208–10

Moody, D. L., 164n

Moody Stuart, A. 163n

Morgan, G. Campbell, 137

Murray, John, 23n, 61, 96, 105,
  114

  Collected Writings, 23n, 61n,
  96n, 105n, 107n, 114n

  *Redemption – Accomplished and
  Applied*, 61n

  Romans, 82n

Narrative of Surprising Conversions
  (Edwards), 4

National churches, 206, 208–9

Neal, Daniel, 137

Nelson, John, 155

  Journal, 155n

Nettleton, Asahel, 193
  Life and Labours, 193n
Nevins, William, 132
  Select Remains, 132n, 193n
Newton, John, 142n, 189, 194–5, 209–10
  *Letters, 189n, 195n
Nicoll, W. Robertson, 42

*Old Paths (Ryle), 89n
Only a Prayer Meeting (Spurgeon), 61n
Orthodoxy and Heterodoxy (Shedd), 213n
Ouseley, Gideon, 152
Owen, John, 2, 19n, 25, 110–11, 120–1, 140, 157–8, 176n, 184n, 186, 190
  *Works, 2n, 19n, 25n, 43n, 91n, 109n, 111n, 113n, 121n, 140n, 147n, 157n, 158n, 164n, 168, 174n, 176n, 186n, 188n, 190n
*Owen on the Christian Life (Ferguson), 184–5n
Owen, John (Thrussington), 32n, 215
  Memoir of Daniel Rowlands, 32n, 215n

Packer, J. I., xiii, 156n, 208
  Collected Shorter Writings, 156n
  Quest for Godliness, xiii
Palmer, Benjamin M., 16–17
  *Life and Letters of, 17n
Parable of the Prodigal, The (Sedgwick), 58n, 60n
Parable of the Ten Virgins (Shepard), 193n
*Pentecost – Today? (Murray), 121n, 185n

Philip, Robert, 21n
Physicians of Souls (Masters), 44n, 61n
*Pilgrim's Progress, 172n, 180
Pink, A. W., 202
Piper, John, 83n, 117n
  'Are There Two Wills in God?', 117n
  Counted Righteous in Christ, 83n
Practical Sermons (Alexander), 165n
Preaching (see also Evangelism):
  and awakening, 1–37
  and Christ's righteousness, 95–6
  for conversions, 60–8
  preaching the cross, 103–33
Preaching and Preachers (Lloyd-Jones), 64n
Presbyterian church order and unity, 211–2
Pulpit and Communion Table (Duncan), 30n
*Puritans: Their Origins and Successors (Lloyd-Jones), 164n
Pyongyang, Korea, 4–5

Rack, Henry D., 141n
  Reasonable Enthusiast, 141n, 188n
Ramsey, J. B., 204n
  *Revelation, Exposition of First Eleven Chapters, 204n
*Redemption – Accomplished and Applied (Murray), 61n
Redemptive History (Vos), 114n, 116–7n
Reeves, William, 129
Real Christian, The (Firmin), 20n
Reformed Dogmatics (Heppe), 43n
Reformed Theological Writings (Finlayson), 192n

Regeneration, 18–24, 43–7,
54–65, 70
Religious Affections (Edwards),
181n, 184n
Reliquiae Baxterianae, 138n
*Reminiscences of the Revival of
1859* 4n
Responsibility and ability, 22–23n
*Revelation, Exposition of First
Eleven Chapters* (Ramsey), 204n
Revivalism, 26–7
Revivals, 3–6, 25–6, 31, 93, 136,
209, 215
Rich Gleanings after the Vintage,
(Duncan), 11–12n, 18n
Richardson, Evan, 81
*Right Comforting of Afflicted
Consciences* (Bolton), 25n
Righteousness of Christ, 71–100
Roberts, William, 125–6
Robertson, William, 210n
Robinson, Thomas, 110
*Suggestive Commentary on
Romans,* 110n
Romans (Haldane), 84–5n, 174n
Romans (Hodge), 84n
Romans (Lloyd-Jones), 9n, 27n
Romans (Murray), 82n
Romans (Robinson), 110n
Romanticizing past times, 3
Rowlands, Daniel, 31–2
Memoir (Owen), 32n, 215n
Rutherford, Samuel, 174–5
Letters, 175n
Ryle, J. C., 81, 89, 142, 181
*Christian Leaders of the
Eighteenth Century,* 142n
Expository Thoughts, xii, 161n
Holiness, 171n, 181n
Old Paths, 89n

Sanctification, 35, 91–3, 162–5,
173, 179, 184
Sandeman, David, 73
Sangster, W. E., 27
Doctor Sangster (Life), 27n
Saviour of the World (Warfield),
111n
Schreiner, T. R., 117n
*Grace of God and Bondage of the
Will,* 117n
Scottish Theology (Macleod), 159n
Scott, Thomas, 35–6, 142
Letters and Papers, 36n, 142–3n
Secession Church, 159–61,
209–10
Second Great Awakening, 26
Sedgwick, Obadiah, 58n, 60n
Parable of the Prodigal, The, 58n,
60n
Sermon on the Mount, Studies in
(Lloyd-Jones), 27n, 69n
Sermons to the Natural Man
(Shedd), 5n
Shedd, W. G. T., 5, 19n, 22, 213n
Dogmatic Theology, 19n, 22n,
43n
Sermons to the Natural Man, 5n
Orthodoxy and Heterodoxy, 213n
Shepard, Thomas, 193
Parable of the Ten Virgins, 193n
Sibbes, Richard, 98, 121
Works, 15n, 92n, 121n, 122n
Simeon, Charles, 14–15, 19, 91
Memoirs (Carus), 99n
Smeaton, George, 89, 103, 136,
138, 155
*Apostles' Doctrine of the
Atonement,* 89n, 103n, 108n
*Christ's Doctrine of the
Atonement,* 111n, 118n

Smith, George, 151, 154
  History of Wesleyan Methodism,
    151n, 154n
Smith, John, 153–4
  Memoirs (Treffry), 154n
Soul-Winner, The (Spurgeon), 21n,
  47n, 52n, 63n
Spiritual Comfort, Treatise on
  (Colquhoun), 192n
★*Spiritual Counsels* (Charles), 164n,
  185n, 194n
*Spiritual Depression: Its Causes and
  Cure* (Lloyd-Jones), 176n
Spiritual Refinings (Burgess), 2,
  181n, 187n
Spurgeon, C. H., xi, xiii, 21, 22,
  26–7, 29–30, 39–68, 92n, 116,
  123, 143, 172, 207
  ★*Advice for Seekers,* 51n, 55n
  ★*Autobiography,* 41n, 48n
  *Cheque Book of the Bank of
    Faith,* 65–6n, 172n
  ★*Commenting and Commentaries,*
    xiii, 143n
  Lectures to My Students, 30n,
    63n, 92n
  Metropolitan Tabernacle Pulpit,
    40, 41n, 44–5n, 48–50n,
    53–4n, 56n, 58–60n, 63n,
    66n, 68n, 123n, 207n
  Only a Prayer Meeting, 61n
  Personal Reminiscences (Williams)
    56n, 65n
  Soul-Winner, The, 21n, 47n, 52n,
    63n
  Sword and the Trowel, The, 27n,
    64n, 206n
  ★*Spurgeon v. Hyper-Calvinism*
    (Murray), 116n, 142n
  State of True Happiness (Bolton)

193n
Stars of Retrospect (Young), 207n
Steel, Robert, 129n
Stoddard, Solomon, 20n, 28
  A Guide to Christ, 20n, 28n
Systematic Theology (Hodge), 43n

Theology and Theologians of Scotland
  (Walker), 161n
Thomas, Owen, 126–7n
  ★*Atonement Controversy in Welsh
    Theological Literature and Debate,*
    126–7n
Thornwell, J. H., 7
★*Thoughts on Religious Experience*
  (Alexander), 22n, 196n
Tozer, A. W., 70
  Renewed Day by Day, 70n
Tyerman, Luke, 25n
Tyler, Bennet, 193n
  ★*Life and Labours of Nettleton,*
    193n

Vaughan, C. R., 52n, 60n
  ★*Gifts of the Spirit, The,* 52n,
    57n, 60n
Venn, Henry, 188n
  ★*Letters,* 188n
View of Saving Faith (Colquhoun),
  161n
Vos, Geerhardus, 114n, 116
  Redemptive History, 114n,
    116–7n

Wallace, R. S., 163n
  *Calvin's Doctrine of the
    Christian Life,* 163n
Walker, James, 161
  *Theology and Theologians of
    Scotland,* 161n

Ware, B. A., 117n
  Grace of God and Bondage of the
    Will, 117n
Warfield, B. B., 44n, 62, 111,
    204
  *Biblical Doctrines, 44n, 62n
  *Saviour of the World, 111n
  Selected Shorter Writings, 204–5n
Watson, Thomas, 20n, 110, 156–7
  *Body of Divinity, 110n, 157n
  *Doctrine of Repentance, 20n
Watts, Isaac, 4
Wesley, Charles, 139, 144n
Wesley, John, xii, xiv, , 26, 135–65,
    170, 187–9, 194, 208, 213
  Appeals to Men of Reason and
    Religion, 152n
  Journal, 188n
  Letters, 26n, 139n, 188n, 189n,
    194n
  Works, 146n, 170n
Wesley, Samuel, 139–40
Wesley, Susanna, 139–41
  Complete Writings, 141n
  Some Remarks on a Letter, 141n
*Wesley and Men Who Followed
  (Murray), 138n, 162n
Wesleyan Methodism, History of
  (Smith), 151n, 154n

Westminster Assembly, 157n
  Minutes, 157n
Westminster Chapel, xiv, 27–8
Westminster Confession of Faith,
    5, 73, 106–7, 156n, 174, 177,
    179, 182, 210–11
Whitefield, George, xiv, 21, 22, 25,
    53n, 122–3, 128, 141, 143,
    156, 194n, 208–9, 213
  *Journals, 123n, 156n
  Life (Tyerman), 25n
  Life and Times (Philip), 21n
  Sermons on Important Subjects,
    53n
White, H. M., 171n
  William S. White, 171n
White, William S., 171
Whyte, Alexander, 36, 73
  Bunyan Characters, 36n
Wilberforce, William, 14
  Life, 14n
Williams, W., 164
Winslow, Mary, 2
Wrath of God, the, 3, 4, 13, 15,
    25, 82, 108n

Year of Grace, The (Gibson), 215n
Young, Dinsdale T., 207n
  Stars of Retrospect, 207n

A Time-Line for Some of the Authors Quoted

'We teach no new thing, but we repeat and establish old things, which the apostles and all godly teachers have taught before us.'
MARTIN LUTHER

THE REFORMATION OF THE SIXTEENTH CENTURY
Martin Luther 1483–1546
John Calvin 1509–64
John Knox c.1514–72

SEVENTEENTH-CENTURY PURITANS (ENGLISH)
Richard Sibbes 1577–1635
Anthony Burgess died 1644
Thomas Hooker c.1586–1647
Thomas Manton 1620–77
Thomas Watson c. 1620–86
William Gurnall 1616–79
John Flavel 1627–91
Joseph Alleine 1634–68
John Bunyan 1628–88
Stephen Charnock 1628–80

SEVENTEENTH-CENTURY PURITANS (SCOTS)
John Brown of Wamphray c. 1610–79
William Guthrie 1620–69
Samuel Rutherford c.1600–61

THE EIGHTEENTH-CENTURY REVIVAL
John Wesley 1703–91
Jonathan Edwards 1703–58
George Whitefield 1714–70